THE QUEEN'S TWO BODIES
Drama and the Elizabethan Succession

Marie Axton

Research Fellow of
Newnham College
Cambridge

LONDON
ROYAL HISTORICAL SOCIETY
1977

The Society records its gratitude to the following, whose generosity made possible the initiation of this series: The British Academy; The Pilgrim Trust; The Twenty-Seven Foundation; The United States Embassy's Bicentennial funds; The Wolfson Trust; several private donors.

Printed in England
by Swift Printers Ltd
London E.C.1.

To the memory of my mother
KATHRYN HORINE

CONTENTS

ACKNOWLEDGEMENTS

For permission to quote from manuscripts in their care I am indebted to the Trustees of the British Library, to the Director of the Public Record Office, to the Curators of the Bodleian Library and to W.W.S. Breem, Librarian of the Inner Temple. Some of the material in Chapter 4 is reprinted from my essay in the *Historical Journal* (1970) with permission of the Editors.

I would like to thank the staff of the Public Record Office, the British Library manuscript room, the Bodleian Library and the Butler Library, Columbia University. In particular I would like to record my gratitude to the staff of the rare books room of the Cambridge University Library, and to the Librarian of the Inner Temple, W.W.S. Breem, for their help.

PREFACE

When the hero of Kyd's *Spanish Tragedy* despairs of justice from his own king, he seeks to redress his wrongs by arranging a play at court, in the course of which he executes his enemies. Hieronymo's entertainment before the Spanish king is far more drastic than anything ever played before an English monarch, yet it is typically Tudor in its premise. Queen Elizabeth's playwrights shared Hieronymo's assumption that the action of a play could decisively alter the course of real events. This book concerns one major species of Elizabethan political drama: the plays that wrestle with the problem of the succession and with the very principles by which government and authority are perpetuated. From the death of Henry VIII to the accession of James I dispute over the succession to the English crown was a principal focus of political instability and unease. During this period, certain lines of legal dispute and public polemic formed a clear and strong tradition, nourishing a vigorous political drama.

In asking the reader to view a line of plays - from *Gorboduc* to *King Lear* - as the medium for speculation and protest, as testing ground for political ideas and situations, I do not mean to devalue the drama to the coinage of propaganda. My purpose is, rather, to recover its contemporary engagement. How could a court as wise and witty as Queen Elizabeth's sit through *Gorboduc*? Many of the court saw it twice. The case of *Gorboduc,* originally played at the Inner Temple and later taken to court, epitomizes the common aspiration of both coterie and popular theatres - the bid for royal audience. Men of law and popular dramatists were alike, too, in their anxiety for the future of England, governed for the first time since before the Conquest by a virgin queen. In formulating advice and offering criticism, in raising ghosts of ancient British kings to lend authority to their arguments or to play out exemplary tragedies, these lawyers had the advantage of their professional training and concerns. In particular, they thought a great deal about the nature of kingship. The circumstances of the Reformation, the antecedent body of ecclesiastical law, the shifts in land ownership relating to the crown, the peculiar circumstances of the Tudor succession were all factors which helped to shape their theories of kingship and to popularize them.

Since Ernst Kantorowicz first drew attention to Shakespeare's use of the theory of the king's two bodies, aspects of Shakespeare's work have been freshly interpreted. In the past few years some familiarity with this Tudor 'doctrine' has become a *sine qua non* for the writer on

Shakespeare's 'political' plays. The time is ripe for an historically based account of why and how this doctrine was so necessary to the Elizabethans. My argument is, briefly, that the development and popularization of the theory are inextricably connected with the Elizabethan succession question, with its polemics and with its reflection in dramatic art. To my knowledge, this observation has not been made before; nor have its important implications been explored. In this book I have tried to bring together the necessary primary material to explain and illustrate how an originally esoteric legal concept became popularized, and how it influenced the themes and conventions of a particular tradition of Elizabethan drama.

The king's two bodies will never, of course, 'explain' a play - even a minor one, but the notion may often elucidate themes, iconography and dramatic techniques not otherwise apparent to a twentieth-century audience. It is with this limited purpose that I have selected the material and have approached some of the notable formal features of the period's drama, such as double plots and the use of twinned characters. Several scholars have seen that 'the king's two bodies', by exalting the immortal and unerring powers of the monarch's body politic, could be used to flatter the incumbent ruler. The element of criticism implicit in the use of the theory has received less attention.

'The king's two bodies' was never a *fact,* nor did it ever attain the status of orthodoxy; it remained a controversial idea. The idea seemed, for a limited historical span, to express a precarious balance of power between the king and the state. This balance could be redefined with each fresh application of the theory to a contemporary situation, to historical or even to fictional example. It follows that a dramatist aware of the terms of the controversy need not be tied to any fixed attitude towards specific issues. Of all the media - lawsuit, parliamentary debate, political pamphlet, stageplay - the stage offered the freest forum for speculation about the succession to the throne and the issues related to it. Drama, far from reiterating homilies and political truisms (which is what many modern scholars would have us believe it did), was, in fact, by virtue of its form and social ambience, ideally suited to *question* the validity of any conceptual explanation of human behaviour. In the best plays of the period between *Gorboduc* and *King Lear* it is precisely the tension between theory and enactment, between ideal political behaviour and the actuality of human life, which compels our lasting interest.

Some of the plays and historical material which I discuss will be familiar to the reader; this is inevitable in any treatment of facts and ideas which concerned Shakespeare. Some texts, like Thomas Pound's two Lincoln's Inn masques, I print from manuscript for the first time. Wherever possible I have used manuscript sources or the earliest printed editions. My synthesis of old and new evidence is intended to provide a fresh perspective on plays, many of which have been much discussed by other writers: *Gorboduc,* Kyd's *Spanish Tragedy,* Greene's *James IV,* Shakespeare's *Comedy of Errors, Henry V,* and *King Lear.* For its intrinsic interest and for its bearing on my main theme, I also discuss Shakespeare's *Phoenix and the Turtle,* placing it in its original context (Robert Chester's *Love's Martyr,* 1601) as the crowning achievement in a collection of political poems. Specific debts are recorded in the footnotes, the most pervasive influences are more like the air one breathes. This study began under the guidance of Muriel C. Bradbrook in 1962, and my debt to her work and knowledge is a lasting one. Leo Salingar has helped me with his perceptive advice. The sympathetic criticism and unstinting scholarly help of Geoffrey Elton have brought this book to completion.

My research was generously supported at various stages by a Fellowship from the American Association of University Women, by Girton College, and by the University of Cambridge.

This book has been the result of a constant and happy collaboration with my husband, Richard. In many ways it is his as well as mine.

Marie Axton
Cambridge 1977

PREFATORY NOTES AND LIST OF ABBREVIATIONS

The Elizabethan year began on 25 March; dates between 1 January and 24 March are indicated with the Elizabethan year, followed by the modern, thus: January 1561/2. Unless otherwise stated Shakespeare quotations are from *The Complete Works,* ed. Peter Alexander; records of election to Parliament from *Parliaments of England 1213-1702* (London, 1878); information about admissions to the Inns of Court from the manuscript and published admission volumes listed in the Primary Sources.

I have retained original spelling in all quotations; standard contractions are silently expanded, other expansion is indicated by italics.

The following abbreviations are used.

BB	*The Records of . . . Lincoln's Inn: The Black Books*
BL	British Library
CIT	*A Calendar of Inner Temple Records*
CSP Rome	*Calendar of State Papers, Rome*
CSP Scot.	*Calendar of State Papers, Scotland*
CSP Span.	*Calendar of State Papers, Spanish: Elizabeth*
Chambers, *ES*	E.K. Chambers, *Elizabethan Stage*
EECT	*Early English Classical Tragedies*
EETS	Early English Text Society
EHP	Irving Ribner, *The English History Play*
Feuillerat, Edward VI & Mary	*Documents Relating to the Revels at Court in the Time of King Edward VI and Queen Mary,* ed. Albert Feuillerat
Feuillerat, Eliz.	*Documents Relating to the Office of Revels in the Time of Queen Elizabeth*
GI	Gray's Inn
Hall's *Chronicle*	Edward Hall, *The union of the two noble and illustre famelies of York and Lancaster*
HLQ	*Huntington Library Quarterly*
IT	Inner Temple

JEGP	*Journal of English and Germanic Philology*
KTB	Ernst Kantorowicz, *The King's Two Bodies*
LI	Lincoln's Inn
MLN	*Modern Language Notes*
MSR	Malone Society Reprints
MT	Middle Temple
MTR	*Middle Temple Records*
Neale, *Eliz.*	J.E. Neale, *Queen Elizabeth*
Neale, *Parliaments 1559-81*	J.E. Neale, *Elizabeth I and Her Parliaments 1559-81*
Neale, *Parliaments 1584-1601*	J.E. Neale, *Elizabeth I and Her Parliaments 1584-1601*
Nichols, *Eliz.*	John Nichols, *The Progresses of Queen Elizabeth*
N & Q	*Notes and Queries*
PMLA	*Publications of the Modern Languages Association*
RES	*Review of English Studies*
SP	State Papers: Public Record Office
SQ	*Shakespeare Quarterly*
SS	*Shakespeare Survey*

                  since your sacred Maiestie
In gratious hands the regall Scepter held
All Tragedies are fled from state, to stadge.

1

THE INNS OF COURT AND THEIR REVELS

Queen Elizabeth's presence at a marriage masque on 1 July 1566 transformed a traditional epithalamion into fine-edged criticism. She was accompanied by the Spanish Ambassador who tried in the course of supper and the succeeding entertainments to elicit the Queen's reactions to the birth of Mary Stuart's son. The young lawyers who danced before the Queen may well have envied the Ambassador's proximity, since they, too, were impatient with their Queen whose disinclination for matrimony and childbearing was becoming notorious.

As 'ambassadors' from Juno, Pallas, Venus and Diana, these masquers entered the Hall to bestow Venus's golden apple, the prize for beauty. The presenter, Thomas Pound, (cousin of the Catholic Earl of Southampton) took upon himself the task of Paris. Surveying the distinguished audience he pronounced cool judgement: the bride is the most beautiful lady in the Hall because she has fulfilled her destiny in marriage; even Diana, goddess of chastity, concurs. This snub to the Queen, so blandly indirect, never found its way into Nichols's *Progresses,* the compendium of courtly entertainments, but remained in manuscript, escaping scholarly attention.[1] The Lincoln's Inn masque which coerces Elizabeth with superior 'Olympian' authority is one forgotten episode in a continuous tradition of political criticism in drama. During her first untried years, outspoken political advice proliferated. England was divided by religion. Parliament, called in 1559, had passed legislation which re-established England as a Protestant power; it pressed the Queen to marry. But her choice of consort had been complicated by its very legislation since the most eligible monarchs of Europe were, like Mary Tudor's detested Philip, Catholic. Parliament met royal resistance whenever marriage and the succession were discussed; Elizabeth deemed these prerogative matters. The same Parliament men, however, found times when Elizabeth would permit the succession to be debated; these occasions, whose licence for advice was even greater than that of the royal entry, were the Christmas entertainments of the Inns of Court. [2]

---

1 Bodley MS Rawlinson Poet 108.

2 George R. Kernodle, *From Art to Theatre* (Chicago, 1944), pp.133-53 suggests the lawyers' debt to civic pageant tradition. For discussion of that tradition see Sydney Anglo, *Spectacle, Pageantry and Early Tudor Policy* (Oxford, 1969); Ernest Talbert, *The Problem of Order* (Chapel Hill, 1962); David Bergeron, *English Civic Pageantry 1558-1642* (London, 1971).

Considerable danger lurked in the lawyers' entertainments. Members of the privy council and judges from the courts at Westminster were often distinguished guests at these revels, and the lawyers regularly performed before their sovereign at court. Mutual involvement of audience and entertainers in the government of England encouraged Inns of Court men to use plays as analogies for political situations created by eminent members of the audience.

During the reign of Henry VIII a lawyer-dramatist and several actors were punished for their part in Christmas celebrations, which began on 25 December 1526 and lasted into January 1526/7, when Gray's Inn acted a play for the King and members of his Council. The author was a man of legal prominence, Serjeant Roo. Archbishop Warham wrote on 6 February that he was sorry such a matter should be taken in earnest and Mr. Roo committed to the Tower for making a play.[1] Both John Foxe and the chronicler Edward Hall agreed that the unsettling impact stemmed from the play's contemporary relevance, though they did not agree about the purpose of its performance. Hall, a member of Gray's Inn, claims it was an old play, refurbished for the occasion, but that Cardinal Wolsey, imagining that it had been designed specially to discredit him, imprisoned Roo and the actors.[2] Foxe brings in current political issues, while insisting that the play was not conceived as an exact reflection of contemporary people or events.[3] Holinshed tells his Elizabethan readers Hall's version of the Gray's Inn incident and adds his own tribute to the political power of the play. 'But what will you have of a guiltie conscience but to suspect all things to be said of him (as if all the world knew his wickednesse) according to the old verse: Conscius ipse sibi de se putat omnia dici'.[4]

Queen Elizabeth understood this tradition when she saw herself as Richard II. Her famous remark 'I am Richard the Second. Know ye not that?' was made to William Lambarde, a distinguished jurist of Lincoln's Inn, and its context makes clear that both Elizabeth and Lambarde saw the play's relevance to the Earl of Essex's rebellion.[5]

As dramatists the lawyers were interested primarily in law, policy and theory. Their masques and plays were socially related to their professional interests. For this reason one can trace in their entertain-

1 SP 1/40 fol. 25.

2 Hall's *Chronicle,* ed. Henry Ellis (London, 1809), p.719.

3 *The Acts and Monuments of John Foxe,* ed. Josiah Pratt (London, 1870), IV, 657, 763.

4 Raphael Holinshed, *Chronicles of England, Scotland and Ireland,* ed. Henry Ellis, III (London, 1807), 714.

5 Nichols, *Eliz.*, III, 552-3.

ments the peculiar impress of contemporary law and theory with unusual clarity. They used fictional or historical play situations much as they would use legal precedents. But these amateur dramatists shared their techniques and belief in the power of the stage with greater writers, some of whom trained at the Inns. Although the Inns' drama touched contemporary problems of state it seems unlikely that the Elizabethan lawyers directly impersonated contemporary politicians. If they differed in this from the practice of civic pageantry, in which children frequently impersonated living royalty, it was perhaps because their own licence for criticism was correspondingly greater and required a greater tact.[1] In 1597/8 a Christmas reveller at the Middle Temple called himself Erophilus 'in sawcy imitation of the great Earle of the time', but at the Inns this sort of thing was apparently the exception rather than the rule.[2] Serjeant Roo and his more careful successors saw in dramatic illusion both a sword and shield. Their plays dealt with issues and situations rather than personalities, and while leaving themselves latitude to escape censure they expected their audience might, as Roo's had, provide the relevant contemporary context for an allegory. Such technique was not, however, confined to allegories; 'Senecan' plays of the 1560s invited the same kind of informed collaboration. Although Elizabethan drama was often political and sometimes vigorously polemical in its function, theatrical conventions developed during this century were a protection to playwrights and performers. To my knowledge the Queen punished no Inns of Court dramatist or actor for displeasing her or her government with a play.[3]

The lawyers' success as political dramatists may be partly due to the particular training they received. During the legal terms they

1 Children impersonated the Pope, Cardinal Wolsey and the French and English kings in a court play on 10 November 1527 and regularly did so in royal entries. Hall's *Chronicle,* p.735.

2 *Le Prince d'Amour* (London, 1660), p.89. An early manuscript version gives the name as Exophilus, leaving no doubt which Earl was intended. However Erophilus was the name of the knight in Francis Bacon's entertainment presented by Essex to Elizabeth in 1596. See 'Noctes Templariae' BL Harley 1576 fols. 556-62, and Francis Bacon, *The Works,* ed. James Spedding *et al,* VIII (London, 1862), p.375.

3 Offences during the reign of Elizabeth are of a different sort. For instance: Recorder Fleetewoode writes to Lord Burghley on 19 January 1582/3 describing the 'great riott' committed by several gentlemen of the Inns of Chancery and one Light, a 'tyrannicall yowthe' indicted for 'singing in the churche vpon Childermas day fallantida dillie &c' (Malone Society *Collections 1:2,* Oxford, 1908, p.160). At Christmas they were complained of as common disturbers of the peace, night walkers, breakers of glass windows. Unruly behaviour was punished by the Inns themselves. See Lincoln's Inn, 1590 (*BB*, II, 16); Middle Temple, 1589/90 and 1590/1 (*MTR*, I, 318, 326-7).

followed judicial business while in the vacations they pursued an informal programme of liberal arts in which learning by imitation led quite naturally to dramatic productions.

Sir John Fortescue, Chief Justice of the King's Bench, described the social composition and educational programme of the Inns as he knew them in the late fifteenth century. Later writers confirm the continuity of traditions sketched by Fortescue, but stress the increasing number of commoners trained at the Inns in the sixteenth and seventeenth centuries.[1] It seems clear that in the Tudor period there was a predominance of what Fortescue's Elizabethan translator called 'gentlemen borne and come of noble stocke'.[2] Men who entered an Inn, if they took the opportunities before them, followed a practical course of legal study dependent on the proximity of the courts of common law:

> The same lawes [of England] are taught & learned in a certain place of publique or comen study more conuenient & apte for attaining to the knowledge of them, then anye other vniuersitie. For this place of study is situate nighe to the kingez courtes where the same lawes are pleaded and argued, & iudgementes by the same geeuen by iudges menne of grauytie, auncient in yeares, perfecte and graduate in the same lawes. Wherefore euery daye in courte [i.e. during term] the studentes in those lawes resorte by greate numbers vnto those courtes, wherein the same lawes are redde & taughte as it were in common scholes. This place of study is set betwene the place of the said courtz & the Citie of London. . . not situate within the citie, where the confluence of people might disturbe the quietnes of the studentes but somewhat seueral in the suburbes of the same Citie, and nigher to the saide courtes, that the studentes maye daylye at theire pleasure haue accesse and recourse thether without weariness. . .there bee. . . tenne lesser housez or ynnes & sometimes moe, whyche are called ynnes of the Chauncery. And to euerie one of them belongeth a C studients at the least, & to some of them a muche greater nomber, though they bee not euer all together in the same. These studentes, for the most part of them, are yong men, lerning or studying the originals, & as it were the elements of the law, who profiting therein, as they growe to rypenes, so are they admitted into the greater ynnes of the same study, called ynnes of court. Of the whiche greater ynnes there are .iiii. in number. [Lincoln's Inn, Gray's Inn, Inner Temple, Middle Temple]. And to the lest of them beelongeth in fourme aboue mentioned twooe hundrethe Studentes or thereaboutes. . .in these greter ynnes there can no studient be mainteined for lesse expenses by the years then xx markes. . .Now by reason of this charges the children onelye of noble menne do studye the lawes in those ynnes. For the poore and commen sorte

1 George Buc(k), *The Third Vniuersite of England,* printed in John Stow's *Annales* (London, 1631); Dugdale, *Origines Juridiciales.*

2 The social composition of the Inns is a subject of recent dispute. See E.W. Ives, 'The Common Lawyers in Pre-Reformation England', *Transactions of the Royal Historical Society,* 5th ser. XVIII (1968), 157, and Wilfred Prest, *The Inns of Court under Elizabeth I and the early Stuarts 1590-1640* (London, 1972).

> of the people are not hable to beare so greate charges for the
> exhibition of theire children. And marchaunt menne can seeledoome
> fynde in theire heartes to hynder theire marchandise with so greate
> yerly expense. And thus it falleth out that there is scant any
> manne founde within the roialm skilfull and connynge in the lawes,
> excepte hee bee a gentleman borne, and come of a noble stocke...[1]

Some men entered the Inns with the primary intention of learning
and practising law as did Thomas Norton (IT 1555) and Francis
Bacon (GI 1576). Social and political reasons seem to have governed
the entries of some of the Elizabethan peers: Robert Dudley
(IT 1561), William, Lord Howard of Effingham (IT 1561), Henry, Lord
Hunsdon (IT 1561),Walter Devereux (IT 1562), Henry Wriothesley, Earl
of Southampton (LI 1565/6), Robert Devereux, Earl of Essex (IT
1588). However, Edward Manners, third Earl of Rutland (LI 1567)
is said to have become proficient in the common law. Thomas
Howard, fourth Duke of Norfolk (GI 1560) did not; writing from
the Tower in 1571/2 to give his last advice to his son Philip, Norfolk
reflects upon the advantages for a nobleman of membership of an Inn
and regrets that he failed to profit by his own:

> If after a year or two you spend your time in some house of the
> law, there is nothing that will prove more to your commodity,
> considering how for the time you shall have continued business
> about your own law affairs; and thereby also, if you spend your
> time well, you shall be ever better able to judge in your own
> causes. I too late repent that I followed not this course that now
> I wish to you, for if I had then my case perchance had not been
> in so ill state as now is.[2]

Christopher Hatton (IT 1559) and Walter Raleigh (MT 1574) were
commoners for whom an Inn provided a suitable entrée into Elizabeth's court. Fortescue describes the multiple advantages the vacation
learning offered such men. Between terms they studied chronicles and
became adept in the arts of the nobility:

> And to speake vprightly there is in these greater ynnes, yea and in
> the lesser too, besyde the study of the lawes, as it were an vniuersitie
> or schole of all commendable qualities requisite for noble men.
> There they learne to singe, and to exercise themselfes in all kinde
> of armony. There also they practise daunsing, and other noble
> mennes pastimes, as they use to doe which are brought vppe in the
> kinges house. On the woorkyedayes the moste parte of them
> applye themselues to the studye of the lawe. And on the holye-
> dayes to the studie of the holye scripture: and out of the tyme
> of diuine seruice to the readynge of chronicles. For there in deed

[1] *A Learned Commendation of the Politique Lawes of England* (London,
1567), fols. 112-14v. Fortescue wrote the work *c.*1467-71. Robert Mulcaster's
translation is printed with the parallel Latin text and dedicated to John
Walshe, Justice of the Common Pleas.

[2] Neville Williams, *Thomas Howard, Fourth Duke of Norfolk* (1964), p.240.

are vertues studyed, and all vices exiled. So that for the endowement
of vertue, and abandoning of vice Knightes and Barons, with other
states and noble menne of the roialme place theire children in those
ynnes, though they desire not to haue them learned in the lawes,
nor to lyue by the practise therof, but only vpon their fathers
allowance.   (fol. 114v-15)

Nicholas Bacon had urged Henry VIII to employ his common lawyers as ambassadors and diplomats. They were well qualified for such
positions of trust not only because they might replace the hitherto
indispensable prelates but because social and artistic accomplishments
acquired at the Inns fitted them for service in royal courts:

> The Readers and Benchers at a Parliament or Pension held before
> Christmas. . .appoint and choose certain of the house to be Officers,
> and bear certain rules in the house during the said time, which
> Officers for the most part are such, as are exercised in the King's
> Highness house, and other Noble men, and this done onely to the
> intent, that they should in time to come know how to use
> themselves. In this Christmas time, they have all manner of
> pastimes, as singing and dancing; and in some of the houses
> ordinarily they have some interlude or Tragedy played by the
> Gentlemen of the same house, the ground, and matter whereof,
> is devised by some of the Gentlemen of the house. [1]

At Christmas the lawyers created a miniature kingdom and chose a
monarch in direct imitation of the government at Whitehall. But
unlike its French counterpart this government terminated at the
beginning of Lent. The French law clerks maintained a permanent and
comprehensive administration, organized as a small kingdom, the
Basoche, which regulated every aspect of their professional lives. The
Basoche had judicial machinery with real though limited power to regu-
late disputes among its members; it was an actual court of appeal for
tradesmen with complaints against law clerks. The English Inns
created regal and judicial courts at Christmas, but the trials held in
their Constable's Court were more like the French *causes grasses,* mock
trials which, in Paris, occurred at carnival time. In these French carnival
trials legal procedure was imitated exactly; humour and frivolity arose
from the absurdity of the case to be tried with such solemnity. Details
of two such English trials survive; both 'law suits' arose directly from
Christmas misrule and were thematically linked with the season's revels.[2]

[1] Bacon's plan is printed in E. Waterhouse, *A Commentary upon Fortescue*
(London, 1663), p.546. John Ramsey's commonplace book contains entries for
his years at the Middle Temple (he entered on 23 March 1606 at the age of 26)
which illustrate those extra-legal studies outlined by Fortescue and Bacon. Ramsey
lists the principal offices of England whose duties were enacted in the Christmas
games; he jots down lyrics without music, 'setts of Madrigalls for violls &
voyces', two pages of steps for 'practise for Dauncinge', then 'Songs and
Dittyes to the Lute and viol de gambo'. 'De vita mea' Bodley MS Douce 280
fols. 193v-194.

[2] The first is in the *Gesta Grayorum* (1594/5) ed. W.W. Greg MSR (1915); the

The tragedies and interludes to which Bacon refers were conceived in the same spirit as the Christmas trials; they were noblemen's pastimes; they, too, constituted sixteenth-century service to a prince. Beyond the obvious niceties of service, cup-bearing and the etiquette of dining in state these Christmas revels gave young lawyers and noblemen practice in the arts of giving counsel on political questions of the day. What is more, within the comfortable and urbane confines of the Inns, imitation provided an important outlet; during the reign of Elizabeth the revels dealt with problems on which the lawyers, in their professional capacity, had been silenced. Two of these plays written during Elizabeth's reign have survived in manuscript; five were printed; of these, three were certainly performed for Elizabeth as were most of the recorded masques.

No texts of earlier Inns of Court entertainments have been certainly identified as such, though a number of the early interludes may have originated at the Inns. It has proved impossible to reconstruct the early history of these legal societies and their customs because many Inns of Court books were burned in Wat Tyler's rebellion.[1] In the fifteenth century professional entertainers came to the Inns at Christmas: Furnival's Inn paid Thomas Thwaits 6s 8d for a Christmas interlude in 1412;[2] by 1498 professionals are clearly distinguished as 'waytes, ministrallis', the Prince's players ('lusoribus') and a singer for a carol at Christmas. Information about the lawyers' own creative mimesis is equally slender. Lincoln's Inn chose officers for Christmas revels in 1455; Inns of Court men participated in a tournament in 1467 by royal command.[3] Appointment of a Christmas Marshal and Master of the Revels seems to have been customary by the time the Middle Temple records begin in 1501 and the Inner Temple records in 1505.

If Serjeant Roo wrote his play twenty years before it caused Wolsey such alarm in 1526/7, as Hall suggests, then there was original drama written by the lawyers during the reign of Henry VII. John Rastell, his son William, John Heywood and Sir Thomas More

second the Middle Temple *Prince d'Amour* (see p.3 n 2), discussed by Philip J. Finkelpearl, *John Marston of the Middle Temple* (Cambridge, Mass., 1969) ch. iv; Desmond Bland discusses the *Gesta* in his edition (Liverpool, 1968).

1 William Dugdale, *Origines Juridiciales* (London, 1666) p.145; Holinshed, *Chronicles,* II, 738.

2 A seventeenth-century transcript preserves this information; it is edited by D.S. Bland, *Early Record of Furnival's Inn* (Newcastle upon Tyne, 1957), p.24. See also Bland, 'Interludes in Fifteenth-Century Revels at Furnival's Inn' *RES,* n.s. III (1952), 263-8.

3 The *Black Books* of Lincoln's Inn begin in 1422 and are the earliest surviving original documents. *BB,* I, 1, 16, 45, 119.

were Inns of Court men, though performances of the surviving interludes of their circle have not yet been traced at the Inns.[1]

The first Christmas Prince whose reign can be enjoyed in any detail is George Ferrers, an eminent, practising lawyer. Ferrers, of Lincoln's Inn, reigned at court as Lord of Misrule to Edward VI. His revels at court are remembered in Holinshed's *Chronicle* as 'learned', and it would seem that this Christmas Prince benefited from just such preparation as Bacon had outlined. Ferrers, together with Baldwin, Sackville and Blenerhasset, is among the best known authors of the *Mirror for Magistrates.* His activities as Lord of Misrule to Edward in 1551/2 and again in 1552/3 suggest a continuum between the court and Inns revels. His appointment came in the midst of an active legal and political career. He had received a bachelor's degree in canon law from Cambridge in 1531; in 1534 he translated Magna Carta and entered Lincoln's Inn. Parliamentary service followed when he was elected burgess for Plymouth and continued under both Mary and Elizabeth. His record of authorship shows the integration of legal, historical and poetic interests suggested by both Fortescue and Bacon. In addition to his translation and work on the *Mirror,* he was praised for writing tragedies and comedies, though only his contribution to the 1575 Kenilworth entertainments seems to have survived.

Ferrers's triumphal progress through London during two successive Christmases was remarked by the London merchant Henry Machyn. In 1551/2 Ferrers landed at Tower Wharf and progressed with his huge company of retainers who drew after them a cart with instruments of punishment - the pillory, axe, gibbet and stocks.[2] Similar items figure in the Elizabethan Inns of Court revels.[3] When they reached the scaffold in Cheap a trumpeter, herald, and doctor of law proclaimed the lineage of the revels Prince, listing his titles. A hogshead of wine was broached; Ferrers and his council drank, and wine was offered to the assembled citizens. From Ferrers's letters to Cawarden (Edward's

---

1 R.J. Schoeck has worked for some time in this period: 'Sir Thomas More and Lincoln's Inn Revels', *Philological Quarterly,* XXIX (1950), 426-30; 'A Fool to Henry VIII at Lincoln's Inn', *MLN,* LXVI (1951), 506-9; 'Satire of Wolsey in Heywood's "Play of Love" ', *N & Q,* CXCVI (1951), 112-14; 'Christmas Revels at the Inns of Court', *N & Q,* CXCVII (1952) 226-9; 'The Date of *The Replication of a Serjeant-at-Law',* Law Quarterly Review, LXXVI (1960), 500-3. See also D.S. Bland, 'Wolsey and Drama at the Inns of Court', *N & Q,* CXCVI (1951), 512-13.

2 *The Diary of Henry Machyn,* ed. J.G. Nichols, Camden Soc. XLII (1848), p.13.

3 Sydney Anglo (*Spectacle, Pageantry* pp.306-17) may exaggerate the sinister implications of the customary revels instruments of punishment which were also used in *Gesta* and *Prince d'Amour.*

Master of the Revels) it appears that for Christmas 1552/3 he planned to send a herald and an ambassador to Greenwich to Edward VI, and to conduct a royal entry on St. Stephen's day by water in a barge decked with his colours. He asked Cawarden to dress up his attendants, at least six counsellors in addition to 'a diuine, a philosopher, an astronomer, a poet, a phisician, a potecarie, a Mr. of requestes, a sivilian [civil lawyer], a disard, two gentlmen vshers besides Iuglers, tomblers, fools, friers & suche other'. Ferrers enumerates his counsellors as 'Chauncellor, Treasorer, Comptroller, Vizchamberlaine', other officers as Admiral, Master of the Horse, and Almoner. Together they entertained Edward with a joust on hobby horses, a hunt and a 'play of cupid'.[1] Evidence has so far seemed too slight to allow more than a few conjectures about the political import of these revels. Ferrers's heraldic device was the holly bush and his motto *Semper Ferians*. In Elizabethan revels the blazoning of the Prince's revels arms was a focal point providing a key to the themes and political relevance of the entertainments. Ferrers's Divine, Master Streamer, delivered a satirical oration recalled (and probably written) by William Baldwin. The puzzling little book *Beware the Cat* (*c.*1553, pr.1570), which is the source of this last piece of information, is set during these revels and its political allegory remains to be unravelled.[2] The close link between Ferrers and Baldwin during these revels and the writing of *The Mirror for Magistrates* suggests an early continuity between these Christmas Princes and the player kings of the later Elizabethan historical drama. It is striking that all the texts of late Elizabethan and early Jacobean Christmas reigns have titles in the style of the chronicle history tradition of the *Mirror*. The *Gesta Grayorum* was announced as the 'History of the high and mighty Prince Henry, Prince of Purpoole, who reigned and died A.D.1594'; the Middle Temple revels of 1597/8 were called 'A briefe chronicle of the dark reigne of the Bright Prince of Burning Love'. Within the revels occasion, then, there were degrees of imitation; the Christmas Prince and his court received ambassadors and dubbed knights, staged councils where the Prince was advised how to rule, received news of rebellion, sat in judgement, waged war; the levels of illusion and reality multiplied as these Christmas 'statesmen' watched a play, or when they took that play to Whitehall and danced before the Tudor monarch.

Motives, beyond the sheer delight of revelling, cannot always be recovered but it is worth reiterating that neither Serjeant Roo nor George Ferrers were students indulging in impromptu larks. They were

1   Feuillerat, *Edward VI & Mary,* pp.89-94.
2   *Beware the Cat,* ed. William P. Holden (New London, 1963).

trained, practising men of law. Ferrers's services had been engaged by the council headed by John Dudley, Duke of Northumberland (IT 1510/11), a man who passed on to his fifth son a lively appreciation of the possibilities of art and politics. This son, Lord Robert Dudley, entered the Inner Temple in 1561 and was chosen by the members of his father's Inn to rule their Christmas kingdom. His revels officers for Christmas 1561/2 included five of the actual governors of the Temple who took it upon themselves to be Dudley's Lord Chancellor, Lord Treasurer, Lord Privy Seal, Chief Justice of the Common Pleas, and Chief Baron of the Exchequer. With little exaggeration these men may be likened to a shadow cabinet. Though Dudley did not achieve his ambition to be king of England, he became governor-general of the Netherlands; the revels Chancellor Richard Onslow was named Speaker of the House of Commons in 1566; Roger Manwood, revels Chief Baron of the Exchequer, was raised to that office in Elizabeth's government in 1578. Dudley's Master of the Game, Christopher Hatton, found favour with Elizabeth almost immediately, and his long career of service culminated in his appointment as Chancellor of England in 1577. These revellers were ambitious men with a shrewd appreciation of the possibilities of imitation; the matter which they treated in 'play' affected the government, safety and future of the realm.

2

SUCCESSION DEBATE AND THE THEORY OF THE QUEEN'S TWO BODIES

The situation throughout Elizabeth's reign was unprecedented: a virgin queen and no immediate heir to the throne. If Elizabeth died childless the crown would go to Mary Stuart, Queen of Scots, according to accepted custom, since she was the heir of the eldest sister of Henry VIII. However, Parliament had given Henry permission to alter the customary succession by his last will, provided this was signed by his own hand. Henry had left a will decreeing that if his own children died without issue the crown should *not* pass to the Stuarts, issue of his eldest sister, but to the Suffolk line, issue of his younger sister. The legal validity of this will was hotly contested. Thus the English succession seemed to be tangled in the coils of law, and England's future apparently lay in the hands of its common lawyers.

Elizabeth, however, made it clear that her lawyers were not to have a *public* voice in the matter. The French Ambassador reported in 1566:

> As for handling the succession, not one of them [her subjects] should do it; she would reserve that for herself. She had no desire to be buried alive, like her sister. Well she knew how people at that time had flocked to her at Hatfield: she wanted no such journeyings in her reign. Nor had she the slightest wish for their counsel on this subject. [1]

The men who felt themselves best able to determine the points of law upon which the nation's future depended were, in their professional capacity, admonished to silence. In the first decade of Elizabeth's reign Mary Stuart and Catherine Grey, the two principal claimants to the throne, were embroiled in legal controversies which might cancel their respective claims. Because both women were so close to the crown neither the disputed marriage of Catherine Grey nor the murder of Henry Stuart, King of Scots, ever came to a free or satisfactory trial. It is not surprising that these two treasonous acts were among those reflected in the plays presented at the Inns of Court.

The Proclamation of 16 May 1559 prohibited plays dealing with matters of religion and also with the 'gouernaunce of the estate of the common weale'. It affirmed that religion and government were 'no meete matters to be wrytten or treated vpon, but by menne of

---

1 La Forêt to Charles IX, 21 October 1566. This is Sir John Neale's paraphrase of a letter in possession of the publisher John Murray; it is printed in Neale, *Parliaments, 1559-81* (London, 1953), p.136.

aucthoritie, lerning and wisedome', nor could they be shown before any audience, but 'graue and discreete persons'.[1] The Inns' plays apparently met both requirements. With gravity and discretion these gentlemen dramatized their dangerous matter in such a way that their loyalty to the monarch seemed never to be in question. In developing their own distinctive kind of politic criticism (which should not be mistaken for offensive or treasonously personal criticism) they made a typically legalistic distinction between the private and public capacities of the monarch. The elaboration of this distinction and its technical and metaphorical language are of the greatest importance to the succession controversy and to the development of techniques of political drama during the reign.

Legal thought and language were in a curious state at this time. For years before the break with Rome, English common lawyers had been borrowing theological concepts and vocabulary to describe the powers of the king and country. Henry VIII's break with Rome served to accelerate this trend. By the beginning of Elizabeth's reign common lawyers had developed a theory about the monarch and state that is best understood as the secularization of a religious concept.

The lawyers were formulating an idea of the state as a perpetual corporation, yet they were unable or unwilling to separate state and monarch. Their concept of the king's two bodies was an attempt to deal with a paradox: men died and the land endured; kings died, the crown survived; individual subjects died but subjects always remained to be governed. Perhaps the lawyers were unwilling to envisage England itself as a perpetual corporation because the law had always vested land in a person. Anyway, for the purposes of law it was found necessary by 1561 to endow the Queen with two bodies: a *body natural* and a *body politic*. (This body politic should not be confused with the old metaphor of the realm as a great body composed of many men with the king as head. The ideas are related but distinct.) The body politic was supposed to be *contained within the natural body of the Queen*. When lawyers spoke of this body politic they referred to a specific quality: the essence of *corporate perpetuity*. The Queen's natural body was subject to infancy, infirmity, error and old age; her body politic, created out of a combination of faith, ingenuity and practical expediency, was held to be unerring and immortal.

This peculiar identification of the nation with the person of the Queen has of course been recognized. What has not been so widely appreciated is that the symbolism and iconography specially pre-

1 Chambers, *ES,* IV, 263.

valent during Elizabeth's reign have an elaborate theoretical underpinning carefully constructed at the Inns of Court.

F.W. Maitland first called modern attention to the metaphor of the king's two bodies, which he found in a case decided in 1561.[1] He based his brief study on evidence in the *Reports* of Edmund Plowden published in 1571 and dismissed the subject as metaphysical nonsense.[2]

> The medieval king was every inch a king, but just for this reason he was every inch a man, and you did not talk nonsense about him. You did not ascribe to him immortality or ubiquity or such powers as no mortal can wield. If you said that he was Christ's Vicar, you meant what you said, and you might add that he would become the servant of the devil if he declined towards tyranny.[3]

Ernst Kantorowicz was not so dismissive; his work focuses on church ritual and canon law, the antecedents of this Tudor concept.[4] *The King's Two Bodies,* a study in medieval political theology, provides a sympathetic introduction. Kantorowicz has now been widely read and can be briefly cited and summarized:

> The tenet. . .of the Tudor jurists definitely hangs upon the Pauline language and its later development: the change from the Pauline *corpus Christi* to the medieval *corpus ecclesiae mysticum,* thence to the *corpus reipublicae mysticum* which was equated with the *corpus morale et politicum* of the commonwealth, until finally. . .the slogan emerged saying that every abbot was a 'mystical body' or a 'body politic', and that accordingly the king, too, was, or had, a body politic which 'never died'. Notwithstanding, therefore, some similarities with disconnected pagan concepts, the KING'S TWO BODIES is an offshoot of Christian theological thought and consequently stands as a landmark of Christian political theology.[5]

The concept was formed to meet a practical need when the Church first began to own and administer lands. Land laws were designed for property which passed from father to son, from man to man. It was perhaps to meet the requirements of these laws that ecclesiastical lawyers wrenched language to insist that, in spite of the demise of its mortal administrators, Church land always remained in possession of a body which resembled a human one in everything but mortality. In the

---

1 The *Duchy of Lancaster Case* was initiated during the reign of Mary Tudor but finally decided in 1561. The case was first printed in Plowden's *Reports* in 1571.

2 F.W. Maitland, 'The Crown as Corporation', *Collected Papers,* ed. H.A.L. Fisher (Cambridge, 1911), III, 249, 251.

3 *Collected Papers,* III, 19.

4 *The King's Two Bodies* (Princeton, 1957).

5 *KTB.* pp.19, 506.

courts where procedures were designed for trial of mortal landowners an abbot or a bishop could represent the mystical body; when one abbot died another was chosen. For the purpose of the law this body successively represented by mortal incumbents was, like Christ, impervious to the powers of time and change.

The realm, like the Church, was a curious aggregation of land and men whose powers and duration exceeded the limits of an individual life. From the earliest years of feudalism the land of the realm was vested in the king and theoretically governed by him. Common lawyers, deciding cases concerning the king and realm, gradually came to recognize the legal usefulness of a concept like the *corpus ecclesiae mysticum*. As Kantorowicz has shown, they began borrowing from theology as early as the twelfth century. The desire to borrow and develop the concept received a boost when Henry VIII appropriated abbey lands, and by the accession of Elizabeth the jurists were talking confidently about their monarch's two bodies. There were, of course, difficulties in adapting the theological notion to the state. An elaborate tradition of ritual and belief justified the Church's share in Christ's immortality. But there were no tenets in either law or theology stating plainly that Christ guaranteed immortality to England. There was only an analogy. Only by metaphor could the king impart immortality to the state and the state reciprocate the gift. Lacking an acknowledged tradition which would make their theory acceptable law, the lawyers attempted to cross the irrational abyss with a bridge of legal logic.

Kantorowicz sees the resultant political theology as an inevitable part of the process which led to the Puritan Revolution. He hears the first rumblings of the Revolution in the language of a judicial opinion of 1560: 'King is a Name of Continuance, which shall always endure as the Head and Governor of the People (as the Law presumes) as long as the People continue. . .and in this Name the King never dies'. He argues that from Plowden's language of 1560 it is only another step to the Puritan slogan, 'fighting the king to defend the King'.[1]

Kantorowicz's analysis of the effect of the theological concept on Tudor and Jacobean theory is suggestive. He notes that in the abdication scene of *Richard II* Shakespeare seems to show familiarity with the jurists' royal Christology. He offers a stimulating discussion of the scene, remarking that Shakespeare may have 'chanced upon the legal definition of kingship. . .when conversing with his friends at the

1 *KTB*, p.23. Kantorowicz is quoting from Plowden's *Reports* in the English translation of 1779.

Inns'.[1] It is not necessary to postulate so fortuitous a conversation to account for this familiarity, since, as I hope to show, the peculiar circumstances of Elizabeth's reign caused diffusion of this legal concept through quite popular channels of print. Kantorowicz, while offering valuable iconographical illustration to support his discussion of the later historical implications of the theory, did not explore the Elizabethan setting in any depth. He relied only on Plowden's *Reports* and assumed that the concept was part of the 'ordinary and conventional terminology of the English jurists of that period and of a generation to follow'.[2] It therefore seems relevant to supply these missing historical links and to consider in more detail the political circumstances in which the concept flourished.

Edmund Plowden (or Ployden, as it was often spelled) was acknowledged by his contemporaries to be one of England's most eminent common lawyers. His teaching and writings influenced students of the law throughout Elizabeth's reign; his influence in the succeeding reign is attested by Francis Bacon, Coke and Blackstone. Despite his remarkable abilities Plowden never became one of Elizabeth's officers or judges, for he was, and continued all his life to be, a convinced Roman Catholic. The Plowden family is said to have possessed a letter containing the religious reasons for Plowden's refusal of the Chancellorship.[3] Plowden's position and convictions were typical of a group of Elizabeth's most eminent subjects.

When she came to the throne, Elizabeth Tudor had in her courts of law the men appointed by her Catholic sister. The situation was delicate and, though the Vatican's informant Nicholas Sander (writing of the first year of Elizabeth's reign) colours the picture rather too vividly, his outline is accurate enough:

> All the judges that exercise criminal jurisdiction with one accord craved of the Queen to be relieved from the obligation to abjure the primacy of the Roman Pontiff, as otherwise, that oath being contrary to their conscience, they could not continue in office; and the Queen, not being able to find among her Lutherans men equal to the duties of this most important order, was fain of necessity to remit the oath.[4]

Edmund Plowden and many other men of his profession were seriously affected by the change of sovereign. Shortly before Queen

1 *KTB*, p.25.

2 *KTB*, p.20.

3 Henry Foley S.J., *Records of the English Province of the Society of Jesus*, IV (London, 1878), 539.

4 *CSP Rome 1558-71*, p.68.

Mary died she had called Plowden to the dignity of Queen's Serjeant at Law. This distinction meant that he would leave the Middle Temple where he had been teaching and become eligible for one of the important judicial posts in the Queen's government. In fact Elizabeth never confirmed Mary's writ and thus one of the ablest jurists of the sixteenth century remained in the Middle Temple, a practising lawyer, teacher and author. It may have been this decision of Elizabeth's which gave us Plowden's copious *Reports*. For, if his religion barred him from an important public position, it probably secured him the leisure needed for completion of his literary labour. Queen Elizabeth in fact retained most of her Catholic judges, but Plowden did not join their ranks.

Keeping in mind the peculiar position of many of the men appointed by Mary Tudor and retained in office to serve her Protestant sister, it becomes significant that Plowden, Anthony Brown, William Rastell and a number of the judges mentioned in Plowden's *Reports* - that is, the men who frequently used the concept of the king's two bodies - personally suffered from the demise of Queen Mary and from the political and religious innovations of her successor.[1] It is understandable that these men should seek to minimize the personal impact of the new sovereign and should emphasize the continuity of the monarchy in their professional work. The *Duchy of Lancaster Case*, decided in 1561, will serve as an example of the way in which the jurists used the theory of the king's two bodies to oppose the wishes of the Queen. The judges affirmed their allegiance by exalting the Queen's body politic while at the same time they frustrated the wishes of her body natural.

The *Duchy of Lancaster Case*, Maitland's first evidence for the existence of the king's two bodies, turns on the following issue. A portion of Duchy land had been granted by Edward VI to one of his subjects. Queen Elizabeth wanted to invalidate that grant and give the land to someone of her own choosing. The lawyers for the Queen argued that Edward's grant was invalid, because made when the king was under-age. By ordinary common law a minor could not grant land.

---

1 The Vatican informant, quoted above, states that Justice Dyer refused the office of Lord Chancellor, saying that he could not execute it in schism. He mentions William Rastell, Justice of the Common Pleas, as one who suffered particularly from the change of sovereigns (*CSP Rome 1558-71*, p.68). Though Plowden mentions Rastell as one of the judges who, in 1561, decided the *Duchy of Lancaster Case*, we know from the Spanish Ambassador (Ch. 4, p.45) that in 1561/2 Rastell chose exile rather than his position under Elizabeth. Anthony Browne, mentioned by Kantorowicz (pp.19, 20) as one of the judges who pushed the metaphor into the 'mystical regions', was demoted by Queen Elizabeth for his overzealous conviction of Protestants during the preceding reign; the Chief Justice of the Common Pleas thus became one of the ordinary judges of that court.

Dyer, Rastell and Browne opposed the Queen and upheld Edward's grant, insisting that the law for minors only applied to *bodies natural.* As king, Edward held within him the body politic; this body could never be under age. The judges' language and reasoning must be sampled to be believed:

> and altho' the natural Body of the King is subject to Infancy, yet when the Body politic is conjoined with it, and one Body is made of them both, the whole Body shall have all the Properties, Qualities and Degrees of the Body politic which is the greater and more worthy, and in which there is not nor can be any Infancy.[1]

The deceptively reasonable language of the law passes what can only be called a miracle:

> And the Person of the King. . .remains always of full Age as well with regard to Gifts and Grants of Lands made by him, as in the Administration of Justice. . .[2] By the common law no act that the King does as King shall be defeated by his nonage. For the King has in him two Bodies, viz. a Body natural, and a Body politic. His Body natural (if it be considered in itself) is a Body mortal, subject to all Infirmities that come by Nature or Accident, to the Imbecillity of Infancy or old Age, and to the like Defects that happen to the natural Bodies of other People. But his Body politic is a Body that cannot be seen or handled, consisting of Policy and Government, and constituted for the Direction of the People, and the Management of the publick-weal and this Body is utterly void of Infancy, and old Age, and other natural Defects and Imbecilities which the Body natural is subject to, and for this Cause what the King does in his Body politic cannot be invalidated or frustrated by any Disability in his natural Body. And therefore his Letters-patent which give Authority or Jurisdiction, or which give Lands or Tenements that he has as King, shall not be avoided by reason of his nonage.[3]

Immortality, perfection, ubiquity all seem to enhance the power of the monarch, but the decision really stresses the continuity of the monarch and reminds Elizabeth Tudor that as Queen she is bound to observe the grants made by the monarchs whose office she holds. Plowden tells us that the Queen in vain asked the judges several times to reverse their decision; but, despite royal pressure, they remained adamant.[4]

At a time when intelligent men worried about the fate of a land governed by a virgin queen, property law was particularly interesting. It was because the future stability of the realm seemed at stake during the succession controversy that a legal metaphor defining the relation-

[1] Edmund Plowden, *The Commentaries and Reports of Edmund Plowden, originally written in French, and now faithfully translated into English* (London, 1779), p.217.

[2] *Reports,* p.221.

[3] *Ibid.* p.213.

[4] *Ibid.* p.220.

ship between sovereign and perpetual state reached out beyond the courts of law to influence writers, polemicists and playwrights. The diffusion of this concept is my theme.

When Shakespeare in *1 Henry VI* set a fifteenth-century succession dispute in the garden of one of the Inns of Court he offered a scene equally familiar during Elizabeth's reign. From the lawyers' training at the Inns arguments and theory can be traced to the succession polemics of the period, to Parliament and to the stage. Through a succession treatise written by Edmund Plowden to support the Stuart claim the concept of the king's two bodies was brought to the attention of men outside the Inns.

In the autumn of 1566, as Parliament sought again, as it had in 1562/3, to move Elizabeth to name her successor, Mary Stuart heard of a succession debate which took place at Lincoln's Inn. Her claim, derived from Henry VIII's eldest sister, Margaret, was strong but she was a Catholic and a foreigner; and at Lincoln's Inn, as in the Suffolk tracts of 1563 and 1565, her title was unfavourably dismissed. She lodged an official protest with Elizabeth's privy council. Secretary Cecil had a word with the lawyers. Mary's Chancellor, Maitland of Lethington, wrote thanking the Secretary, interpreting his intervention as an indication that he favoured the Catholic Queen of Scots.[1] Maitland wrote again in January 1566/7 apparently in response to a request that he state clearly the arguments which might refute objections to Mary's foreign birth. The Scotsman referred Cecil to the English chronicles. The most telling argument, put forward rather tentatively in this letter, was that 'Manye lawes made for subjectes take no houlde in the case of the prince, and they have soch privileages as other persons enjoye not, as in cases of atteynders and other penall lawes'.[2] He went on to say that experts in the English common law could be called upon to explain the difference between the legal cases of a prince and a subject. That is exactly what happened.

In January after Parliament had again failed to bring the Queen to name a successor and had been dismissed, Edmund Plowden wrote a treatise supporting the claim of Mary Stuart. Prudence confined Plowden to manuscript and for this reason the tract is little known today and has only recently been rediscovered and identified.[3] Influential in its own time, it was praised in the seventeenth century

---

1 *CSP Scot. 1547-1603,* II (Edinburgh, 1900), p.304.

2 *The Egerton Papers,* ed. J. Payne Collier, Camden Soc. (London, 1840), pp.43-5.

3 See Axton, 'The Influence of Edmund Plowden's Succession Treatise', *HLQ.* XXXVII (1974), 209-26.

by Sir Matthew Hale as 'Mr. Plowden's learned tract touching the right of succession of Mary Queen of Scotland'.[1] Four manuscript copies are known of 'A treatise of the two Bodies of the king, vis. natural and politic. . .The whole intending to prove the title of Mary Quene of Scotts to the succession of the crown of England and that the Scots are not out of the allegiance of England'.[2] Here is a fresh document by Plowden, which Kantorowicz did not use, expounding the concept of the king's two bodies, designed to show Englishmen the difference between the legal cases of a monarch and those of his subjects. It sheds new light on the history of the legal metaphor and suggests that under the aegis of the succession controversy this technical concept was popularized.

The prologue to the Harley manuscript of the treatise shows that Plowden believed that he was the first common, or as he says 'temporall', lawyer to undertake a written defence of the Scottish Queen's title to the English crown. I have suggested elsewhere the process by which his arguments were simplified and adapted by his friend Sir Anthony Browne and published in 1569 by John Leslie, Mary Stuart's English Ambassador and chief polemicist.[3] In his first prologue Plowden writes for Browne, Justice of the Common Pleas, describing the reasons which have moved him to defy the Queen's wishes and give an opinion on the succession. At the same time he makes clear his own reluctance to publish.[4]

> Your earnest request cam to me of whom you (highly learned) haue conceived an opinion of learning in the temporall lawe greater than there is cause, earnestly moving me to showe unto you myn oppinion in the said pointe and that my knowledge might helpe you to conceive the righte way in this darke myste: And that for the more conceiving therof I woulde wryte to you the causes and reasons of the lawe approving thopinion I shoulde conceive. Your request being so earnest, your frendshipp so great, and your leisure to study the poynte so lytle made me nowe in this vacation tyme having some leisure to take delyberation therupon; and finally I resolved so to do. . .and therfore aswell for the satisfaction of myselfe as of you I have serched the reasons and groundes of the lawe in the pointte

1 *Pleas of the Crown* (London, 1736), I. 324.

2 There are three anonymous 16c manuscripts: BL Cotton Caligula B IV fols. 1-94 does not contain the prologues or section on the will of Henry VIII to be found in BL Harley 849 fols. 1-38 and Bodley Rawlinson A 124 fols. 1-47. The early 17c copy Bodley Don. c.43 has a unique prologue written by Francis Plowden and a version of Edmund Plowden's first prologue which differs in several important respects from that of the earlier BL Harley 849.

3 Axton, 'Plowden's Succession Treatise', 209.

4 BL MS Harley 849, fol. 1. Folio numbers are those of the individually paginated treatise. It is bound with other items and the whole volume paginated by a modern hand; the Plowden treatise begins according to that notation, on fol. 173.

and have spent a great parte of this christmas 1566 about the same. And the rather because this parliament nowe ended hathe left this pointe undiscuste, albeit that occacion was ministered therin to have decyded it. Which reasons and groundes I have here putt in wryting, not to thintent to publishe the same, but to satisfy myselffe and you, bothe whom it behovethe to be resolved in opinion in the point, and armed with the righte reasons therof, to bothe whom many will resorte for thintellegence of the Lawe in the pointe if our Soveraigne Ladie the quene should faile without yssue in our tyme which god prohibit. for you knowe right well that in dealing in tytles of kyngdomes there is mutche danger, and specially to the subiects, and in these cases I thinke the surest waie is to be sylent, for in silence there is saufftie but in speache there is perill, and in wryting more. therfore I wilbe silent in wordes and wryting unles I be urged and oughte to utter.

Bishop Leslie later acknowledged his indebtedness to both Plowden and Browne. Even allowing for transmission by word of mouth (which, to judge from the extreme caution of Plowden's preface, was the only safe way) it is evident that Browne and Leslie worked with written source material at their elbows. In his *Defence of the honour of Marie Quene of Scotlande and Declaration* (1569) and in subsequent editions, Leslie repeats verbatim whole paragraphs and pages of Browne's simplified legal arguments. Through Leslie's printed pamphlet Plowden's interpretation of history by means of the king's two bodies reached a wide range of English readers. Plowden's contribution to the Stuart cause was more significant than Leslie admitted when imprisoned and questioned during the Ridolfi plot.[1] The accession of James Stuart in 1603, nineteen years after Edmund Plowden's death, brought safety, and the family disclosed the Catholic lawyer's authorship. Plowden's son prepared a handsome copy of the treatise for presentation to the King.

In the troubled year of 1571 Plowden published his law reports, the work for which he is best known, and which has been acknowledged as the chief Elizabethan source for the metaphor of the king's two bodies. Once published, the *Reports* became a textbook for young law students. Plowden began compiling them, he tells his readers, in the thirtieth year of the reign of Henry VIII (1539), when he was a young man of twenty; originally for his own use, they remained in manuscript until he was persuaded to publish them. The *Reports* contain a number of cases argued by Anthony Browne, showing Browne to be as facile in his use of the king's two bodies as Plowden himself. The volume includes a Latin elegy commemorating Browne.

Plowden, when he wrote his succession treatise in 1566/7, was not educating Browne in a new ideology. He was influential because he had

1 *Burghley Papers,* ed. William Murdin, II (London, 1759), p.122.

kept a voluminous record, then unpublished, of the cases in which this legal theory had been used. Men like Maitland of Lethington, Browne and Leslie knew this theory might further Mary Stuart's claim. Plowden, who had been excluded from a high judicial position because of his religion, was the man with both learning and leisure to assemble in written form the legal arguments and historical material which supported them.

Plowden's name became synonymous with the common law during Elizabeth's reign. In Marston's *Jacke Drums Entertainment* a gallant, disappointed in love, turns to legal studies with these words: 'Therefore Gentlemen, I leave love, and fall to the (puffe) Lawe, I will interre myselfe in Ploydon's Coffin and take an eternal Conge of the world. And so sweete gallants farewell'.[1] Whilst the *Reports* educated law students to use the theory of the king's two bodies, Plowden's succession treatise, adapted by Browne and Leslie, reached a wider audience. His arguments and legal examples supporting the Stuart succession were used in the scurrilous and widely circulated attack on the Earl of Leicester, published in 1584 and commonly known as *Leycester's Commonwealth* or *Father Parson's Greencoat.* Plowden died on 6 February 1584/5. The book takes the form of 'a Leter Wryten by a Master of Arte of Cambridge' and records a discussion which took place at Christmas between the author, a gentleman and 'an ould Lawyer' who was 'a Papist yet. . .with. . .moderation and reservation of his duty towards his Prince and Country'.[2] The Queen and council took vigorous measures to suppress *Leycester's Commonwealth,* but it was widely copied and many contemporary manuscripts of it survive. So persistent was its circulation that the Queen found it necessary to issue a letter denouncing it to the magistrates of Cheshire. Sir Philip Sidney's reply to the book is well known. Sir John Harington, in his own succession treatise, gives an amusing account of the popularity of *Leycester's Commonwealth* among Elizabeth's courtiers.[3]

Arguments by Plowden, Browne and Leslie were adapted by Peter Wentworth in the nineties to support the claims of James Stuart. They were put to use by Thomas Craig, Sir John Harington, John Hayward, by Jacobean polemicists and lawyers who, on James's accession, argued for the legal union of Scotland and England. *Calvin's Case,* the

1 *The Plays of John Marston,* ed. H.H. Wood, III (London, 1939), p.210.
2 *Leycesters Commonwealth,* ed. Frank J. Burgoyne (London, 1904), pp.172-95 and p.6.
3 *A tract on the succession to the crown A.D. 1602,* ed. C.R. Markham, Roxburghe Club (1880), p.44.

Jacobean law suit cited frequently by F.W. Maitland and Ernst Kantorowicz in their discussions of the king's two bodies, is by no means a random or isolated example of the theory, but rather the crystallization of Stuart succession polemic into Stuart law. Theoretical arguments for James's succession seemed in 1603 to be vindicated and the new king pressed for a legal union of his two kingdoms first in Parliament and, when that failed, in a judicial decision, *Calvin's Case*. Early Jacobean application of the theory will conclude this study when James, expecting unanimous approval for Plowden's arguments, unwittingly re-opened the disputes and old wounds of the succession controversy.

Bitter opposition might have been expected, for James invoked arguments from a notorious book. Leslie's treatise ran to five editions published in England and abroad between 1569 and 1587. When it became clear during Mary's captivity that Elizabeth would not declare the Scottish Queen heir to the English crown, the Bishop exaggerated the Scots claims. His first edition of 1569 fully acknowledged, as Plowden and Browne had done, the rightful sovereignty of Queen Elizabeth, but subsequent editions, published after the Pope's Bull of Excommunication in 1570, implied Mary's immediate, superior claim to England.[1]

Thus the English lawyers who had written in all innocence in 1566/7 of the *future* succession found their arguments used in a printed tract which, after 1571, was treasonable. Leslie's treatise was used as evidence in the treason trial of the Duke of Norfolk, when Elizabeth's Council made strenuous inquiries about the English lawyers who had assisted the Bishop; the book was discussed in the Parliament of 1572.[2] Leslie's challenge to Elizabeth's sovereignty infinitely complicated the position of loyal Englishmen who believed that the *future* Scottish claim was clear and certain. Plowden had contributed to a dangerous, popular and influential work.

In his own prologue Plowden reviews the succession polemics he had read by January 1566/7.[3] These are fully discussed in Mortimer Levine's useful study of the subject, *The Early Elizabethan Succession Question,*

---

1 A full discussion of the various editions may be found in 'The Editor's Preface to the Defence of Queen Mary's Honour', James Anderson, *Collections MQS,* I, pp.v-xvi.

2 William Cobbett, 'Tryal of the Duke of Norfolk', *A Complete Collection of State Trials,* I (London, 1809), p.1016. Also see Sir Simonds D'Ewes, *A Compleat Journal of the. . .House of Lords and. . .Commons* (London,1693). p.215.

3 Harley 849 fol. 1.

though he does not share my view of Plowden's priority.[1] Each of the tract writers had made use of the English chronicles, beginning with John Hales who in 1563 initiated the pamphlet war with his treatise supporting Catherine Grey, the Protestant candidate preferred by the will of Henry VIII. Plowden is no exception but he, unlike his less learned adversaries, interprets history and classical myth by means of the legal theory of the monarch's two bodies.

From the comfortable vantage point of the twentieth century we can see that these lawyers were dealing with a legal problem which had never before occurred. They turned confidently to a past history which held absolutely no precedent for their dilemma.[2] Undeterred, they re-interpreted both history and myth in the light of contemporary legal theories; to enlist these revered authorities they argued by analogy. From its very outset, then, the succession debate churned up controversial exempla and suggested plot material for the early English classical tragedies and the history play.[3] Catholic and Protestant contestants were supported by totally different theories which inspired conflicting versions of the same classical stories, historical events, legal cases and, ultimately, plays which offer radically distinct interpretations of incidents crucial to the succession settlement.

The Elizabethan religious settlement and the question of the Queen's successor were, of course, inextricably connected. In 1566 no one could foresee that Mary Stuart's son, James, would reject his mother's Catholic faith; in those early years Mary's claim to the English throne was therefore opposed by Englishmen who wanted independence from Rome. These men, like John Hales, favoured the Protestant Suffolk line. Curiously neither early Catholic nor Protestant succession polemicists argued about religion in their treatises. Religious objections were subsumed in disputing foreign or native claims. However, in the nineties, when James Stuart declared his Protestantism, he was accepted by Protestant polemicists who immediately dropped their objection to his foreign birth.

Suffolk arguments

Suffolk polemicists were first in the field and turned as a matter

1 Stanford, 1966.

2 Levine, p.107.

3 Ernest W. Talbert (*The Problem of Order,* Chapel Hill, 1962, pp.66-7) makes a similar point when discussing the late Elizabethan treatises: the conflicting succession theories of Peter Wentworth and Robert Parsons. His analysis of *Richard II,* showing how Shakespeare balances the Yorkist and Lancastrian interpretations of events, is particularly valuable.

of course to the chronicles to find arguments against a foreigner. Such was the disagreement among chroniclers that a good polemicist could find support for the pretensions of any of the principal claimants. William Baldwin in the 1563 edition of *Mirror for Magistrates* laments 'the varyaunce of the cronycles. . .This disagreynge of wryters is a great hinderaunce of the truthe, & no small cumbrauns to such as be diligent readers, besides the harme that may happen in succession of herytages. It were therefore a wurthye and a good dede for the nobilyte, to cause al the recordes to be sought, & a true and perfecte cronicle therout to be wrytten'.[1]

The alien Scots Queen

Hales, against whom Plowden chiefly argued, placed his faith in the validity of Henry VIII's will. He then attacked the Scots Queen's claim of primogeniture with a maxim of the common law (based on 25 Edward III, stat. 1). According to this maxim, common laws of inheritance applied only to Englishmen, not to foreigners born in another realm of alien parents. Mary was born in Edinburgh of a French mother and Scottish father. Hales maintained that Edinburgh was outside the *allegiance* of the kings of England; Mary was foreign born and therefore unable to inherit anything according to the laws of England.[2] Only children of a king of England were excepted from this maxim and Hales interpreted this exception in its narrowest sense. He made public a controversy about who could be called 'king's children'. Did the phrase include grandchildren of the king (and thus Mary, grandchild of Henry VII) or did it simply mean the sons and daughters born to a reigning monarch? Cancelling the potential precedent of two famous foreign-born kings, Hales pointed out that the Angevin Henry II was the child of an English Queen, and that Richard II, though born in Bordeaux, had English parents.[3]

Bastardy

Next came the vexed question of legitimacy. Bastardy in Elizabethan drama often unobtrusively challenges or affirms these succession arguments. After the death of James IV, Margaret Tudor had married again and produced, on English soil, a daughter, Margaret Lennox. Hales dealt swiftly with the claim of Margaret Lennox and her

---

1 *The Mirror for Magistrates,* ed. Lily B. Campbell (reprint New York, 1960), p.267.

2 George Harbin, *The Hereditary Right of the Crown of England Asserted* (London, 1713) prints Hales's Treatise in Appendix VII, pp.xxix-xxx.

3 Harbin, p.xxxii.

sons Henry and Charles Stuart by remarking that Margaret Tudor's second husband was a bigamist; that line was thus illegitimate. But the charge of illegitimacy could also be raised against the Suffolks. Hales anticipated possible objections by tracing Charles Brandon, husband of Henry VIII's younger sister Mary, through his various precontracts and annulments to a triumphant vindication.

Scotland as foreign realm

Another Suffolk tract, which Plowden believed to be indebted to Hales for its main lines of argument, was printed in December 1565. It, too, exploited the traditional English enmity with Scotland and insisted that Scotland was a foreign realm; in war the Scots were enemies not rebels; the English king sent *ambassadors* to Scotland as to a foreign realm. Surely then the common law maxim excluded the foreign Mary Stuart. King John was enlisted as precedent; born in Oxford he lawfully ascended the throne of England because young Arthur, the Plantagenet next in blood to Richard I, was excluded from the crown by his foreign birth.[1]

By the time Shakespeare came to learn his genealogies of kings, certain figures had been marked as guarantors of the future English succession.

---

1 *Allegations Against the Svrmised title of the Qvine of Scotts* (n.p., Dec. 1565) (now extant only in MSS Ashmolean 829 fols. 23-31; Cambridge Univ. Lib. Dd ix 14 fols. 53-64; BL Harley 4627 no. 2. fols. 1-32.

3

PLOWDEN POPULARIZED

Politically engaged Elizabethans knew this much of Plowden: he made much of the distinction between kings and subjects and the law pertinent to each case. The Catholic lawyer disagreed with 'Suffolk' history and he wrote ostensibly outraged that Hales, a member of the House of Commons, should have so mistaken the laws of England. Treating three major succession issues (the maxim against alien inheritance, Scotland's independence from England, and the validity of the will of Henry VIII), Hales had failed to see that the common law made a distinction between bodies politic and bodies natural.[1] Settlement of the succession turned upon conflicting views of the legal standing of king and commoner. Stuarts throve upon absolute legal discrimination between heir apparent and subject; Suffolks strove to abolish this distinction. 'King as common man' history plays follow this debate and form a distinct genre from 1561 to 1642; they are persistently anti-Stuart.[2] Plowden's discrimination between king and common man was by no means new in the sixteenth century, but the circumstances of Elizabeth's reign encouraged him to interpret historical precedent and custom as immutable legal theory. Accordingly he suggested that the monarch's body politic had existed even in Trojan times, and he traced its shadow in history through startling incarnations in Greek, Roman, British, Saxon and English monarchs. He defined its dubious divinity in theory and illustrated it in stories. In Plowden's hands Ovid's sacrifice of Iphigenia becomes a tragedy of the conflict between the king's two bodies, showing how parochial classicism at the Inns of Court could be. When Agamemnon heard that Diana demanded the sacrifice of his daughter for the welfare of his state, he

> was angrie with heaven and earth. *Atque in Rege pater est.* for albeit he was a king, and oughte to do as seemely was for that estate, yet in the king was a father saith the poet, and in his body politicke there was a body naturall. The body politicke respecting tharmyes comoditie woulde she shoulde be killed in Sacrifice. the body naturall whiche begatt her and loved her inteerely wolde she should be preserved. the scepter moved her slaughter earnestly, but nature impugned it vehementlye; and as faste as thone body willed, so faste thother body nilled.

1 Harley 849, fol. 17.

2 Some of these are discussed by Anne Barton in 'The King Disguised: Shakespeare's *Henry V* and the Comical History', *The Triple Bond*, ed. J.G. Price (London, 1975); 'He Who Plays the King', *English Drama: forms and development,* ed. M. Axton and R. Williams (Cambridge, 1977).

Plowden stages the king's decision as a judgement scene. Ulysses speaks for the goddess Diana, pleading for the sacrifice and the good of the commonweal; Agamemnon, the father, sits as judge:

> The cause was harde and the Iudge unequall. for he muste make the father to be judge whether his owne inocent doughter shoulde be putt to deathe. Ulisses with eloquent wordes moved him. . .but nature without somme of wordes did vehemently counterpleade him in every poynte. Greate was the contention in this sely king touching the duety of his bodye politicke, and his affection in his body naturall, and which he shoulde preferr in their desyres but in thende (as the poet saithe) *pietatem, publica causa / Rexque, patrem vicit.* And so the common cause prevayled before the private. and Agamemnon as king overcame himselffe as father. . . And thus we see how this poet showeth that there is in a kyng two bodyes of dyvers distincte natures, and that they be conioyned together. (fols. 6v-7).

Plowden re-works his classical source expressing tension between the king's two bodies by the conflicting demands of a goddess and a fallible king.

Theorizing about the two bodies of the king never spread far beyond the Inns of Court, but the stories, cases and histories used to illustrate this double vision of monarchy did. The twinned person of the monarch appears frequently in the art and iconography of the period. Plowden's historical examples, discussed below, will serve to introduce the principles and ramifications of the theory, whilst occasional reference to the treatises of Browne and Leslie will illustrate its popularization.

The common law maxim

Death vs. demise

Plowden attacked Hales for his assumption that the crown passed from one king to another as land and chattels passed from an ordinary man to his son. There was a vital difference: in the eyes of the law the king and his successor were the same person; the crown and its possessions could not be bequeathed by will because the king never died. In this respect the monarch and crown resembled other corporate bodies. Plowden argued that Hales confused the cases of king and subject because the crown usually passed in the blood royal from father to son. To prove how radically royal *succession* differed from ordinary *inheritance* Plowden proposed legal cases and historical episodes showing the finality of a subject's death as opposed to the momentary disjunction of the king's body natural from the body politic which was then instantaneously vested in his successor. Demise, in legal terminology, was not equivalent to death. A single legal term described both the extinction of Henry VIII and the deposition of Richard II for 'every removing of the state Royall from one body naturall to another is called in lawe *Demise Le Roy'* (fol. 3).

For Plowden the perpetual, changeless crown symbolized the monarch's body politic. A crown case implied the presence of 'a body not visible nor tangible. . .voyde of infancy and of age. . .constituted and devysed by reason and pollicy and of mere necessitie for preservation of the people' (fol. 2). In his cases the crown works legal miracles which are often no more than deceptively reasonable *post facto* justifications of history by political expediency.

A subject was freer than a king and might dispose of his property by will as he pleased. Conversely, however, there were many common law maxims impeding his son's receipt of this inheritance: the law demanded his son's age, his legal status, his crimes and natural impediments. These common law maxims could not impede the crown which passed by succession because with it passed the invisible perfect body politic which altered the identity of the heir to that of his predecessor.

A man who received the crown of England was immediately released from his former legal commitments and impediments. For 'that body politicke is lyke an addamant attractyve that draweth all to himselffe'. Once he received the crown a man could no longer do service for lands held from another Englishman; jointures were severed; his former English titles had to be discarded or given to his eldest son, for 'the majestie of the state Royall setled in the body naturall doth make the same body naturall more pretios. So as to kill it yea to attempt to kyll it is treason. and it. . .altereth him in qualitie. . .And extolleth him so highe that it will not suffer him to beare base tytles, as duke or other lyke' (fols. 4v, 6). Reading these arguments in Plowden's treatise or in his *Reports* one understands rather better the meaning of the Elizabethan proverb ' "The case is altered", quoth Plowden'. How many of his contemporaries he convinced one cannot say; they certainly became aware of the distinction he was trying to make. The proverb is not always used, of course, with the legal nicety observed by Shakespeare in *3 Henry VI* where Warwick deliberately shows that he no longer recognizes Edward IV as king in addressing him by the lesser title, 'Duke':

> Warwick: . . .here is the Duke.
> K. Edw.:   The Duke! Why, Warwick, when we parted,
>   Thou call'dst me King?
> Warwick: Ay, but the case is alter'd.
>   When you disgrac'd me in my embassade,
>   Then I degraded you from being King,
>   And come now to create you Duke of York. (IV. iii. 29-34)

Shakespeare indicates unmistakably in the next scene that Warwick has removed from Edward the greater of the king's two bodies: Edward has suffered 'the loss of his own royal person' (IV. iv. 5).[1]

Currency of the proverb gives some sense of the lawyer's repute, but unless its context shows the author's familiarity with one of Plowden's actual arguments, the proverb no more reveals a reader of Plowden than the expression 'Freudian slip' indicates a disciple of Freud. Some such proverb existed before Plowden wrote and is used in the fifteenth-century *Nut-Brown Maid*, when a supposed outlaw reveals himself to be the son of an earl with the words, 'The case is changed new'. It is not clear when Plowden's name was first linked with the saying. Proverb experts suggest a recusant scene in which Plowden's logic saved unfortunate Catholics caught hearing Mass. He asked whether the priest would swear he had been ordained. The priest could not, whereupon Plowden exclaimed, 'The case is altered - no priest, no Mass, no violation of the law'. I have not so far found the saying in a religious context. The instances known to me sometimes comment on a simple change of circumstances but more often indicate a change of identity which the law would recognize. George Whetstone employs the proverb in this latter sense in 1 *Promos and Cassandra* (V.v.1), explaining that the whore Lamia cannot be prosecuted because her patron is the government lawyer Phallax.[2] It recurs in Lyly's *Mother Bombie* (V.iii.40), in Dekker's non-dramatic *Batchelors Banquet,* in a Medley in the *Roxburghe Ballads* as a comment on a cuckolding:

> There was a man did play at Maw
> The whilest his wife made him a daw,
> Your case is altered in the law
> quoth Ployden.

Thomas Heywood reveals changed identity occasioned by the death of the king in 2 *King Edward IV* by reference to the proverb.[3] Ben

---

1 Plowden explained carefully in the *Duchy of Lancaster Case,* as he did in the succession treatise, that because of the dignity of the body politic the Lancastrian kings, though possessors of the Duchy of Lancaster, could never be called Duke in their own realm. The same legal point applied, of course, to the Yorkist kings: 'after he [Henry IV] had deposed King Richard 2. and had assumed upon him the royal Estate, and so had conjoined to his natural Body the Body politic of the King of this Realm. . .then the Possessions of the Duchy of Lancaster were in him as King, and not as Duke, for the Name of Duke being lower than the name of King was drowned by the name of King, and by the accession of the Estate royal to him who was Duke, for the King could not be Duke in his own Realm, though he might out of it'. *Reports,* p.214.

2 Printed in Geoffrey Bullough, *Narrative and Dramatic Sources of Shakespeare,* II (London, 1958).

3 *The Complete Works of John Lyly,* ed. R.W. Bond (Oxford, 1902), III;

Jonson chooses it as a title for a comedy which reveals a commoner to be noble and vice-versa. Father Parsons, who probably received his information from Elizabeth Southwell, one of the Queen's maids of honour, hears the proverb from Queen Elizabeth's lips shortly before she died. What is important in this last case is not the veracity of the report but Parsons' belief that the saying was appropriate to the death of a monarch:

> [The Queen] willed my Lord Admirall to stay, to whom she showke her head, and with a pitiful voice said unto him, 'My Lord, I am tied with a chaine of iron about my feet;' he alleging her wonted courage, she replied, 'I am tied, tied, and the case is altered with me'. [1]

Browne and Leslie do not talk of the monarch's body politic; they summarize Plowden's conclusions, sink his theoretical argument, popularize the historical episodes and cases which demonstrated the operation of the body politic, and attribute its miracles to the crown. [2] These succession exempla attracted Elizabethan dramatists with a keen sense for plots of unique contemporary interest.

Attainder for treason

Plowden's exempla permeate Heywood's Edward IV plays, Shakespeare's 3 Henry VI and Richard III; as we shall see, the accessions of Edward IV and Henry VII were legal precedents for the Stuart claim. Plowden discussing the common law impediment of attainder distinguished between subject and sovereign in the following manner, using history to support his theory. A subject has two sons. The eldest is attainted of felony. When the father dies his land cannot descend to the attainted elder son nor to the younger because the elder is still

---

The Non Dramatic Works of Thomas Dekker, ed. Alexander B. Grosart (reissue New York, 1963), I, 235; 'An excellent new Medley, To the tune of the Spanish Pauin', The Roxburghe Ballads, ed. Charles Hindley, (London, 1873), I, 77; The Dramatic Works of Thomas Heywood (London, 1874), I, 150.

[1] The ascription to Lady Southwell (wife of Leicester's son) is in Father Parsons' hand in Stonyhurst MS Ang. A iii. 77, entitled: 'The relation of the Lady Southwell of late Q. death, primo Aprilis, 1607'. This document is published by Charles Dodd in his Church History of England, ed. M.A. Tierney, III (London, 1840), 72.

[2] Leslie describes the peculiar conjunction of the crown and king which makes common law maxims inapplicable: 'It doth plainely appeare, that the King is incorporate vnto the Croune, and hath the same properly by· succession, and not by Descent onely. And that is likewise an other reason, to proue, that the King and the Croune can neither be saide to be within the wordes, nor yet within the meaning of the said general rule or Maxime'. A Treatise Touching the Right, Title and Interest of. . .Marie, Queene of Scotland, to the succession of the croune of England (Louvain, 1571), fol. 21. He took this from Browne as one can see on fol. 190v of his treatise extant in BL MS Lansdowne 254.

alive and worthiest of blood. It therefore returns to the lord from whom it was held. In contrast, when a king dies there is no superior lord to whom the land may be returned. Common law therefore gives the realm to the king's eldest son. Why? Because the body politic purges his attainder (fol. 7v). Plowden buttressed political expediency with historical precedent; he reminds his readers that both Henry VII and Edward IV were attainted of treason. Suffolk polemicists would agree that both kings were able to receive the crown despite their attainders; therefore the maxim on attainders could not apply to royal persons. By analogous logic the maxim about foreign birth could not prevent the accession of Mary Stuart. Henry VII and Edward IV are legally transformed as the 'disability of the body naturall is wasshed away by accesse of the body politicke to it' (fols. 16, 9). Browne and Leslie use the accessions of Henry VII and Edward IV as legal precedents for Mary Stuart.[1]

Division of the realm

A king could not legally divide his realm whereas a subject might divide his lands. Plowden compares a monarch and a subject who have daughters and no son; his arguments are crucial for *Gorboduc* and the Lear plays. An ordinary man's inheritance would be shared equally by his daughters. However, a king's daughters could not receive a divided crown or crown lands: 'the crowne shall discende only to the eldeste & thother shall haue no parte of thinritance [sic] thereof.' Sound political reasoning lies behind the assertion that 'the crowne goeth not after the maxim, for where it is there is a body politicke', for if the crown were shared out as common inheritances are, 'then shoulde the subiects haue dyvers rulers, and then woulde one rule one waie, and an other an other waye. *Et nemo potest duobus divis servire.* and perchance if the lawe were so they shoulde haue sixe or seven Lordes or soueraignes...they would devyde the realme into vi or vii partes and so muche inconvenience should ensue'.[2] Royal primogeniture was essential to the Stuart argument; departure from it would split the realm; past strife over primogeniture called to the minds of these polemicists the folly of Henry VIII who had preferred the younger to the elder and thrown the succession into confusion.

Foreign birth

Plowden, Browne and Leslie all list further common law maxims which apply to subjects but not the crown, coming in due course to the

---

1   Leslie (1571) fol. 12; Browne fol. 188.
2   Harley 849 fol. 16; Leslie (1571) fols. 10v-11; Browne fol. 188.

crucial maxim about alien inheritance. Plowden argues that alien bishops received the land of English bishoprics in right of their corporation, and, building on an argument that must have seemed a little shaky in Protestant England, he affirms a predictably Stuart conclusion: 'then I thinke no man cann doubte but the higheste body politicke of all whiche conteigneth the crowne of the realme is not interrupted by forreyne birthe from setling in the nexte of bloude royall'. Chronicles are suborned to witness: William Rufus was born in Normandy, Henry II in France.[1] Plowden conveniently omits the essential qualification to these precedents: the Angevin Empire had made these boundary distinctions quite irrelevant at that time.

Plowden's treatment of King John is pre-eminent. Suffolk polemicists advanced the sovereignty of Oxford-born John as a precedent for their maxim against alien inheritance. Mary Stuart's team condemned John as a usurper. The crown should have gone to the best blood royal, the foreign born child of the eldest brother of Richard I. Arthur Plantagenet became a precedent for Mary Stuart. Plowden writes: 'King John toke the kingdome upon him uniustly. . .and would never ceasse untill he had founde the meanes to distroy Arthure. . .whiche he neded not so diligently to haue practised if Arthure had ben an alien and disabled to the kyngdome by Lawe'; and he is echoed by Browne and Leslie.[2]

Lily B. Campbell drew attention to the comparison between Arthur and Mary Stuart in Leslie's tract but did not stress the intense controversy this Catholic interpretation of John's reign immediately aroused in the rival tracts and later on the stage.[3]

Edward III and Henry V claimed France and yet were not born there; these hero kings challenge the common law maxim and sound the clarion call of the Stuarts: 'kingdomes go by discente to the next of bloude, & proximitie of bloude is the generall lawe for kynges throughe the worlde. And so I conclude that no more then our tytle to Fraunce was taken away by forreine birthe out of the ligeance of fraunce, no more shall this. . .Scottishe. . .tytle to the kingdome of Ingland be taken away by forreyne birthe out of the ligeance of England'.[4] With disarming certainty Plowden reviews the miracles performed by the body politic: it washed away legal impediments, purged bodies natural of crimes, exalted, extolled, drew like an

---

1   Harley 849, fol. 17v.
2   Harley 849 fol. 18; Leslie (1571) fol. 15; Browne fol. 189.
3   *Shakespeare's Histories* (San Marino, California, 1947) p.142.
4   Harley 849, fol. 18; Leslie (1571) fol. 39v; Browne fol. 197.

adamant attractive; the crown, its miraculous talisman, would remove
the impediment of foreign birth from Mary Stuart.

Scotland subjected

Homage and allegiance

History could attack the Suffolk maxim from another angle,
proving that Scotland was not a foreign realm. English chronicles all
testified to a feudal relationship between the two kings. On this
point they disagreed with the Scottish chronicles. Plowden selected
material from chroniclers who showed the strongest legal ties between
the two monarchs and supported his argument that the Scottish
Queen was not an alien. The Suffolk tract of 1565 dismissed the
English kings' title to Scotland as one briefly gained by the sword and
subsequently lost. Plowden thought otherwise; insisting that Scotland
belonged within the allegiance of the English kings, he revives
the historical figures of Locrine, King Arthur, Edward the Confessor,
Edward I and Henry VII to prove his point. Plays set in those reigns
dealt, then, with both the past and the future since confrontations
between ancient kings of England and Scotland might carry tacit legal implications about Elizabeth's successor.

Plowden explains the legal significance and appropriate ceremony
of the three possible feudal bonds. Any one of these formal gestures on
a pageant or theatre stage might suggest that the Scots king was, or was
not, within the allegiance of the king of England, and thus wordless-
ly broach the matter of Queen Elizabeth's rightful successor. The
greatest bond is allegiance; this makes the Scottish monarch a subject
of the English crown. He refers to the English king as his liege lord and
receives the maximum protection from the laws of England, being liable
to the greatest service in return. The next degree of affinity is the oath
of homage for the whole realm of Scotland: it admits that originally
Scottish kings received their land from the kings of England. The
Scottish monarch calls the English king his superior lord and promises
not to oppose him; in return the English king promises to uphold his
homager's title to the throne of Scotland and to aid him in defence
of his land. The third and weakest tie is the one admitted by the Scots
themselves, that kings of Scotland had in times past done homage to
the southern king for some small holdings of land in England itself. This
limited homage bypasses any admission of inequality between sovereigns
but also encourages the notion that the Scots are indeed aliens.
Plowden's logic posed a dilemma for Mary: should she insist on *de
facto* independence or gamble with the greater bond of homage to
catch a greater crown? Plowden himself has no doubts; he is sure the

Scottish monarch owes homage for the whole realm of Scotland. He even found one document giving a Scottish king's oath of allegiance sworn to Henry III; but he does not insist on this highest bond and builds his case instead on the second.

As illustration of this principle Plowden lists occasions both before and after the Norman Conquest when homage had been done for the realm of Scotland; he recalls how the dying Brute, first king of the island, gave Scotland to his second son Albanact, to hold it of Locrine, the eldest son, who became king of England. Ever since that time Scottish kings have done homage to the kings of England for their realm of Scotland (fols. 19v-20). This feudal bond is established in the second scene of the anonymous play *Locrine*. For Plowden, ceremonies recorded in the chronicles 'correctly' interpreted showed the strength of this bond. Geoffrey of Monmouth had described King Arthur's feast at Caerleon, where Auguselus, king of Scots, bore the sword before King Arthur, a ceremonial role required as 'service due for the kyngdome of Scotlande' (fol. 21v). Feudal subordination of Scotland to England is enacted in Gray's Inn's *Misfortunes of Arthur* (1587/8) and in Greene's *James IV*. St Edward performed the legal duty of an English king to his chief homager when he set Malcolm on the throne. In Shakespeare's *Macbeth* King Edward responds with immediate recognition of Malcolm as rightful heir; old Siward and the army of ten thousand Englishmen have been ordered to Scotland before Macduff arrives to ask for them. Edward's soldiers make possible the recovery of the throne for the true claimant. This episode in Acts IV and V of the play no doubt delighted James I, seated comfortably in 1606 on the throne of St Edward, as an historical sequence which had carried him to that much contested seat. Edward I had decided the rival claims of John Balliol and Robert Bruce to the crown of Scotland. When Peele dramatized the scene in *Edward I* Balliol acknowledges this authority in his superior lord. At the conclusion of Greene's *James IV* the Scots 'humble' themselves and the erring Scottish king offers just such ceremonial subjection to the English king. Plowden alerts one to the political importance of such stage directions. The ceremony of homage contained four 'pointes or signes of humblenes' requisite by law. Seated, the superior lord receives homage:

> And so we see that the homager by his kneling, by his being ungyrded by his handes being stretched out and putt betwene the Lordes knees, and by his being bareheaded doth abase himselffe all he maie and renownce in respecte of the Lorde all power and force and humble himselffe to him as lowly as he can, and therby he dothe asmuche as he can extoll and magnify his lorde.
> (fols. 27-8)

Still seated, the lord kisses his homager, signifying the conjunction of their hearts in amity.

Unfortunately for Plowden's argument, Henry VI had been the last king to receive Scottish homage. Undeterred he insisted that because a king's body politic was unchangeable, the bond of homage remained perpetual:

> Shall we saie the chiffe homager of the crowne of England. . .is a mere stranger? Phye, Phye, that is to Farr oute of the way. the Subiection by homage counter pleadeth it. And albeit homage were not don by the kyng of Scottes father, or her selffe, that is no matter. . .sithens it oughte to be don and the doer and he to whom it oughte to be don be bothe bodyes politicke. . .And so I muste conclude that the quene of Scottes and her father were homagers to Inglande, and borne within the Fee and sayniory of England. (fols. 28, 29)

The will of Henry VIII

Henry's will was another matter. Plowden, Browne and Leslie believed that Henry, as king, had no power to determine the succession by testament, since legally speaking, he never died. However, they agreed, reluctantly, that Parliament had bestowed upon Henry VIII an extraordinary power to settle the succession by means of Letters Patent or by his last will signed with his hand. But they did everything in their power to invalidate this will which gave the crown to the cadet Tudor line. Leslie, by a series of outrageous hypotheses, places Henry VIII with kings like Lear and Gorboduc whose bias against primogeniture and erratic provision for the succession brought ruin to the kingdom.[1] Leslie's faith in primogeniture leads him from Troy to Rome to pre-Conquest Britain, seeking examples of succession controversy that demonstrate the propensity of men in all ages to seek the fruits of power and fall into sins of political disobedience. He writes of Eteocles and Polynices, of Pompey, of the disasters which followed the rule of Gorboduc, and of Richard III. Not logic but a common pattern unifies his examples which are shaped to influence the future succession. Stories of civil disobedience in Leslie's vigorously polemical work are, as in Plowden's more moderate treatise, contrasted with the prophecy of a Scottish redeemer foretold by Henry VII.

Suffolk polemicists had put their faith in Henry VIII and used the will as their standard in the succession battle. Plowden and Leslie met the challenge by arming Henry's father to champion the Stuarts. Polydore Vergil supplied the text and Henry VII became a prophet of true succession as he decreed the marriage of his eldest daughter

1   Leslie (1571) fols. 55v, 56.

Margaret to James IV of Scotland. Greene dramatized such a marriage in *James IV* with a good deal of scepticism for this prophecy of universal peace. Leslie wrote:

> For what time King James the fourth sent his ambassadour to king Henry the seuenth to obteine his good wil, to espouse the said Lady Margaret, there were of his Counsaile not ignorant of the lawes and Customes of the Realme, that did not wel like vpon the said Mariage, saying, it might so fal out, that the right and Title of the Croune might be deuolued to the Lady Margaret and her children, and the Realm therby might be subiect to Scotland. To the whiche the prudent and wise King answered, that in case any such deuolution should happen, it would be nothing preiudicial to England. For England, as the chief, and principal, and worthiest part of the Ile, should drawe Scotland to it, as it did Normandie from the time of the Conqueste. Which answere was wonderfully wel liked of al the Counsaile. And so consequently the mariage toke effect. . .I say then, the worthly wise Salomon foreseeing, that such deuolution might happen, was an interpretour with his prudente and sage Counsaile for our cause. For els, they neaded not to reason of any such subiection to Scotlande, if the children of the Ladie Margaret might not lawfully inherite the Croune of England.[1]

When Plowden and Leslie presented Henry VII as prophet and used him to announce the advent of a Scottish Prince of Peace, they drew on a venerable church tradition. Figural patterns permeate their succession arguments. So, too, in many Elizabethan plays choice and re-patterning of episodes was often determined not by artistic caprice, but by what one might call rival political theologies.

The mirroring or shadowing of present political events in past historical situations, which Lily B. Campbell defines in *Shakespeare's Histories* (pp.106-16), can, since the work of Erich Auerbach, be seen as the political adaptation of a much older scholastic device.[2] Figura developed from, and was well suited to, controversy from its first use in Christian proselytizing. Elements of faith and irrationality in Plowden's techniques need not be explained away; they belong to the religious context from which both the theory of the king's two bodies and the method of argument developed.

In the tracts of Plowden and Leslie certain reigns and stories acquired legal importance as analogues for a Stuart succession. This method of culling authorities gave ingenious lawyers of rival persuasions considerable freedom for interpretation and enabled them to create levels of reference and allusion in their intriguing political art. Julius Caesar, Brute, Gorboduc, King Arthur, King John, Edward I,

---

1 Leslie (1571) fol. 30; Harley 849 fol. 29v.

2 Erich Auerbach, *Scenes from the Drama of European Literature* trans. R. Manheim, C. Garvin (New York, 1959).

Edward III, Richard II, Henry IV, Richard III, Henry VII and
Henry VIII became as important to Tudor politics as the Old
Testament prophets were to medieval Christianity. Prefiguration
neatly avoided confusing Queen Elizabeth with King Gorboduc,
King Arthur or even Henry VIII. It was an article of faith that
where the old kings failed, Elizabeth would triumph. A flawless
image of the Queen demanded that she should live up to it. Elizabeth's
reign as the lawyers knew it, was nevertheless not the 'ultimate
fulfilment' (to use the words of Erich Auerbach), but a 'promise of the
true kingdom' in a political sense.[1] Plowden's stories of old kings
of England applied by analogy to Elizabethan England, yet pointed
beyond Elizabeth, further still, into the future when the Queen would
be as unerring as her body politic, and the succession would be
perpetual. Such a prophetic view could only be achieved by faith.
Meanwhile, in their treatment of the old kings, lawyers and dramatists
warned that the mistakes of history might be avoided only if the
monarch's body natural were mortified as Plowden's Agamemnon
had been, for the sake of his body politic.

Plowden's theory and figural technique - his miracles of the crown -
have important implications for the Elizabethan theatre where a
remarkable number of gods, goddesses, faeries, magicians and friars
drew attention, not simply to the imaginative realm of faerie, but to
this irrational theory of state. Plowden's analysis of the sacrifice of
Iphigenia as a tragedy of the king's two bodies, a conflict between the
goddess Diana and erring Agamemnon, belongs as surely to the
tradition of political figura as his interpretation of the conflict
between Arthur and King John. In the early Elizabethan drama
use of classical stories as legal analogues initiated rivalry between
entertainers; caught up in controversy a handful of myths
and gods were continually reshaped and re-interpreted to express a
conflict between the Queen and her lawyers. This literary game with
classical myths was most fashionable during the period of the Queen's
active courtships. Though it never entirely ceased it is more typical
of courtly entertainment than of the public theatres. On the public
stage more use was made of political analogues drawn from English
chronicles. Nevertheless this courtly-classical tradition helps to account
for the presence and meaning of gods and supernatural agents in the
history plays. It will therefore be considered in some detail in the
next two chapters. Mythical and historical figura are mutually
dependent in the Inner Temple revels of 1561/2.

1 *Ibid.* pp.59-60.

4

THE CHOICE OF A GODDESS
Entertainments of the 1560s at Court and the Inns of Court

The Queen's metaphors

Oblique allusion and analogy were the lawyers' strongest cards; the Inns of Court risked no tragedies of virgin queens plagued by clamorous female rivals; they conjured up two unnatural sons of Oedipus (*Jocasta,* 1566), an ancient British king and his warring sons (*Gorboduc,* 1561/2), King Arthur and his bastard (*Misfortunes of Arthur* 1587/8). They urged Elizabeth to marry in the voices of Desire, Lady Beauty and the goddess Pallas (*Desire and Beauty* 1561/2), in a quarrel between Juno and Diana (1564/5). They pressed her to accept the marriage of her heir by the cautionary tragedy of a selfish Italian king and his distracted daughter (*Gismond of Salerne* 1567/8). Thus the Queen's own vein of political metaphor runs through these entertainments and carries their contemporary significance.

The lawyers were not slow to recognize Elizabeth as a master of their own forensic art. She was well acquainted with their theory of kingship, as she showed in one of her first speeches to her council:

> My Lordes, the lawe of nature moveth mee to sorrowe for my Sister, the burthen that is fallen uppon me maketh me amazed. . .And as I am but one bodye naturallye considered though by his [God's] permission a bodye politique to governe, so I shall desyre yow all my Lordes (cheifly yow of the nobilyty, every one in his degree and power) to bee assistant to me, that I with my Rulinge and yow with your service may make a good accoumpt to Almighty God, and leave some comforte to our posteritye in earth.[1]

She, too, could twist language to her own ends. Time and again she relied on metaphor to avoid the necessity of irrevocable action. Previous monarchs had spoken figuratively of themselves as 'father' of their subjects; a king had been called 'husband of the realm'. Evasive Elizabeth justified her single life by claiming the kingdom as her spouse:

> To conclude, I am already bound unto an Husband, which is the Kingdome of England, and that may suffice you: and this (quoth shee) makes mee wonder, that you forget yourselues, the pledge of this alliance which I haue made with my Kingdome. (And therwithall, stretching out her hand, shee shewed them the Ring with which shee was giuen in marriage, and inaugurated to her

1 SP 12/7: 'Wordes spoken by the Queene to the Lordes'.

Kingdome, in expresse and solemne terms.) And reproch mee no
more, (quoth shee) that I haue no children: for euery one of you,
and as many as are English, are my Children, and Kinsfolkes. [1]

Instead of marrying and producing children she did so verbally,
declaring (when it suited her) that either Mary Stuart or Catherine
Grey was her child for example: (January 1560) 'The Queen calls Lady
Catherine her daughter, although the feeling between them can hardly
be that of mother and child. . .She even talks about formally adopting
her'. [2] Marriage by Catherine Grey or Mary Stuart would affect the
English succession and Elizabeth exercised considerable power and
ingenuity to thwart their respective courtships. She intimated in
1564 that if Mary would accept a husband chosen by the Queen
of England, Elizabeth would 'declare her, Her Sister, or Daughter, and
Englands Heretrix, by Act of Parliament'. [3] Since the Queen had a
body politic she might also have a family politic. Leslie had a happy
phrase for it: 'children of the Crown'. Depending on the occasion Elizabeth might 'adopt' all her subjects or only the rival claimants as her
children. In either case they were not flesh of her flesh; the family
relationship was in that sense unnatural.

A Speaker of the Commons, John Puckering, trained at Lincoln's
Inn, urged the Queen to protect her subjects and not her cousin Mary
Stuart, addressing Elizabeth as mother and spouse of the realm:

She is only a cousin to you in a remote degree. But we be sons and
children of this land, whereof you be not only the natural mother,
but also the wedded spouse. And therefore much more is due from
you to us all than to her alone. [4]

The Commons played her metaphor game; the dramatists went much
further. Gentlemen of Gray's Inn, impatient for a real child born
of their Queen, pointed out the disastrous implications of her claim to
be both spouse and mother of her realm by presenting the tragedy
of state consequent on the unnatural marriage of Jocasta. In the
context of this protracted wrangling with figurative language, Inns
of Court classical plays of the sixties were no more 'classical' than
Plowden's Agamemnon.

Pallas

Gorboduc is the earliest survivor, written and played during the Christ-

1 William Camden, *Annales* (London, 1625), p.28.
2 *CSP Span 1558-67,* p.122.
3 Camden, *Annales,* p.100.
4 This quotation is taken from the version printed in Neale, *Parliaments
1584-1601,* p.116.

mas season 1561/2. A scarecrow in a lavish field of entertainments, it contrasts starkly with the tilt, tourney and masque performed consecutively at the Inner Temple before Lord Robert Dudley. This revels prince was potentially the most powerful man in England; with him, as members of his council, sat five of the governors of the Inner Temple and eight members of Elizabeth's Parliament.[1] Dudley took the tragedy and the masque to court on 18 January 1561/2 and offered advice on two of the most controversial questions of the day: the Queen's marriage and the succession. A single theme links these entertainments: the masque presses the Queen to marry and, through the myth of Pallas, Perseus and Andromeda, offers the Christmas Prince, an English Perseus, as royal consort. In this myth both bodies of the Queen are represented. Pallas symbolizes the monarch in council - the Queen's body politic; Andromeda (or as they called her Lady Bewty) her body natural. Consent of both is necessary if the marriage is to preserve the realm. *Gorboduc,* by contrast, chronicles the destruction of a realm in which the king's two capacities are at variance; the king-in-council (no longer a personification but a group of argumentative men) is powerless to restrain Gorboduc who, as doting father, abrogates primogeniture, divides his realm and gives power to his ruthless younger son.

These 1561/2 entertainments can only be pieced together through several witnesses. Thematic unity in the revels' classical and historical iconography can be suggested but not extensively proved because the surviving evidence is allusive and fragmentary. We may begin with Henry Machyn, whose diary is now partially destroyed by fire:

> The xxvij day of Desember cam rydyng thrugh London a lord of mysrull, in clene complett harnes, gylt, with a hondered grett horse and gentyllmen rydyng gorgyously with chenes of gold, and there horses godly trapytt, unto the Tempull, for ther was grett cher all Crystynmas tyll [blank], and grett revels as ever was for the gentyllmen of the Tempull evere day, for mony of the conselle was there.
> .... of myssrule ....
> playhyng and syngyng unto the [court with my] lord, ther was grett chere at the. . .gorgyusly aparrell(ed) with grett cheynes. . .
> The xviij day of January was a play in the quen('s) hall at Westmynster by the gentyll-men of the Tempull, and after a grett maske, for ther was a grett skaffold in the hall, with grett tryhumpe as had bene sene; and the morrow after the skaffold was taken done.[2]

---

1 See Appendix.

2 *The Diary of Henry Machyn,* pp. 273-5. It seems clear that *Gorboduc* was performed in Whitehall Palace in the Queen's Hall and not in the meeting room of the Court of Requests, the White Hall of Westminster Palace. The 1565 quarto states that *Gorboduc* was performed 'in her highnes Court of Whitehall'.

Machyn's observations are amplified by the printer of the second quarto of *Gorboduc* (1570/1).

> ...this Tragedie was for furniture of part of the grand Christmasse in the Inner Temple first written about nine years agoe by the right honourable Thomas now Lorde Buckherst, and by T. Norton, and after shewed before her Maiestie, and neuer intended by the authors therof to be published.[1]

Gorboduc was performed twice that Christmas; a pirated edition appeared in 1565; the authors agreed to an official printing in 1570. The marriage masque, and the description of Dudley as Prince Pallaphilos, on the other hand, were immediately printed in Gerard Legh's *Accedens of Armory*. Tottel brought it out on 30 December 1562; it reached a wide public and was reprinted at least five times, in 1568, 1576, 1591, 1597 and 1612. The Christmas charade, backed by men as influential as Richard Onslow, Anthony Stapleton, Robert Kelway, William Pole, Roger Manwood and Richard Sackville, was splendid propaganda.[2] The lawyers channelled their hopes into their revels iconography and gave Dudley a role commensurate with their esteem. These governors of the Inner Temple threw their weight behind their revels Prince, anticipating the change in his fortunes which came on 26 December 1561 when Queen Elizabeth reinstated the treason-tainted heirs of the Duke of Northumberland by giving Ambrose, the eldest, his father's former title, Earl of Warwick; Lord Robert expected even greater eminence. His sole distinction in 1561 was the Mastership of the Queen's Horse, which gave him

Machyn, too, seems to refer to Whitehall Palace when he writes 'the quen's hall at Westminster' for on p.61 he calls it 'Her Grace's Palace at Westminster, called the White Hall'.

1 *EECT*, ed. Cunliffe. Paul Bacquet (*Thomas Sackville,* Geneva, 1966, p.231) suggests that publication in 1565 coincided deliberately with news of Mary Stuart's pregnancy. This edition was pirated and both authors disclaimed it. Bacquet further suggests that the authorized edition of 1570/1 was printed at a time when both authors had been actively engaged in putting down the Northern Rebellion.

2 Dudley incurred the gratitude of the Inner Temple when he used his influence with the Queen to settle a dispute between the two Temples over jurisdiction of Lyons Inn. Details will be found in: Inner Temple MS Acts of Parliament 1505-89; badly damaged by fire the original French reads: 'per un gran & solemyne Cristmas en lynner Temple en [   ] officers/ le hon Robert Duddely ft or Governor Mr. Oneslowe or Chancellor, Mr. Basshe Seneschall, Mr. Coppeley Marshall, Mr. Patten Butler'. Inderwick translated from the MS before it was damaged; the titles, Lord Governor, Lord Chancellor etc. are rendered as in the original; Inderwick gives 'steward' for 'seneschall'. F.A. Inderwick, *The Calendar of Inner Temple Records 1505-1603*, I (London, 1896), p.219. Also see pp.216-18, 286; Marie Axton, 'Robert Dudley and the Inner Temple Revels', *The Historical Journal*, XIII (1970) 365-78; J.G. Nichols, 'Gerard Legh's *Accedens of Armory'*, *The Herald and Genealogist* I, (1862), 42-68, 97-118, 268-72.

a public proximity to the Queen, as he rode immediately behind her leading the palfrey of honour. But his office carried none of the political importance of its continental counterpart, Constable of France. (There had been no High Constable since the attainder and death of Edward Stafford, Duke of Buckingham, when Henry VIII decided the office too closely rivalled that of the King.) When Elizabeth raised Dudley to the peerage in 1564 he became Earl of Leicester, a title borne by sons or heirs of English kings. From the outset of her reign Elizabeth thus made no secret of her preference. The revels fiction - Pallaphilos - the second Perseus, patron of the order of Pegasus, the horse of honour - gambled on the Queen's affection and made the most of Dudley's meagre office, effacing his treason-lopped family tree with a fictitious classical genealogy.[1] This dodge into Olympian fiction when English history became 'awkward' is characteristic of Inns of Court literature throughout the reign.

Legh treats Dudley's masquerade with perfect seriousness, writing as a herald who had visited the court of a real monarch. Introducing his Prince he tells two stories, as a herald would before the entry of costumed knights at a tournament or masque. The history of Pallas, Perseus and the Gorgon Medusa interprets the Prince's arms and his 'high parentage'; the tale of Desire and Lady Beauty is a wooing allegory which neatly dovetails with the myth when Desire and Beauty are joined in marriage by command of the goddess in the Temple of Pallas.

The tilt, tourney, masque and knighting ritual described by Legh are all ceremoniously offered by the lawyers to the crowned Pallas; the goddess, on this occasion, is symbolic of 'the inseparable conjunction of counsel with kings'; her attributes are secret counsel and policy (fol. 216). Francis Bacon, active in later Inns of Court revels, records this allegory in his essay *On Counsel:*

---

1 Pegasus is the device of the Inner Temple to this day; it has not been traced with absolute certainty to a time earlier than these revels though F.A. Inderwick suggests a derivation from the horse of the Knights Templar (*CIT*, pp.lxvi-lxvii). R.J. Schoeck assumes its early use when discussing an Inns of Court setting for Chaucer's *House of Fame* (*University of Toronto Quarterly*, XXII [1954] pp.185-92.) George Buc in his *Third University*, first printed in 1615, reports that the Inner Temple adopted Pegasus 'in the Raigne of the late Queene of immortall memory'. In a prefatory poem to John Bossewell's *Workes of Armorie* (1572), Nicholas Roscarroke alludes to Legh's account of the origin of the device, 'The auncient Pegasus, which earst Minerua dame diuine/ To Inner Temples martyall gaue'. Certainly Pegasus was invested with a special significance during and after the revels of 1561/2, and to this both Buc and Roscarroke allude. In 1969 D.S. Bland reopened this question; using Buc as his authority he concluded for origin in 1561/2, suggesting it might have honoured Dudley as Master of the Horse (*N&Q*, CCXIV [1969], 16-18).

The ancient times do set forth in figure both the incorporation and inseparable conjunction of counsel with kings, and the wise and politic use of counsel by kings: the one, in that they say Jupiter did marry Metis, which signifieth counsel: whereby they intend that Sovereignty is married to Counsel: the other in that which followeth, which was thus: They say, after Jupiter was married to Metis she conceived by him and was with child, but Jupiter suffered her not to stay till she brought forth, but eat her up; wherby he became himself with child, and was delivered of Pallas armed, out of his head. Which monstrous fable containeth a secret of empire; how kings are to make use of their counsel of state. That first they ought to refer matters unto them, which is the first begetting or impregnation; but when they are elaborate, moulded, and shaped in the womb of their counsel, to grow ripe and ready to be brought forth, that then they suffer not in their counsel to go through with the resolution and direction, as if it depended on them; but to take the matter back in their own hands, and make it appear to the world that the decrees and final directions (which, because they come forth with prudence and power, are resembled to Pallas armed) proceeded from themselves; and not only from their authority, but (the more to add reputation to themselves) from their head and device. [1]

Blazoning the arms of Prince Pallaphilos, Legh calls him the nation's champion against tyranny and Gorgon nations (fol. 219). He bears a crystal shield stamped with the snake-wreathed head of his enemy, the Gorgon Medusa. Ovid's story (*Metamorphoses* IV) succumbs to political allegory when Legh tells of the origin of the shield - a classical mirror for magistrates - and identifies the enemies of Pallas. Medusa was a queen who profaned the temple of Pallas by committing in it 'filthy lust with that fome god Neptune'. For thus polluting a sanctuary for holy rites the gods changed the beautiful queen into a beastly monster, a 'myrror for Venus mynions'. Then Pallas gave Perseus a crystalline shield and bade him kill this monstrous woman. Looking in the shield Medusa beheld the outward manifestations of her sin: her golden hair transformed to foul and hideous serpents, she saw herself bereft of all 'dame Bewties shape' (fol. 221). Perseus, gazing only on the mirror shield, slew Medusa; the reflection of her severed snaky head remained forever on his shield. Springing from the blood of Medusa, Pegasus, the winged horse of honour, flew to heaven and struck Mount Helicon; and the fountain of the Muses gushed forth. According to Legh, drops from the ancient fountain flowed over the Inner Temple transforming it into the kingdom of Pallaphilos. This is the closest he comes to acknowledging the agency of art (of which Pallas was also patroness) in the creation of the Christmas kingdom where Templars honour a second Perseus whose 'zealous affeccion preseruith religion, whose chast disposicion defendeth places consecrate to goddes from filthie prophanacion. And thoffendors

1 Francis Bacon, *Works,* VI, 424.

therein with distruccion of themselues as monstres of nature' (fol. 222).

Pallas's temple profaned by Medusa's lust is a fiction rich in suggestion: a temple of the law, of government. Defending it, Pallaphilos preserves religion against Gorgon *nations*. It therefore enshrines a particular policy established by the conjunction of monarch and council. The image has widened, and Pallaphilos has become the champion of the Protestant religious settlement made by the Queen in her High Council of Parliament. As Prince, Dudley binds himself to twenty-four Templars in the order of Pegasus when they swear to protect the Temple of Pallas against further outrage. Rape in the temple, as a figure of speech, focuses a national threat to religion and quiet government: the menace of Catholicism, memories of the civil strife under Mary and Philip, the threat of Mary Stuart's religion, and of course the danger of a Catholic consort for Elizabeth. Snakes writhing on the head of the Gorgon are serpents of division.

(As an emblematic warning against national discord, the snaky head appears in Thomas Sackville's celebrated contribution to the *Mirror for Magistrates*, the 'Induction to the Complaint of Buckingham' where the targe of War is described. In the centre of the shield 'there we founde Deadly debate, al ful of snaky heare,/That with a blouddy fillet was ybound,/Outbrething nought by discord euery where'.[1] Paintings surrounding this monstrous head depict the fall of kings and the destruction of Troy.)

In the received myth Perseus slew the Gorgon and later found the beautiful Andromeda chained to a rock, killed the monster who threatened her, sacrificed to the gods and married the lady he rescued. Legh's allegory of Desire and Beauty deftly corresponds to this section of the myth. I think it probable that some parts of the story were enacted. Despite its aptness to Dudley's bid for Elizabeth's hand the story of the allegory of Desire and Beauty did not originate in 1561. It comes from Stephen Hawes's *Pastime of Pleasure,* of which the most recent edition was Tottel's in 1555. As in earlier and subsequent Inns entertainments the impact lay not in the originality of the story but in its relevance to the historical moment chosen for its presentation.

It is not a simple love affair the herald tells, for in order to win his lady Desire trains in political virtues, passes into a great chamber in the House of Chivalry hung with tapestry - a stitchery succession controversy - depicting the siege of Thebes; the war between the sons of Oedipus confronts the hero. Desire receives traditional moral armour from Trouthe and Courage and knighthood from Honour;

1 *Mirror for Magistrates,* ed. Lily B. Campbell, 2nd edn (New York, 1960) p.312.

mixing Greek and English traditions, he vanquishes a serpent with nine allegorical heads 'whereon weare carectred these ix seuerall names, Dissimulacion, Delay, Shame, Misreporte, Discomfort, Variance, Enuye, Destraction and doublenes' (fol. 210v). Welcomed at last in the Temple of Pallas Desire gets the goddess's permission to wed Lady Beauty. This temple is precisely located; it is 'my Princes Temple' (fol. 210v). The Temple of Pallas in the court of the second Perseus suggests this allegory as part of the Ovidian story. Elizabeth might be Andromeda, in need of rescue, but the analogy is never explicit.

Audacious advice is couched in impeccable legal terminology: politic and natural bodies are consulted in a love story every way antithetical to the lust of Neptune and Medusa - the first of many Elizabethan political 'rapes'. A sixteenth-century context is provided for these lustful enemies of Pallas when Pallaphilos arms his knights and reviews the bitter lessons of recent English history, 'thonour gained with losse of so many Frindes, bludd of mightie Enemies, distruccion of so manye riche regions' (fols. 215v-16). The keynote of the first dumbshow of *Gorboduc* is sounded, as the politic Templars are bound to their Prince:

> For thinges deuyded, carry theyr onely strength, which being together, double theyr enduring. . .Thys vnion, perfectlye rooted, maye so throughly woorke with euerye of you, as with the fathers Patrimonye, the same maye dyscende to the posteritie. (fols. 216v-17)

His knights wear the mantle of Pallas whose colours betoken 'simple trouth, secret counsel and good advice' (fol. 224), qualities the counsellors of Gorboduc most conspicuously lack.

The Spanish Ambassador, de Quadra, writing on 17 January 1561/2 the day before the royal performance of the British tragedy, gives a vivid though biased glimpse of the tense political situation in which the Templars' tragedy and mask were performed. He releases the news of the flight of William Rastell, one of the Catholic judges who defied Elizabeth in the Duchy of Lancaster decision. Rastell fled in order to avoid signing an opinion 'which seven or eight lawyers are to give on the succession to the crown, declaring as it is suspected that there is no certain heir. All this is to exclude the Scotch Queen and Lady Margaret [Darnley's mother] and declare that the selection of a King devolves upon the nation itself'.[1] Dudley probably hoped to benefit from such a declaration. At the repeat performance at Whitehall the Inner Templars offered advice in the succession impasse.

---

1 *CSP Span 1558-67* p.224.

Marriage was their answer. Emblem and classical allegory demonstrated the Templars' unanimity in the choice of a Prince. As they
were servants of Pallas so the choice of consort would be settled by
the Queen in Council. The British tragedy drew a sharp contrast: a
dynasty destroyed by the discord between Gorboduc and his council.

Because Dudley had everything to gain from contrast between masque
and tragedy he consented to take to court a play which might be
interpreted as favourable to the claim of Catherine Grey.[1] If the
Queen refused to marry, Sackville and Norton, at least, seem to have
been prepared to push the claims of Catherine, who had sought Dudley's
aid in the previous summer (August 1561) when her pregnancy made
inevitable the revelation of her secret marriage to Edward Seymour,
Earl of Hertford. She stated in her testimony (BL Harley 6286 fol. 37)
that on the Sunday night before she was committed to the Tower she
confided the secret of her marriage and pregnancy: 'she declared the
same to my Lord Robert by his Beddes side requyringe him to be a
meane to the Queenes Highness for her'. Dudley could indeed provide
a solution to her plight (imprisonment and separation from her
husband) simply by pursuing his own self-interest and achieving the
marriage which would remove Catherine from the centre of the
political arena. The pointed advice of *Gorboduc's* last act recommending
native not foreign claimants is subordinate to the masque's more
pressing proposal.

Sackville and Norton re-worked their British history to emphasize the
legal importance of the monarch in council; they had no chronicle
warrant for Gorboduc's advisers whose discord allows the king to
proceed unchecked in his mad plan to divide the realm and alter the
principle of primogeniture. Untrammelled, the king's inordinate love
for his younger son destroys the dynasty. The initial travesty of monarch
in council repeats itself at the sons' rival courts. Porrex the younger
son, as King of Scotland, is encouraged to win the English crown from
his elder brother Ferrex. One by one the royal family is killed. Only
the counsellors remain at the beginning of Act V. The play's
protagonist has been and continues to be the king in council. This

---

1 *Gorboduc* has long been considered a Suffolk play. H.A. Watt made an early,
full study of *Gorboduc* and its relation to the succession question (Madison,
1910). English scholars have long been indebted to his work. Sir John Neale
referred to the play's succession implications (*Queen Elizabeth*, London, 1934).
More recently Mortimer Levine devotes a chapter in his *Early Elizabethan
Succession Question* to consideration of *Gorboduc* as a succession tract. Ernest W.
Talbert has refuted the earlier notion that the play reflects conflicting political
views held by the two authors, ('The Political Import and the First Two Audiences
of Gorboduc' in *Studies in Honor of DeWitt T. Starnes,* ed. T.P. Harrison,
Austin, 1967, pp.89-115).

legal body, in the course of the play, is as surely dismembered as Pentheus or Hippolytus in their greater tragedies. No effective legal body remains in Act V. Gorboduc's helpless counsellors turn out of the play to exhort Elizabeth to settle her succession in conjunction with the High Council of Parliament before similar fragmentation occurs in her state. Only by the union described figuratively by Bacon, enacted by the knights of Pallaphilos, could policy spring forth fully armed to assure the perpetuity of England and defeat the power of the enemies represented realistically in the tragedy by Porrex, the northern king, and the rebellious Duke of Albany, and symbolized in the revels by the destructive Gorgon. A serpent-haired horror makes a brief appearance in the dumb show of Act IV. Powerless to stem the disasters he has initiated, Gorboduc calls down heaven's thunderbolt to punish his usurping younger son. His metaphor is mimed in the dumb show which follows. A woman clad in black, sprinkled with blood and flames, her body girt with snakes, carries a flaming firebrand - her head twists with serpents. The menace of division is visualized; Gorboduc's younger son has become a monster. In the subsequent dialogue Porrex is hysterically described in the same terms as Medusa. Gorgon and Fury merge: he is 'traitor to the gods, cruel tyrant, changeling and monster of natures worke', whose lust can only be appeased by blood and death (IV.i.1-80).

Within the context of the revels the shadow of Pallas dwarfs the British king; Gorboduc is judged by a political morality which will not pardon or tolerate error; he cries out against an ideal which demands that men act as gods:

> Many can yelde right sage and graue aduise
> Of pacient sprite to others wrapped in woe,
> And can in speche both rule and conquere kinde,
> Who if by proofe they might feele natures force,
> Would shew them selues men as they are in dede,
> Which now wil nedes be gods. (IV.ii.159-64)

There are moments, such as this, when our sympathy is engaged for the old beaten king. Nevertheless, the authors of *Gorboduc* were more interested in the political remedy than in the sufferings of a defeated monarch and his sons, just as Plowden was more concerned with the political sagacity of Agamemnon's sacrifice than with the suffering it caused. Emblems and icons of political conflict are deployed with skill though no corresponding dexterity animates the human scene.

Emblems and icons were more tractable than the human heart, more receptive vessels for legal thought. Samuel Daniel reminds us that these coterie authors were at liberty to interpret the gods to suit their present purpose, 'nor were tied by any laws of heraldry to range them

48

otherwise in their precedences, than they fell out to stand with the nature of the matter at hand'.[1] Unlike the more predictable English vices and virtues whose dramatic traditions they sometimes usurped, deities at the Inns had 'diverse significations'. Even Pallas was a chameleon, changing significance to suit each new occasion. In 1561/2 she was a compromise figure. Elizabeth had announced her preference for a virgin life to her first Parliament in 1559.[2] Diana was clearly a royal choice, but her sylvan chastity seemed inimical to the perpetuation of the English body politic. Pallas, on the other hand, as patroness of Athens, was both politic and martial; chastity was incidental, not central to her identity; in the 1561/2 revels her statesmanlike qualities were 'worshipped'.

If Elizabeth sat on the stage for Inns of Court performances at Whitehall, as she did at Oxford and Cambridge, the 'show' involved constant comparison of goddess, player king and Tudor Queen. Her regal chair, in full view of the audience, surmounted by an embroidered canopy, was known simply as 'the state'. Even when it was unoccupied, as it was when Leicester celebrated St George's day in Utrecht in 1587, the Queen's presence was assumed and ceremony performed as though she were seated on it.[3] When the Queen was in 'the state' ambassadors, peers and lawyers could analyse her reactions as she watched a play. Year after year castles, mounts, armed champions and deities passed before her, yet each fresh occasion gave new relevance to familiar props and myths.

Pallas was chosen again in the summer following the Temple revels to arbitrate in masques prepared for a meeting of Elizabeth and Mary Queen of Scots at Nottingham. Such an occasion posed questions about homage and equality. This masque author shows his awareness of the legal implications behind every ceremonial gesture; he solves problems of political etiquette with double personae.[4] Although Inns of Court men like Dudley or Nicholas Bacon might suspect that Pallas, riding on the Scottish unicorn, suggested the supremacy of England over Scotland the author never overtly equates Pallas with Elizabeth. Pallas is merely supreme arbiter between two estranged virtues: Prudentia (riding a crowned English lion) and Temperantia (riding a crowned Scottish red lion). Equality between two virtuous *ladies* is tactfully stressed. The snaky figure of Discord enters but is quite separate from the lady on the

1 *English Masques,* ed. H.A. Evans (London, 1897), p.3.
2 Neale, *Parliaments 1559-81,* p.49.
3 John Stow, *Annales,* p.717.
4 BL MS Lansdowne 5, fol. 126; printed in Malone Society *Collections I.2,* pp.144-8. Discussed by Wickham, *EES,* II.

Scottish lion. Allegorical analysis of conflict keeps the figures in a morality play suspension, encouraging a hope that discord between the two nations may be resolved. Nevertheless the difference between the masque world and the hard reality of the council table has no more eloquent testimony than the cancellation of this carefully planned meeting of Elizabeth and Mary.[1]

Pallas may have again provided a tactful compromise in a Gray's Inn entertainment given at Whitehall on 5 March 1564/5. 'Diana, pallas' is the laconic title given in revels records which call for chariots and clouds for the goddesses.[2] De Silva, the Spanish Ambassador, saw the shows and describes Elizabeth's reaction to a debate between Juno and Diana. Tartly admitting 'This is all against me', she nevertheless offered her services as expositor and urged the Ambassador to remain to see the rest of the day's 'rejoicing' before Lent began:

> On the 5th instant the party of the earl of Leicester gave a supper to the Queen in the palace, which was the wager their opponents had won of them on the previous day. . .There was a joust and a tourney on horseback afterwards. The challengers were the Earl of Leicester, the Earl of Sussex and Hunsdon. . .The tourney was a good one, as such things go here, with four and twenty horsemen between challengers and opponents. . .When this was ended we went to the Queen's rooms and descended to where all was prepared for the representation of a comedy in English, of which I understood just as much as the Queen told me. The plot was founded on the question of marriage, discussed between Juno and Diana, Juno advocating marriage and Diana chastity. Jupiter gave the verdict in favour of matrimony after many things had passed on both sides in defence of the respective arguments. The Queen turned to me and said, 'This is all against me'. After the comedy there was a masquerade of satyrs, or wild gods, who danced with the ladies, and when this was finished there entered 10 parties of 12 gentlemen each, the same who had fought in the foot tourney, and these, all armed as they were, danced with the ladies - a very novel ball, surely.[3]

Quite another tone was reserved for Parliament in 1566 when it petitioned the Queen to marry and declare the succession. Elizabeth lacerated thirty members of each House:

1 '15 July, Greenwich: Declaration and accord by Queen Elizabeth postponing the proposed meeting with the Queen of Scots, until next year' (*Calendar of SP Domestic 1547-80*, p.202).

2 Feuillerat, *Eliz.*, p.117. It appears from these accounts that the Queen's revels costumed these shows. This would correspond to the practice recorded at King's College, Cambridge in 1564 when the students presented *Aulularia* 'for the hearing and playing whereof, was made, by her Highnes surveyor and at her own cost. . .a great stage' (Nichols, *Eliz.*, I, 166). Another night, however, during the same royal visit a play *Ezechias* was 'played by the King's College, and the charges thereof by them born' (Nichols, I, 171).

3 *CSP Span 1558-67*, pp.404-5.

There hath been some that have ere this said unto me they never required more than that they might once hear me say I would marry. Well, there was never so great a treason but might be covered under as fair a pretence.[1]

The texts of two surviving Lincoln's Inn masques establish the tone these lawyers adopted in Elizabeth's presence; perhaps from these the nature of their Olympian ventriloquism in 1561/2 and 1564/5 may be inferred. Thomas Pound wrote and presented both masques.[2] Elizabeth was not present at the first, a fictional embassy from the gods at the marriage of the young Earl of Southampton on 12 February 1565/6.[3] As servants of Diana the masquing Lincolnians dress in white but their devotion to chastity seems strictly temporary; the virgin goddess does not represent the Queen. The knights pay regular visits to another altar to sing orisons to Hymeneus, god of marriage (fols. 24v-25).

Elizabeth did watch the second masque at the marriage of Frances Radcliffe and Thomas Mildmay (LI 1558/9) on 1 July 1566.[4] The groom's fellow Lincolnians carried Gorgon shields and dressed as servants of Pallas. Elizabeth was not the primary focus of the masque but the fact of her presence altered the tone, which was no longer simply complimentary, as Southampton's masque had been. The Spanish Ambassador attended and describes the occasion:

> On the 1st of this month a sister of Sussex was married. . .I being asked to supper, as the Queen was invited. There was a masquerade, and a long ball, after which they entered in new disguises for a foot tournament, in which there were four challengers and thirty-two adventurers. The principal of the challengers was Ormond. The statement of the cause of the tourney and the conditions were read first in Spanish and afterwards in English. . .The tourney lasted till daybreak, and I was with her [Elizabeth] the whole time.[5]

Pound introduced himself at Bermondsey by reminding the Queen of a previous Inns of Court entertainment in which he had performed

1 Text from Neale, *Parliaments 1559-81*, pp.146-8.

2 Bodley MS Rawlinson Poet 108, fols. 24-37.

3 The knights enter on horses from 'the country of Lincossos', bordering the land of Portpulia (the location of Gray's Inn). Their Prince is called Troposonte 'so named long ago' (fol. 24v). This is the earliest reference I have found to the name of the Lincoln's Inn Prince. Prince de la Grange was the seventeenth-century title of the Lord Lieutenant of Lincoln's Inn. See *Universal Motion* (1662); John Evelyn mentions 'the solemne foolerie' of the Prince de la Grange. Perhaps the title was 'Troposonte, Prince de la Grange', as it was 'Pallaphilos, Prince of Sophie' at the Inner Temple.

4 E.K. Chambers, who briefly notes the existence of these masques (*ES*, I, 162 and III, 468) assumes Elizabeth's presence at both, but gives no evidence for her attendance at Southampton's. The text does not support his conjecture.

5 *CSP Span 1558-67*, p.565.

as one of Pallas's knights 'Counte Phylos' - either the Dudley revels of 1561/2 or subsequent ones continuing that fiction.[1] By recalling the revels in which Pallas shadowed the Queen's politic capacity the masquing lawyers identified themselves as the Queen's public servants. Yet although the conceptual framework of the earlier festivities is invoked, the allegorical content of the 1566 masque is distinctly different. They enter to bring gifts from the gods. Pallas sends her Gorgon shield to the bride; the severed head is, here, simply a warning to all who distain virtue. Venus sends her golden apple. Pound lingers for two pages praising the goddess born from the sea foam; she is 'dame bewtye right in ded' (fols. 32v-33), and her prize for beauty is given to the bride. Pound hastily adds:

> I tell but what the goddes saye
> Lothe were I to offend
> I come to gratyfye you all
> And to no other end   (fol. 33)

He admits that there might be a fairer lady in the hall and turns to the Queen to excuse himself:

> but as for that I wyll appeale
> for pardone to here grace
> I must suppose she is not here
> as thoughtes (we saye) be free
> And then I do here grace no wronge
> no faulte there is in me
> I do but my commission
> which I may not transgrese
> for seynge that I come from the godes
> nowe I cane do no lesse
> but lyke a messenger to shewe
> what they dyd byd me saye   (fol. 33v).

Juno chid Pound for remaining a bachelor; he, in turn, conveys the goddess's blunt advice to Elizabeth:

> for wedlocke I lyke best
> it is the honorablest state
> it passethe all the rest
> my Jove saithe she doth knowe this ioye
> this bodye is his owne
> And what swete use I haue of his
> to men may not be knowen   (fol. 34).

Diana receives the hardest treatment. Lineaments of the elegant huntress

---

1 Pound recalls that he conquered Envy while Templars and men of Gray's Inn looked on in approval; Legh's nine headed dragon had 'envy' written on one of his nine heads; Pound refers to himself as a knight 'to pallas bownde by former othe' (fol. 31v) and then paraphrases the verse oath sworn by Dudley's knights in 1561/2 (Legh fol. 224v; Pound fol. 34v).

of later Elizabethan verse are scarcely discernible in these back-handed compliments to a hearty, red-faced virgin:

> thowghe venus fayrer was then she
> yet was her grace so good
> that she semde all as aimiable
> thowghe somewhat full of blude
> but that became here passinge well
> importinge to me styll
> that huntynge kept here coloure good
> in runnynge uppe the hill
> Suche exercyse preservethe healthe
> I note it for no harme
> that nature dothe reioyce the more
> to fele the bodye warme   (fol. 35v).

Diana is resigned to the loss of her nymph and sends platitudes about maids being born to become wives.

The continuity of convention is particularly apparent in this masque, but the function of the gods is constantly being redefined. A single cipher will not serve.

Richard Edwards's reputed masterpiece *Palamon and Arcite* dramatized Chaucer's story of the fight between the knight of Venus and the knight of Mars for the hand of Emilia, the votaress of Diana. Edwards, best known as Master of the Children of the Queen's Chapel, is not usually remembered as an Inns of Court man. He was, however admitted to Lincoln's Inn on 25 November 1564 and was responsible for at least two entertainments there.[1] He moved freely from Court to the Inns in a career which illustrates the continuity of coterie theatrical conventions in this period. Edwards (like Pound) devised entertainments and sometimes performed. He appeared as herald for 'stranger knights' at the marriage of Ambrose Dudley on 11 November 1565 announcing to the Queen an entry by Christopher Hatton and the Earl of Leicester who were accompanied by elaborately costumed Amazons.[2]

Elizabeth sat on the stage at Oxford to watch *Palamon and Arcite*; the audience included her council and the ubiquitous Spanish Am-

---

[1] *BB*, I, 418. It has been suggested that *Damon and Pithias* was performed at Lincoln's Inn in the winter of 1564/5; if so another performance at Court may be noted when the Queen's revels accounts refer in 1564 to 'Edwardes tragedy' (Feuillerat, *Eliz.*, p.116). The prologue to the printed edition of *Damon and Pithias* (1571) explains that although entitled 'the excellent comedie' it is more suitably a 'tragical Commedie', that it was presented at court and that it was Edwards's first play in this more sober genre. (MSR, Oxford, 1957) Edwards and his Chapel boys performed again at Lincoln's Inn on the Feast of the Purification in 1565/6. (*BB*, I, 352).

[2] John Leland, *De rebus Brittanicis collectanea*, ed. T. Hearne (London, 1770), II, 667-8.

bassador. The show was performed in two parts on 2 and 4 September 1566. The script is lost but one of the audience tells of a spectacular hunt, sacrifices at the temples, a tourney and a judgement scene arbitrated by Saturn.[1] Venus pleads and the victorious servant of Mars, Arcite, is struck by subterranean fire. Only a fragment of text survives - Emilia's song mourning the death of Arcite.[2] Her devotion to Diana, too, is clearly transient for she sings not of her miraculously preserved chastity but a lament more suitable to the court of Venus:

> I wyle & want my new desire
> I lack my new delight. . .
> Why could not I embrace my ioy?
>   for mee that bidd such woe   (fol. 106v).

Promptly King Theseus gives her to Palamon, the knight of Venus. Intriguing levels of dramatic illusion reveal themselves even in these fragments. As in Chaucer's *Knight's Tale,* Saturn is supreme and carries the day for Venus against Mars and Diana; Theseus, the player king, and his council implement the god's decision. This verdict against Diana is given political point by the Queen's presence and elicits spontaneous approval from an Oxford audience.

While Elizabeth procrastinated, both her potential successors married and gave birth to sons. Catherine Grey was immediately at the Queen's mercy, yet she bore two sons in the Tower before being more effectively separated from the Earl of Hertford. Elizabeth refused to recognize the legality of this marriage, branding the children as bastards. Catherine remained in custody until her death in 1568. Mary Stuart impetuously married Henry Darnley in 1565, deliberately flouting Elizabeth and uniting the two strongest Stuart claims. The birth of James in June 1566 consolidated her strong position in the succession contest. But not for long. Mary's rapid disillusionment with Darnley, whom she had ennobled as Duke of Albany and then King of Scotland, culminated in his murder and her ill-judged marriage with the chief suspect, the Earl of Bothwell. Her flight from Scotland and imprisonment in England put the Scots Queen effectively in Elizabeth's power in 1568.

These kaleidoscopic changes in the Queen's 'political family' are reflected at the Inns of Court in entertainments whose theme might, with *Gorboduc*, be called 'unhappy families'. The lawyers' originality

1 Printed in Charles Plummer, *Elizabethan Oxford* (Oxford, 1887). Bereblock's Latin is translated rather freely by W.Y. Durand in 'Palaemon and Arcyte. . .1566', *PMLA,* XX (1905), 502-28. Staging is discussed by Glynne Wickham, *EES,* I, 355-9.
2 Hyder E. Rollins discovered this song in BL MS Additional 26737 ('A Note on Richard Edwards', *RES,* IV, 1928, 204-6).

may be seen in the framework of prologues, dumbshows and commentary which encapsulates these old tragedies - mediating between inevitable catastrophe and the Elizabethan present, demanding of the audience both a double perspective and an act of silent judgement. The lawyers gestured toward eventual solution in their choruses and left it to a politically acute audience to decide whether player kings were types or anti-types of majesty. Choruses continue the masque experiments with different gods who might satisfactorily represent the Queen's body politic.

George Gascoigne (GI 1555) admits the vital importance of prologues which alert an audience to the desired contemporary perspective. Describing a play about Reformation politics he hesitates, 'And I the prologue should pronounce, but that I am afraide'.[1] His own prologue to a translation of Ariosto's I Suppositi given at Gray's Inn in the winter of 1566/7 acknowledges that his audience expected this opening speech to 'discipher vnto you some queint conceiptes which hitherto haue bene onely supposed as it were in shadowes'.[2]

For the same revels George Gascoigne also translated Lodovico Dolce's version of the Thebaid and set this contention between Eteocles and Polynices for the throne of Oedipus within his own framework. The Templars had asked for a similar contemporary application of the Theban conflict in their 1561 revels when Desire, the natural mate for Lady Beauty, stood beside a tapestry depicting the miseries brought to Thebes by Oedipus' unnatural marriage.[3] In Gascoigne's Jocasta a marginal gloss to Oedipus' last speech in Act V labels the sightless king as a 'mirror for Magistrates'. The translators are concerned to show a 'blind' Elizabeth the dangers of her metaphorical marriage with the realm and by implication to urge a real marriage, producing her own children not unnatural heirs. In the union polemic of the early seventeenth century both Jocasta and Gorboduc's queen Videna explicitly represent the strife-torn realm.[4] Gascoigne's Jocasta often speaks as the morality figure, Lady Respublica, and

---

1 Complete Works, ed. J.W. Cunliffe, I (Cambridge, 1907), 69-70.

2 Supposes, lines 8-11, Early Plays from the Italian, ed. R.W. Bond (Oxford, 1911).

3 In 1569 the University of Oxford prepared an entertainment on the same subject for their Chancellor, Leicester. Thomas Cooper wrote to ask whether the Earl would be pleased to see 'a playe or shew of the destruction of Thebes, and the contention between Eteocles and Polynices for the gouernement thereof'. He asked Leicester's 'healpe for prouision for some apparaile and other thinges needefull' (Collections II.2, Malone Society, Oxford, 1923, p.146).

4 Thomas Craig, De Unione Regnorum Britanniae Tractatus (1605), trans. C. Sanford Terry (Edinburgh, 1909), pp.232-4.

this idea of political perpetuity which heightens her significance, inspires the choric optimism. For the Grayans Dolce's fatalism is not the last word. Their choric remedies are not directed at the Greek queen. Looking beyond the player king and queen, these translators see Oedipus and Creon as 'types and fygures' of monarchy. Achievement of the politic ideal lies in the future, for this reason the Chorus in Act IV delivers its startling praise of Concord with perfect English decorum turning away from the horrors of incest to the personification of that divine force which ensures perpetuity of kingdoms: [1]

> O blisful concord, bredde in sacred brest. . .
> Thou doest inspire the heartes of princely peeres
> By prouidence, proceeding from aboue,
> In flowring youth to choose their worthie feeres,
> With whom they liue in league of lasting loue,
> Till fearefull death doth flitting life remoue,
> And loke how fast, to death man payes his due,
> So fast againe, doste thou his stocke renue.   (1-35).

Theban legend as dramatic metaphor makes a powerful criticism. If the Queen did not like what was shadowed in the mirror she had only herself to blame for indulging in the equivocation of metaphor in high places. Gradual spread of Inns of Court techniques and allusions may be inferred by a comparison of the elegant manuscript version of this tragedy prepared for Elizabeth's maids of honour (BL Additional 34063), and printed editions of Gascoigne's works (1573, 1575, 1587). In the last two editions certain words not in common use are glossed 'at the request of a gentlewoman who vnderstode not poetycall words or termes'. [2] Gascoigne finds it necessary to explain, for instance, that 'the type of Tyranny' means 'fygure' and that the Gorgon Medusa is 'one of the Furies' (Argument 14 and II.i.275).

Comedy, tragedy and romance were suffused with current political meaning at the Inns. Shakespeare must have seen this as he paged through *Supposes* (a source of the Bianca plot in *Taming of the Shrew*) and through *Romeus and Juliet,* the tragic poem by a young Inner Templar, Arthur Broke. Broke entered the Inner Temple in 1561 as a protege of Sackville and Norton.[3] His *Romeus* (a translation from Boaistuau) was printed by Tottel on 19 November 1562 at a time when England was intensely interested in the fate of two English star-crossed lovers - the imprisoned Catherine Grey and the Earl of Hertford. Broke's preface refers to a recent stage version of the

1 *EECT;* quotation from this edition.

2 *EECT* p.159.

3 Desmond Bland, 'Arthur Broke, Gerard Legh and the Inner Temple' *N&Q,* CCXIV (1969), 453-5.

story,[1] and he was recompensed in the Pallaphilos revels for 'certain plays and shows at Christmas last set forth by him'.[2] These words do not tell us that Broke was author of a stage version, but evidence for Broke's collaboration in the Temple revels highlights an interesting discrepancy in his published tragedy. Broke condemns the lovers in his *Epistle to the Reader*; their example will 'teache men to witholde themselves from the headlong fall of loose dishonesty'. Romeus, Juliet and the Friar who married them are moral debauchees. Yet in the poem itself the Friar is vindicated; he paces forth an honest supporter of the common weal and counsellor of his Prince. The lovers appear in simple innocence. This same discrepancy between official condemnation and sympathetic poetic treatment of the lovers can be seen in the Inner Templars' tragedy *Gismond of Salerne*.

Gismond of Salerne was performed for Elizabeth during Christmas 1567/8 written not by one but by five Templars.[3] Its fourth act comes from the pen of the future Lord Chancellor, Christopher Hatton. Two manuscripts preserve this early version of the play (BL Lansdowne 786 and Hargrave 205). It was later completely re-written and printed between 1591 and 1592 when the Earl of Hertford was trying (unsuccessfully) to get his sons legitimised.[4] *Gismond,* as it was presented to Elizabeth in 1567/8, is a tragedy caused by a sovereign who will not allow the heir to the throne to marry an earl worthy to be her husband. The authors' alterations in their source material (Boccaccio, Dolce and Seneca) create a tragedy of state by strengthening the analogy between the play and the contemporary political situation and

1 *Romeus and Juliet* ed. J.J. Monro (London, 1907), p.lxvi.

2 *CIT* I, 220. The context suggests that Broke is being reimbursed for money spent in connection with the revels; 'set forth' seems to mean 'costumed, staged and produced'. It is in this sense that William Baldwin used it when he offered his play *Love and Live* to Sir Thomas Cawarden, Master of the Queen's Revels, to be 'set furth' in 1556. The play he offered Cawarden was to be performed for Queen Mary; it had already been cast and the actors were learning their parts when Baldwin wrote his letter. He adds 'there be of the Innes of court that desyr to have the setting furth therof, but because your mastership now thre yeres passed offered in a sort to set furth sum of my rude devises, I thought it good to know your mynde herein, before I gave answer to any other. The settyng furth wil be chargeable because the matter is stately' (Feuillerat, *Edward VI & Mary,* p.215).

3 The first performance has been dated from the epistles to the first printed version, where the author Wilmot refers in 1591 to his involvement with the heroine as 'The loue that hath bin these 24 yeres betwixt vs'. This, as the editor suggests, should indicate a first performance in 1567.

4 As *Tancred and Gismund,* MSR (Oxford, 1914). This text is the revised printed version of the play. I have not seen the Yale Ph.d. dissertation by Kyoko I. Selden: 'A Comparison of the Two Versions of *Gismond of Salerne',* 1965.

by giving the three principal characters significant rank.[1] Cupid speaks the prologue and his obsession with his audience betrays a very English 'classicism'.[2] This prologue may have been modelled on that of Euripides' *Hippolytus,* but whereas Aphrodite precipitates the Greek tragedy because the chaste Hippolytus scorns her, the Templars' Cupid, directing attention outside the play, seeks vengeance on the contemporary audience who disdain him. The Inner Temple tragedy will demonstrate Cupid's power and bring members of the English audience to their knees: 'This royall palace will I entre in' (I.i.61).[3] Had Cupid been accorded his rightful place in 'Royal palaces', had Elizabeth not thwarted the marriage of her most likely successors, tragedies would have been averted. Cupid disdained is a blind god, angry and deadly. Catherine Grey lay dying in the winter of 1567/8; Mary Stuart's marriage ended in violent death and imprisonment.

King Tancred forbids his widowed daughter Gismond to remarry; she defies her father by taking an earl as lover; the king discovers their illicit affair, tries and executes the earl for treason, whereupon Gismond commits suicide and the king dies of grief.

Diana makes her first appearance as a redemptive figure in the fourth chorus of the tragedy. Here she is contrasted to the tyrant Tancred who, within the play, enforces chastity upon his heir and brings his dynasty to an end. Hatton, consigning Gismond and her earl to the dubious company of Venus and Adonis, Paris and Helen, holds up for admiration the chaste love of Hippolytus and Diana. Seizing on a variant of the myth to assure us that Diana restored her mangled devotee to life, Hatton cautiously suggests that the body politic can work miracles. Sympathetic presentation of the lovers is at odds with such choric condemnations. In Act V the messenger, who bears the heart of the dead earl, meets the Chorus and his speech indicts the king:

> Is this Salerne I see?
> what? doeth king Tancred gouern here, and guide?
> Is this the place where ciuile people be?
> or do the sauage Scythians here abide?   (V.i.21-4)

This question presses beyond the play world asking the audience to

1 The literary, but not political, implications of these alterations are discussed by Cunliffe in the Introduction to *EECT* and in *'Gismond of Salerne' PMLA,* XXI (1906), 435-61, and by David Klein in 'According to the Decorum of These Daies', *PMLA,* XXXIII (1918), 244-68.

2 The *Gismond* prologue follows Dolce for the first 16 lines. Dolce's Cupid reappears at the beginning of Act II of *Didone.*

3 Line references from *EECT,* the early MS version.

examine their state, pushing the audience toward the conclusion that 'the king's to blame'.

Tactfully, the epilogue readjusts this perspective, forces Cupid back into the play, reassuring the ladies that this blind god and his snaky Fury (who provided a fine spectacle in Act IV) will not come amongst them, for this actor finds no signs in Britain of rebellion against Cupid. His dead-pan irony testifies to the difficulties of playing tragedies of state before an audience of statesmen.

Elizabeth might see her policy reflected in the miracle of the chaste goddess or the tragedy of the player king. The choice was hers but when the two are held in perspective the criticism is unmistakable.

John Puckering (LI 10 April 1559) who, as Speaker of the House of Commons, challenged Elizabeth with her own marriage metaphor to protect her realm and not Mary Stuart, may well be the author of the 'classical' morality play *Horestes*. J.E. Phillips has suggested that the play originated at Lincoln's Inn in 1567/8 and identifies the author John Pikeryng with the Speaker of the House and later Lord Keeper in Elizabeth's government.[1] Certainly the Parliamentary returns refer to the Lord Keeper as Pickering, Puckering and Pyckering. It has long been recognized that *Horestes* reflects the issues which surrounded the murder of Henry Stuart, King of Scots, and Mary's precipitous marriage with the Earl of Bothwell. Bothwell's trial was a legal farce. In November 1567 Murray and the lords who represented James VI were in London showing Elizabeth's council the notorious casket letters, which revealed the guilt of both Mary and Bothwell.

Interesting details linking this morality printed in 1567, 'divided for VI to play', with Lincoln's Inn need not detain us. Its author (whether or not a lawyer) shows an easy familiarity with the English 'classical' mythology of Sackville and Gascoigne and invites common players to take his script into the provinces. He is aware of the topical relevance of the legend, exploited that year by Robert Sempill, a Scottish politician and ballad writer who used Orestes' story to shadow the dilemma of Murray and the Scottish government; a play of *Orestes* (either Pikeryng's or someone else's) was performed for Elizabeth in the winter of 1567/8.[2]

The morality play conventions implicit in *Gorboduc* and *Jocasta*

1 'A Revaluation of *Horestes*', *HLQ*, XVIII (1955) 227-44.

2 *The Semphill Ballates 1567-1583*, ed. T.G. Stevenson (Edinburgh, 1872). See especially 'The Nobell and Gude inclination of our King' (1567) and 'The testament and Tragedie of umquile King Henrie Stewart of gude memorie' (1567); Feuillerat *Eliz.*, p.119.

are quite explicit in *Horestes*. Pikeryng, like Plowden, is more interested in legal theory than the tragic potentialities of his legend and he offers political solutions. Yes, he replies to the searching question Aeschylus had first asked, revenge can be called justice. Such certainty is only possible within the morality play framework Pikeryng has chosen. Acknowledging in his title the dubious nature of revenge - *A Newe Enterlude of Vice Conteyneinge the Historye of Horestes with the cruell reuengment of his Fathers death upon his one naturall Mother* - he nevertheless makes Plowden's distinction. The Vice, Revenge, has a purely evil effect upon commoners such as Rusticus and Hempstring: two scenes of rough comedy precede the Vice's meeting with Horestes. When Revenge approaches an heir to a throne the case is quite altered. Pikeryng has no difficulty reconciling the laws of gods and men because his gods are metaphors; they uphold a limited, man-made legal theory. When the Vice assures Horestes that 'god Mars' will aid his revenge he means simply that King Idumeus and his council will provide an impressive army and permission for war. The god of war never appears, but his power can be successfully invoked by the correct legal ritual. Accordingly, Horestes enacts the ceremony of homage. Kneeling before Idumeus and Council, he addresses the king as 'my leege' and asks permission to recover his own kingdom. This ceremony appropriate to a king of England and his chief homager, the king of Scots, affirms the feudal bond which *requires* English military aid to solve a Scottish succession problem. Idumeus reviews Horestes' troops and sends him on his way with the requisite ceremonial kiss. 'God Mars' will not fail him.

Pikeryng's pre-occupation with the English scene is most apparent in the duet he provides for his outrageous Clytemnestra and her lover. Oblivious of the approaching army, they sing in their citadel; they liken their flame to the love of Paris and Helen and anticipate the gods' approval of their deeds. Their adulterous treason is celebrated to the tune of a song which, in 1559, had acclaimed the accession and ancestry of Queen Elizabeth, its refrain - 'Lady, ladye/A Queene and ladye unto me,/My dear ladye'.[1] Their punishment is immediate.

When Revenge ceases to act in the interests of King and Council, and stirs Menelaus to revenge, Pikeryng separates him from Horestes; Vice is exiled by the state. Horestes, therefore, never becomes a personification of revenge; because he is among allegorical characters he differs from his counterpart in Aeschylus's tragedy or from a Jacobean revenge

[1] 'A New ballade', R.M. (London [1560?]) printed in *Ancient Ballads and Broadsides,* ed. Henry Huth (London, 1867), pp.43-6.

hero like Vindice. Horestes is politicly married to Menelaus's daughter, acclaimed by Nobles and Commons and crowned by Truth and Duty. Truth warns the audience that 'much prophet may aryse' from the old story and promises punishment for certain reckless persons when Time and Truth have discovered the crime to all.[1] Duty prays for Elizabeth and her council hoping that they too will set up virtue and correct vice.

Pikeryng wrote to urge the legal punishment of Mary Stuart and he simplified his legend to this end. His hero chooses cleanly between Nature and Duty. When Shakespeare wrote *Hamlet* both the personal and public aspect of Orestes' situation became fully dramatic. Shakespeare's achievement should not, however, obscure the effective synthesis of forms which enabled Pikeryng to present the classical dilemma as a political situation relevant to his own time. Pikeryng, Sackville, Gascoigne brought policy and legal theory to the stage and accustomed audiences to believe that theoretical justice might become reality. On their stages with startling frequency legal theory staunched tragedy. It is against the background of such theatrical wish-fulfilment that Shakespeare's realism works. Hamlet, waiting for a clean choice to be offered him between vice and virtue, is destroyed.

The Inns of Court gods of the 1560s voiced a demand for continuity in the monarchy which was pressed both in Parliament and in the courts of common law. Hatton stood apart from his fellows with his gallant suggestion (albeit sharply qualified) that the chaste Diana might transmit perpetuity akin to that of Plowden's body politic. As Elizabeth grew older and hope for offspring faded, Diana or Cynthia as a public image found reluctant acceptance. Though the virgin huntress eventually found her way to the playing place, she did not immediately silence protest.

---

[1] *Horestes*, MSR (Oxford, 1962), lines 1402-9.

5

TRIUMPHS OF DIANA

Court Entertainments 1575-1590

No easily identifiable Inns of Court entertainments survive between *Gismond of Salerne* (1567/8) and *Misfortunes of Arthur* (1587/8). However, the activities and influence of Inns of Court entertainments may be followed in the interim. Their astringent criticisms of royalty, their peculiarly English classical myths, persist in plays and pageants shaped by the Queen's courtships.

These may be contrasted with two works which avoid the marriage question and use classical *figurae* for simple flattery: Thomas Blenerhasset's non-dramatic Olympian fantasy *The Revelation of the True Minerva* (1582) distinguishes between the Queen's two bodies without exploiting the contrast for criticism; Peele's *Araygnement of Paris* dramatizes this Trojan's judgement without exploring its darker implications. By these two, the critical thrust of the Kenilworth entertainments (1575) and the work of John Lyly may be gauged.

Several conclusions may be drawn from the *Princely Pleasures* seen in the context of Inns of Court traditions. David Bergeron's picture, drawn in *English Civic pageantry,* may be amplified in two ways. First he sees Kenilworth in 1575 as 'the beginning of the crucially important relationship between dramatists writing not only for the regular theatre but also for the pageant theatre' (p.30). This seems a late date to establish such a link. 'Regular theatre' is a problematic term before 1576, but Inns of Court men had been writing plays for at least fifty years and producing Christmas pageantry for the amusement of the London populace; witness the careers of Richard Edwards and George Ferrers. Bergeron secondly sees praise of Elizabeth in episodic, diffuse Kenilworth pageants. I think this is only half the picture. Elizabeth does indeed bring to Kenilworth power to charm and free; she acts as a regenerating, liberating force (p.35). But from what situations is she to liberate Leicester's actors? Surely fictionalized versions of a predicament caused by her mortal self and the aging Earl, who because of this interminable courtship had no legitimate heir. Kenilworth reveals its coherence and critical edge, as a sequel to the Templar's marriage bid, first expressed through personification of Desire, Lady Beauty and the Olympian body politic.

In the summer of 1575 Leicester's protégés gathered at Kenilworth to entertain the Queen. These men who penned verses and dressed as

Hercules or Sylvanus were Oxford dignitaries, Parliament and Inns
of Court men, proud to serve, though their set piece might be followed
by an Italian tumbler or a rustic morris dance. George Gascoigne
of Gray's Inn, translator-producer of *Jocasta* and *Supposes,* wrote and
supervised many of these shows. He published *Princely Pleasures* in
1576 with descriptions and texts.[1] Another eye-witness version
survives in *Laneham's Letter* (1575).[2] Laneham writes familiarly
of Lady Sidney and of Sir George Howard, Master of the Queen's
Armoury.[3] George Ferrers of Lincoln's Inn, Howard's Christmas
Prince in 1552/3, wrote some of the verses of welcome.

Ferrers's earlier career has been briefly sketched in Chapter I. By
1575 he was an old man. His recent political ventures had brought him
close to treason. This former Christmas Prince had been linked with
Plowden, Barker and Ridolfi in evidence taken by the council in the
Ridolfi plot: in October 1571 John Leslie, Bishop of Ross, confessed
that Ferrers of St. Albans had not only seen his succession treatise but
had given advice 'to amend som thyng towching the stories of the
Books; as for the law, he said it was well'. Ferrers had shown Leslie
a Latin treatise which he had made 'of the deducing of the Lyne from
the Red Rose and the White, and so he thought to bryng it to the End
of the Scots Quene's title'. Mary's Bishop disclosed that Ferrers had
long favoured the Scottish claim which he talked over with Maitland
of Lethington in former times, and that Ferrers, who was of the lower
House, had 'brought hym Intelligence, from Tyme to Tyme, of suche
Matters as weare propounded in the Parliament'.[4] That both Ferrers
and Plowden escaped punishment after the Bishop's confession is
perhaps due as much to the clemency of Elizabeth as to their agility in
their profession. In 1575, Ferrers used his knowledge of chronicles to
create an Arthurian pedigree for Leicester that might match the
Queen's own supposed descent from that British Worthy.

Leicester's wooing depended, as it had in 1561, upon an Olympian
fiction. Fifteen years of cold answers had, however, caused Leicester to

1 This has survived only in later Elizabethan editions of his works. Nichols (*Eliz.,*
I) prints Gascoigne's text from the 1587 edition. All Kenilworth page references
from Nichols.

2 M.C. Bradbrook has suggested that the author is not Robert but John
Laneham the actor, one of Leicester's Men and colleague of James Burbage (*Rise
of the Common Player,* London, 1962, pp.141-61).

3 *Laneham's Letter* printed in Nichols *Eliz.,* I, 482. All references to this edition.

4 *Burghley Papers,* II, 30, 51. The Parliamentary returns are not complete for
this period, and though none survive to indicate which constituency Ferrers represented in Elizabeth's early Parliaments there is no reason to doubt that
Ferrers, who sat for Plymouth in 1544/5 and 1552/3 and Brackly Borough in
1554 and 1555, was a burgess of the House.

alter the literary presentation of his suit. In the interim it had become clear that when the Queen thought of marriage there was no happy concurrence of her two capacities. Elizabeth might love him, but the Queen could not marry her subject. Leicester's poets did what they could to equalize the disparity in degree by again providing their patron with Olympians to match the Queen's immortal office. But marriage was only one of the possibilities put forward.

Elizabeth's policy of prolonged non-decision was a strain on her favourites. It is understandable that Leicester should have held her largely responsible for it. The pageants show that he was also aware his enemies blamed him; they believed that the Earl kept her a prisoner for his own ambitions, preventing with Machiavellian diplomacy more suitable matches. The Spanish Ambassador in February 1565/6 recalled the Duke of Norfolk's advice to Leicester:

> All those who wished to see the Queen married, the whole nation in short, blamed him [Leicester] alone for the delay that had taken place. So great would be the hatred aroused against him that evil could not fail to befall him, and this could only be allayed in time by his joining the rest of the nobility and helping forward the Archduke's suit with the Queen. Leicester replied that he would do as he advised if it could be so arranged that the Queen should not be led to think that he relinquished his suit out of distaste for it and so turn her regard into anger and enmity against him which might cause her, womanlike, to undo him.[1]

Several Kenilworth entertainments press for marriage; two suggest disengagement as an alternative: free an enchanted suitor; free an imprisoned virgin. The Queen is asked to intervene and justly remedy the destructive effects of her own beauty by delivering first the Lady of the Lake held prisoner by Sir Bruse Sans Pité, and then that wretched worthy, Deepdesire, enchanted by Zabeta. These two shows are carefully linked with allegories of the gods whose Olympian fiction carries the positive bid for marriage.

Leicester's poets provided Olympian and Arthurian pedigrees, a double fiction. Ferrers wrote verses of greeting spoken by the Lady of the Lake as the Queen entered the castle. The maiden, a shadow of Elizabeth's virgin peril, stood alone upon a floating island and described the antiquity of the castle which since Arthur's days had been held by Earls of Leicester, whose names she recounted. She hailed the Queen as her protector and as descendant of King Arthur. Neither Arthurian pedigree could bear prolonged scrutiny. A second greeting was given by Olympians. By these pageant metaphors a second, immortal capacity for the Earl was suggested. Laneham explains the

---

1 *CSP Span. 1558-67*, p.518.

greeting gift of Mars's protection, armour supported by Leicester's heraldic device, a ragged staff; Jupiter's fireworks signify the thunder god's pleasure at his princely guest. Publication of *Laneham's Letter* (1575) provided an occasion to explain the pageant metaphors to a wider public; at Kenilworth the Queen found an Olympian host, a protector worthy of majesty:

> Thus partly ye perceyve noow, hoow greatly the Gods can do for mortals, and hoow mooch alwey they loove whear they like: that what a gentl *Jove* waz thys, thus curteoosly too contrive heer such a treyn of Gods? Nay then rather, Master Martin, (to cum oout of our poeticaliteez, and too talk on more serioous terms), what a magnificent Lord may we justly account him, that cold so highli cast order for such a Jupiter and all hiz Gods besid (p.471).

Leicester's aspirations were voiced through gods but he directed his poets to provide an alternative for heavenly demands. To avoid offending the Queen he calculated that the mask should slip occasionally and the man behind the gods be frankly revealed.

The more frequently accepted double person of the Queen is the basis for a little play prepared by Gascoigne: a search for political identity, cast as a debate between Diana and Iris, messenger of Juno. Diana appears in the forest, seeking her nymph, Zabeta, who she fears is transformed by Juno's gift of sovereignty. Sovereignty has made Zabeta a goddess. Diana refinds her nymph in the person of Queen Elizabeth. But what goddess has she become? Has power changed her devotion to chastity? Gascoigne relies on the diverse significations of Juno, goddess of empire and of marriage, to imply that, having accepted the gift of one, Elizabeth must accept the other. With a few harsh reminders of the 'nymph's' imprisonment under Queen Mary, Iris insists that Diana was powerless then to aid her nymph: sovereignty altered the case and now must work a further transformation:

> How necesserie were for worthy Queenes to wed,
> That know you wel, whose life alwaies in learning hath beene led.
> The country craves consent, your virtues vaunt themselfe,
> And Jove in heaven would smile to see Diana set on Shelfe,
> His Queene hath sworne (but you) there shall no mo be such. . .
> Then geve consent, O Queene, to Juno's just desire,
> Who for your wealth would have you wed, and, for your farther hire,
> Some Empresse wil you make, she bad me tell you thus;
> Forgive me, Queene; the words are hers; I come not to discusse (p.514).

But this little play was not presented. Possibly its conclusion was too hopeful for 1575. In it Leicester still resists identifying the Queen's majesty as Diana. Gascoigne's distinction between Zabeta and the unnamed goddess is functional in two of the shows which propose release. The unerring body politic must judge two suppliants, one of whom reflects Elizabeth's embattled chastity.

The first, an Arthurian version of the struggle between Diana and Juno, (the theme of the unperformed Zabeta play) concerns the imprisonment of the Lady of the Lake who had greeted the Queen on her arrival at Kenilworth. Immediately after the Queen entered Leicester's castle (we are told) the Lady of the Lake was made prisoner by Sir Bruce sans Pité. Verses place gods thematically behind corresponding Arthurian figures: Sir Bruce is only a harsher face of Mars who gallantly offered Elizabeth his protection as she crossed the bridge to Kenilworth; the Lady, alone upon her island, another metamorphosis of Diana's nymph, Zabeta; moreover Juno, goddess of marriage and empire, and 'all the crue of cheefest Gods' support Sir Bruce. Only the Queen can decide the Lady's fate:

> that yrefull Knight Sir Bruce had hyr in chase;
> And sought by force her virgin's state full fowlie to deface.
> Yea, yet at hand about these bankes his bands be often seen;
> That neither can she come nor scape, but by your helpe, O queene:
> For though that Neptune has so fanst with floods her fortresse long,
> Yet Mars her foe must needs prevaile, his batteries are so strong.
> How then can Diane Juno's force and sharpe assaults abyde?
> When all the crue of cheefest Gods is bent on Bruse his side. (p.499).

In this case the Queen obligingly freed the virgin prisoner, overruling Leicester's marriage gods.

As she hastened away from Kenilworth the ageing Gascoigne, dressed as Sylvanus, trotted on foot beside her Majesty's departing train. He extemporized, salvaging what he could of the Zabeta play which had not been performed, altering it to suit the circumstances of departure. As he ran he wove themes of the Kenilworth entertainments into a sylvan fantasy. Her Majesty 'stayed her horse to favour Sylvanus, fearing least he should be driven out of breath by following her horse so fast'. But Sylvanus besought her to go on, declaring that 'if hys rude speech did not offend her, he coulde continue this tale to be twenty miles long' (p.517). As he protracted the Queen's leave-taking, Gascoigne asked her to provide a happy ending for his story. He tells how the mortal Zabeta most cruelly rejected all her suitors. The language is blunt:

> All which she hath so rigorously repulsed, or rather (to speake playne English) so obstinately and cruelly rejected, that I sigh to thinke of some of their mishaps. (p.518).

This nymph of Diana's has effected monstrous transformations in her suitors, turning them to 'fishes. . .foules. . .huge stony rocks and great mountains'. Chief among Zabeta's victims is Deepdesire, Gascoigne's patron, metamorphosed into a prickly holly bush:

> So is he now furnished on every side with sharpe pricking leaves,

66

to prove the restlesse prickes of his privie thoughts. Mary there are two kinds of Holly, that is to say, He-Holly, and She-Holly. Now some will say, that She-Holly hath no prickes; but thereof I intermeddle not. (p.520).

At this point Gascoigne and the Queen arrived at an arbor of holly and the Principal Bush addressed her, linking Leicester's old allegory of Desire with his Olympian fiction. Desire, as spokesman of the gods, pleads, lightly alluding to the aptness of Leicester's holding Crown lands:

> O Queene commaunde againe
> This Castle and the Knight, which keepes the same for you. . .
> Live here, good Queene, live here. . .
> Give eare, good gratious Queene, and so you shall perceive
> That Gods in heaven, and men on earth are loath such Queenes to leave.
> (p.522).

But he got no reply from the departing Queen.

Clearly the conventions used by Gascoigne and his colleagues could convey both criticism and compliment. The Queen's chastity was in many respects incompatible with her office; it prejudiced the judgements she was called on to make at Court and in 'play'. She had tried to thwart the marriage of Mary Stuart and Darnley, had succeeded in the case of Catherine Grey, and showed a marked predilection for freeing pageant virgins whose deflowering would produce heirs. Time and again Elizabeth exercised a judgement in the marriages of her courtiers that was biased by her own choice. Chastity was a virtue which could hardly admit of compromise (though married chastity is a subject both Spenser and Shakespeare pondered). In her responses to models of her own situation in dramatic art Elizabeth would seem to compromise if she favoured the cause of marriage or of the male pursuer of virgins. The complexity of her situation called for multiple images so that she is figured as impervious goddess, jealous tyrant who does not wish anyone to marry or beget heirs, enchantress and helpless nymph pursued by would-be ravishers: Elizabeth's situation as it appears to the world and as it appears to herself. The criticisms inherent in such fictional explorations were usually mitigated by the suggestion that the Queen, when she remembered the perfections of her higher person, would somehow reconcile the conflicting demands of chastity and justice (virtues for which she was famed) and solve the problem of perpetuity.

It may sound odd to speak of the 'school of Gascoigne' but, for men like George Whetstone, Thomas Churchyard or Thomas Blenerhasset, Gascoigne's proximity to Leicester and the Queen was a mark of dazzling success. He had his disciples and imitators. Whetstone is more often remembered because Shakespeare thought his *Promos and Cassandra* worth rewriting. His story of the judge who punished lechery but seduced his suppliant has been traced to French sources; nevertheless Shakespeare's debt is chiefly to Whetstone. Whetstone's connection with the Inns of Court traditions is therefore worth tracing.

There is some reason to think that Whetstone was for a time at Furnival's Inn, although contemporary registers of admission do not survive. He signs his *Rock of Regard* 'from my lodgings in Holborn, October 25, 1576'; it contains poems addressed to young men who were members of neighbouring Inns of Court or Chancery, and one poem addressed 'to my friends and companions at Furnival's Inn'.[1] *Promos,* dated 29 July 1578, is dedicated to William Fleetwoode, Recorder of London. In 1583 in his *Heptameron of Civil Discourse* Whetstone offers a non-dramatic version of *Promos* but, unlike Arthur Broke who had circulated a post-performance poem of *Romeus,* Whetstone remarks that his play has not yet been performed. No Broke or Hatton had stepped forward to defray the expenses of a production. Whetstone seems to stand, hat in hand, on the very edge of the sphere of influence.

Another figure at the periphery of the Leicester circle and possibly connected with the Inns of Court is Thomas Blenerhasset who in 1582 published his *Revelation of the True Minerva,* a work indebted to Spenser's *Shepheardes Calendar* (1579) and dedicated to Leicester's sister-in-law Lady Leighton.[2] Blenerhasset is remembered chiefly for his contribution to *The Mirror for Magistrates.* His *Revelation·* describes a search for the most suitable symbol for the Queen's majesty. The printer describes it as a 'Poetical description of a deuise'. Possibly the book is an embroidered account of Inner Temple revels, since in its tournament and coronation ceremony Blenerhasset announces the appearance of Pallaphilos:

> The Poets P[r]ince, and Harauldes chiefest king
> Mightie Palaphilos you might persaue
> To place ech one appointing euerie thing
> As it shoulde bee: the gods were bounsing braue,
> No goddesse there, no muse nor Nymphe was graue,
> All did with ioyfull Iubilie reioyce
> Shouting Minerua liues with often voyce   (E2)

The allusion may, on the other hand simply be a complimentary way of recalling Leicester's earlier fictive role and referring to his duties as Master of the Horse during a tournament.

1 Thomas C. Izard, *George Whetstone* (New York, 1942), p.13.

2 *A Revelation of the True Minerva,* ed. J.W. Bennett (New York, 1941). The editor traces the debt to Spenser. References to this edition.

The title page announces the book's theme: its author's wish to discover, 'Who on earth be gods: and by what means men may be made immortall'. Its pilgrim narrator, who relates the tangential episodes (including a pastoral, tournament, songs and a coronation), is reminiscent of Legh and the narrator of Peele's later *Poly-hymnia*. Blenerhasset supposes, as Sackville and the authors of the *Mirror* had done, that magistrates are gods by virtue of their office - a parochial blend of English morality and euhemeristic traditions:

> when. . .a god is rehearsed, not the man, but the vertue which made him of so great estimation is to be regarded, and in this place the author with great admiration, finding all vertue, goodnes and godlinesse, to concurre in a woman his intent is that they whoin [sic] vertue made goddes, shoulde create this goddesse. . .(*4v-5)

He makes a distinction between the Greek and Roman goddesses of wisdom. Minerva is greater than Pallas, goddess of mere human knowledge; Minerva (as is appropriate to the shadow of a Queen who is also supreme governor of the Church of England) is 'euen shee who had the knowledge of heauenly wisdome'.

The inferior goddess Pallas complains in a council of the gods that she cannot continue to exist unless a new Minerva is found on earth. Blenerhasset's legal point here is that knowledge, customs, decisions, laws of a realm must be incarnate in a particular person. Mercury is despatched to seek a new Minerva. Classical figurae are unfolded: Troy, Greece, Rome and Europe are desolate and waste; Mercury reports his fruitless search and delivers the oracle of a new Troy where they will find an English Minerva. She is first described as the Phoenix:

> Yet I am sent that Phoenix rare to finde
> Whom all in vaine I seeke and can not see,
> And yet shee liues, and is of Saturns kinde,
> Begot by Mars, preserued by Ioue, and shee
> Remaynes aliue, in place not knowne to mee. . .
> Yet her to finde the Oracle hath taught. (A3)

The ideal promised by this oracle is imaged as Neptune's diadem, a crown-circled island rising from the sea. Symbolism of the crown expounded by Plowden and Leslie is visualized in pageant. We are shown sovereignty in at least three forms: as the protective golden circlet girdling England to hold back the sea; as two bodies, a woman and an angel; as a line of kings from classical times to the Elizabethan present. Trojan Brutus appears as guarantor and stands beside the lady enthroned upon her island. Aided by the angel who 'did his misse amende' he recounts a perfect genealogy from Aeneas leading to the enthroned Virgin Queen (A4). This iconography appears on Elizabethan coins and state portraits, on book plates, wherever the Queen is portrayed in her legal complexity as body natural and body politic: on one side of a coin a state portrait of Elizabeth, on the other an island with a sacred tree symbolizing the succession; on another coin, the Queen's portrait and on the reverse a Phoenix; on another the Queen matched by Minerva.[1]

The *Revelation* gods journey to England to greet their new Minerva, who thus sees her own virtues pass in pageant before her. She recognizes the procession of deities as the qualities of a good governor and accepts them as an expression of the divinity of the body politic:

> And then the Queene, my seruants? no, my saints,
> Copertiners of my crowne and dignitie:
> Let them leaue off their heeretofore complaintes:
> Bid them come rule this mightie Realme with mee (B4v).

Subservient Pallas weaves another crown for the Queen from symbolic plants and gems brought by familiar pageant figures, by the nine Muses, nine Worthies, seven sages and three Graces. This crown of immortality celebrated in songs confirms the revelation of a true Minerva; a Faerie Queene guarantees that the plants and herbs of the circlet shall never wither. The natural virtues of the Queen have been immortalized, first in legal theory in Neptune's crown, then by poesie in the crown of Pallas. Thus Blenerhasset fulfils his promise to show 'Who on earth be gods: and by what meanes mortall men may bee made immortall'.

Trojan legend reappears in a similarly complimentary and reassuring design in George Peele's *Araygnement of Paris*.[2] Paris, enticed away from pastoral idyll to judge among the goddesses, is made to suggest a political fall of man. Whereas the young Trojan prince spurns Juno's tree decked with golden crowns and Pallas's masque of knights treading a warlike dance, he is tempted by the vision of Helen and bestows the golden apple for beauty upon Venus. Act III ends with angry goddesses decreeing destruction for Troy. The last two acts, in which Paris is arraigned before Diana for his offense against chastity, assume the audience's knowledge of the fall of Troy and subsequent wandering which led survivors from Troy to Rome to Britain. As in the 1561 revels, lust and chastity are political alternatives. In Peele's denouement his rival goddesses are guided to harmony by chaste Diana; earlier in the reign in Pound's marriage masque, Venus and Juno had coerced the virgin. Peele excludes troublesome bodies natural; Diana finds redemp-

---

1 Roy Strong, *Portraits of Queen Elizabeth* (Oxford, 1963).

2 *The Araygnement of Paris* MSR (Oxford, 1910). See H.G. Lesnick 'Myth and Flattery in Peele's *Arraignment of Paris', Studies in Philology*, LXV (1968) 163-70.

tion for Troy. Chastity is seen as a national virtue - England inviolate against European rapists. England's Eliza, combining in her person the powers of the three goddesses, will transform the tragic destiny of Troy into a *felix culpa,*

> The place Elyzium hight, and of the place,
> Her name that gouernes there Eliza is,
> A kingdome that may well compare with mine.
> An auncient seat of kings, a second Troie,
> Ycompast rounde with a commodious sea:
> Her people are ycleeped Angeli,
> Or if I misse a lettre is the most.
> She giueth lawes of iustice and of peace,
> And on her heade as fits her fortune best,
> She weares a wreath of laurell, golde, and palme;
> Her robes of purple and of scarlet die,
> Her vayle of white, as best befits a mayde.
> Her auncestors liue in the house of fame. . .
> In state Queen Iunos peere, for power in armes,
> And vertues of the minde Mineruaes mate:
> As fayre and louely as the queene of loue:
> As chast as Dian in her chast desires.
> The same is shee, if Phoebe doe no wrong,
> To whom this ball in merit doth belonge.   (1246-71)

Two decades after Pound's snub at Bermondsey Elizabeth finally gets her apple. The actors hail her,

> Liue longe the noble Phoenix of our age,
> Our fayre Eliza, our Zabeta fayre.   (1338-9)

Venus's power to destroy kingdoms is exorcised and England appears a paradise regained, perpetually assured by the maiden Phoenix.

Peele's pattern of figura and fulfilment and his use of political metaphor distinguish this play from Pound's marriage masque and an earlier pageant of Paris and the three goddesses devised by Nicholas Udall for Anne Boleyn's coronation in 1533. Udall's pageant, with its devout prayer for an heir, was not concerned with Paris as a prince nor with the historical link between Troy and England. Peele's pattern of sin and redemption stands out clearly by contrast.

The primary value of both Blenerhasset's *Minerva* and Peele's *Araygnement* for this study of political myths is the clarity of their typological patterns and the fund of metaphor they supply for more complex and allusive works of art. In themselves, as solutions to the perpetuity of the realm, they offer a typically Elizabethan answer answerless.

John Lyly, writing at the same time and in the same courtly tradition, probed the paradox of rival goddesses and the partiality of Cynthia or Diana as judge. Two of his best plays (probably written in the 1580s) *Woman in the Moon* (pr. 1597) and *Endimion* (pr. 1591) explore the discrepancy between the two bodies of the monarch. Lyly's use of myth is vigorous and original, his purpose critical as well as complimentary, and it is hard to escape a suspicion that he wrote as much for Elizabeth's exasperated courtiers as for the Queen herself.

The Woman in the Moon proposes that the Queen, who is first in all their hearts, bears resemblance to the first woman - infuriatingly self-contradictory until her magpie's nest of perfections is seen in a proper perspective. Nature creates Pandora so that the shepherds of Utopia can perpetuate themselves; her virtues are taken from the seven planets. The process whereby these planets jealously seek domination of Pandora's perfection is a delightful spoof of the conventions of moral heraldry. In similar terms Peele's Diana had described Eliza (lines 1266-71) and the herald had proclaimed Dudley's virtues as Christmas Prince:

> And as the Torse is by nature wrethid with pure colours of wise Ioue and Pale Luna, Manteled of the first dubled of the secounde, so it vttereth the naturall hasty behauiour of the bearer neyther aboundyng in hote desire, nether oppressed with qwamy colde apte to vnwelde slouthe. But with interchaungeable gouernement of eche disposicion, suppresseth the growynge pride of bothe.[1]

Consecutive descent of each god to exercise influence from the gallery makes Pandora the despair of all mortals. By turns she is imperial, humble, martial, scornful, loving and inconstant. When the play ends her shepherds are as far from propagating their kind as they were before she was created. Finally this baffling creature is taken up to the moon and set to rule in Cynthia's place 'to make the Moon inconstant like thyself'. Pandora rejoices and reminds the audience that the Moon has a multiple persona which she and Cynthia will now share. While Pandora rules the Moon, the goddess may appear as Diana on earth, or as the ambiguous and dreaded Hecate:[2]

> Say Cynthia, shall Pandora rule thy starre,
> And wilt thou play Diana in the woods,
> Or Hecate in Plutos regiment?   (V.i.296-8)

Compensation for Pandora's beloved shepherd Stesias is far from satisfactory. In the course of the play Stesias has finally doubted Pandora's perfection and for this he receives the punishment of comedy; he must become the moon's slave, a ridiculous figure with

---

1 Gerard Legh, *Accedens of Armory,* fol. 222.

2 John Lyly, *The Complete Works* ed. Richard Warwick Bond (3 vols. Oxford, 1902), III.

lantern and hawthorn bush. Amusing as it is, this resolution is even less satisfactory than Hatton's restored Hippolytus. (ch. 4 p.57).

One myth suggested that Cynthia was not only a seductress but the mother of fifty daughters.[1] Lyly dramatized that story and coped with its erotic element in the manner of Gascoigne's Kenilworth shows; he produces a double image. Endimion is enchanted by the mortal and released by the immortal aspect of Cynthia.[2] Contrast between these two bodies is expressed as different phases of the moon; the dark phase when the goddess deserts heaven and walks on earth is represented in the play by Tellus, a lady of Cynthia's court. Tellus and Cynthia struggle for possession of the hero. In scenes with Endimion, who tries to offer a chaste love to Cynthia, Tellus functions quite simply as the vice of the play, evoking and reciprocating weaknesses of the flesh. She is the agent of Endimion's fall into a dream of desire from which the majesty of Cynthia finally awakens and releases him at the end of the play. Endimion is freed of the imperfections of his mortal state; his long white beard falls from him after a kiss bestowed by his sovereign; the heavenly body of this goddess works a stage miracle worthy of Hatton's Diana.

Michael Drayton followed Lyly. While Lyly needed only the dumb shows to direct his coterie audience to see a rivalry between the two bodies of the moon, Drayton in his poem *Endimion and Phoebe* (1595) left nothing to inference. Writing for the general reading public he explains why and how Phoebe appeared as a mortal rival to herself to test Endimion's love. He states that Endimion's sleep was caused by his 'melancholy passion' for this earthly nymph. In a still later version of the myth, the poem *Man in the Moon* (1606) he spells out the imagery which appears in Lyly's dumb shows, offering neo-Platonic explanations for the threefold power of Phoebe, Diana and Hecate, and men's attempts to alter the dark phase of the moon. Lyly dramatized the conflict between an earthly and a heavenly mistress and left his audience to choose the truest likeness.

---

[1] Ovid *Heroides* XVIII, 65; Pausanias, *The Description of Greece* V.i, 3-5, Loeb (Cambridge, Mass., 1935).

[2] For a fuller discussion of *Endimion* see my essay 'Tudor mask and Elizabethan court drama' in *English Drama: forms and development,* ed. M. Axton and R. Williams (Cambridge, 1977).

6

HEIRS AND TWINNED PERSONS
'Gesta Grayorum' 1587/8 and 1594/5

The Theatre, established by James Burbage in London in 1576, created a permanent London base for the popular touring company known as Leicester's Men. The following decades saw a shift in theatrical initiative from the Inns of Court to the public stage. Patrons such as Leicester were an obvious link between occasional and professional drama; common players could reach a much wider audience. The interests of a powerful patron may well have thrust both coterie and professional play texts into print for reasons which were not primarily theatrical. In any case, texts such as *Damon and Pithias, Tancred and Gismund* and *Horestes* survive to suggest ways in which coterie themes and conventions could be adapted 'for six to play' and made available for the public in the provinces and regularly, after 1576, in London.

Festive occasional theatre continued, of course, but its most vital contribution to Elizabethan drama came before 1590. The Inns of Court legacy of dramatic 'cases' and political icons seems a more vital and lasting contribution to English drama than the plays themselves. Professional actors had their own strong traditions and had regularly played morality and social-morality plays through the century; their plays readily absorbed the small stock of enacted political metaphor which was the hallmark of Inns of Court drama. The tension which we have seen sporadically in the lawyers' plays, where men embodied metaphors, was if anything heightened in the popular theatre. Even when appearing for a public audience, the Olympians still seem to embody moral or superhuman political power in a fairly straightforward way, but there was already a supply of stock characters in the popular drama whose dramatic powers were analogous to the Olympians but whose entertainment value was greater - magicians, jugglers, friars, faeries, shapeshifters and quack doctors. These - and Suffolk scepticism of the mysterious differences between king and ordinary man - often explode into nonsense the 'miracles' of the body politic.

The historical and classical figurae chosen at the Inns in the early days of the succession controversy and impressed with contemporary legal meaning passed straight into the popular repertoire; Plowden's ancient kings often appear in the plays of Henslowe's *Diary* and in playlists of the Stationers' Register. The London-based public theatre had a continuity and singleness of purpose - entertainment worth the price of admission - which by its very professionalism rivalled and quickly surpassed the Inns of Court as a creative nucleus. In the 1580s university men and provincial wits thus found another outlet for their talents. Although some like Francis Beaumont and John Marston based themselves at the Inns, their major contribution was to a politically engaged professional, not coterie, theatre.

This shift in the focus of dramatic activity may be seen in a comparison of the two *Gesta Grayorum:* one on the eve of the Armada in 1587/8 and one in 1594/5 just after the plague year which closed all theatres, when Shakespeare is said to have brought the *Comedy of Errors* to Gray's Inn. Some of the implications of this shift from coterie to popular political drama will be looked at in this and the following chapters whose principal subject is the Elizabethan 'history' play.

Coming freshly from the earlier political masques and plays to a study of the history play one must question Irving Ribner's careful distinction between history play and historical romance drama. He rightly says that authenticity of source material is not a good test of an Elizabethan history play, but his assumption that didactic intention is paramount is certainly open to question.[1] Inns of Court masques and plays, however pre-occupied with legal theory, were always speculative because their subject matter, historical or fanciful, was shaped to influence the future. The same may be said of many of the 'romantic' and 'comical histories' of the public stage. Robert Greene's heroes, Prince Edward (later Edward I) in *Friar Bacon* and James IV in the play of that name, are crucial figures in the succession; each is juxtaposed in his respective play to a character with supernatural powers (a magician friar and a faerie king), and the resolution of each romance conflict reveals an important historical figura; I think, therefore, that a knowledge of Inns of Court traditions compels one at least to consider the seriousness of Greene's political engagement. The very improbability of some of the 'magical' solutions to knotty problems of state can be seen as testimony to political awareness and scepticism.

When Edmund Spenser visualized the English succession he placed beside his chronicle of Elizabeth's Trojan, Roman, British, Norman and English predecessors another tree of faerie lineage. This and the title

---

1 *The English History Play* (Princeton, 1957; rev. 1965) Ribner says that histori-cal romance plays have 'no political significance' pp.25, 50. R.B. Sharpe (*The Real War of the Theaters*, Boston, 1935, p.235) says on the other hand: 'It was simply impossible for the Elizabethan writer to keep off the succession problem, whether dealing with history as in *Edward II*. . .or with romance'.

of his Arthuriad should widen our view of Elizabethan 'history'. A damsel from the Queen of Faeries had petitioned Elizabeth at an Accession day tilt in 1571.[1] The Faerie Queene herself appeared at Elvetham in 1591 when the Earl of Hertford entertained Elizabeth and tried for the last time to win her consent to the legitimation of Catherine Grey's sons. Spenser's double genealogy in II.x of the *Faerie Queene* and his further genealogies in III.iii and ix were seized by his contemporaries who annotated with equal care[2]

> A chronicle of Briton Kings,
> from Brute to Vthers rayne,
> And rolles of Elfin Emperours,
> till time of Gloriane.   (II.x)

History, 'faerie' and legal precedent were united in the figure of King Arthur. Elizabethan lawyers did not argue about Arthur's existence; according to their need they simply assumed it. Polydore Vergil had questioned Arthur's historicity in the early years of the Tudor reign but only under the Stuarts were his arguments systematically vindicated. Arthur had served no overlord and had ended tribute to Rome; these precedents vital to Reformation England gave Arthur a legal 'existence' which has sometimes been forgotten.[3] 'Events' in Arthur's reign were cited as early evidence for the oath of fealty; Plowden remembered Arthur's feast at Caerleon as a precedent for homage due from the Scottish monarch.[4] William Lambarde in his *Apxaionomia* (1568) credits Arthur with the custom of *folcmote,* the meeting in which fealty was sworn by all princes, counts, soldiers and freemen to the king in the presence of the king's bishop.[5] Lambarde's precedent and Plowden's arguments were adduced by Edward Coke and Francis Bacon to establish the legal unity of England and Scotland in 1608. Working in unaccustomed concord, these two lawyers showed that a king had always had two bodies and that ever since the time of Arthur allegiance had been sworn to the king's body natural.[6]

---

1 BL MS Ditchley fol. 2.

2 *The First Commentary on the Faerie Queene,* Graham Hough (privately published, 1964), pp.13-14. Professor Hough prints a sample of the annotations made by John Dixon in 1597 to a copy of the 1590 edition of Books I-III, in the possession of Lord Bessborougn.

3 A fine, if sceptical, re-appraisal of the Tudor Arthurian myth is Sydney Anglo, 'The British History in Early Tudor Propaganda' *Bulletin of the John Rylands Library,* XLIV (1961), 17-48; he discusses Arthur as a pageant figure in *Spectacle, Pageantry* pp.44-6, 55, 56.

4 BL MS Harley 849, fol. 21v.

5 William Lambarde, *Apxaionomia* (London, 1568), fol. 135v.

6 Edward Coke, 'Calvin's Case', *The English Reports: King's Bench Division VI,* LXXVII (London, 1907), p.385.

Bacon affirmed Arthur's legal importance twenty years earlier in the Armada year when he wrote dumbshows for *The Misfortunes of Arthur,* a Gray's Inn play which anticipates the conflict of loyalties in Elizabeth's Catholic subjects posed by Philip's Catholic 'crusade'. In this Inns. of Court tragedy, as in earlier entertainments, historical and classical figurae were adapted to express the new and constantly shifting political scene.

Arthur, Astraea and political bastards

Mary Stuart was executed a year before the Arthurian tragedy was presented (February 1587/8) to Elizabeth.[1] Her claim and not her person remained as a burning issue.[2] Her son, James, a Protestant, had been either unwilling or unable to negotiate her release from prison or to prevent her final trial. In despair and with dubious legality, therefore, Mary had finally offered her claim and commended the Catholic cause to Philip of Spain. It was expected in England, and rightly, that Philip would enforce this doubtful claim by arms, as he had successfully done in Portugal, and that he would look for support to Elizabeth's Catholic subjects.

What would James Stuart do under the threat of invasion? Would he join forces with English Catholics and make a bid for Philip's foreign support to gain immediate possession of the crown of England for himself? Or would he remain loyal to Elizabeth and Protestantism, trusting to the due course of succession? James as well as Elizabeth's Catholic subjects faced a conflict of loyalties. The smouldering antagonisms between Scotland and England and between Catholic and Protestant threatened to break out under the threat of Spanish invasion. Statesmen in the audience for *Misfortunes of Arthur* did not know in February of 1587/8 whether a greater peril lay beyond the sea or within the island.[3] Not until 5 August 1588 did James declare himself. Finally, braced by the promise of an English Duchy which

1 Robinson's quarto dates the Greenwich performance 'the twenty eighth day of Februarie in the thirtieth yeare' of Elizabeth's reign. Leslie Hotson points out that this would mean a performance during Lent, which began that year on 21 February. The Queen's revels accounts state that Elizabeth was entertained by Gray's Inn 'betwixt Christmas and Shrovetide' (Feuillerat, *Eliz.,* p.388). The most probable emendation would be 'twentieth day', as Hotson suggests (*Mr. W.H.* London, 1964, p.228).

2 I agree here with Ribner (pp.229-35) that the play should not be seen as a representation of actual persons and events of recent occurrence. E.H. Waller ('A Possible Interpretation of the *Misfortunes of Arthur', JEGP,* XXIV 1925, 241) finds Elizabeth and Mary Stuart in Arthur and Mordred; G. Reese, ('The Political Import of *Misfortunes of Arthur', RES,* XXI 1945, 91) sees James Stuart and the younger Bothwell.

3 BL MS Vespasian C.VIII, fol. 12.

would fortify him against the maxim against alien inheritance, and by the promise of a pension of five thousand pounds and a royal guard, the Scots King proclaimed his eleventh hour hostility to Spain. It was characteristic of Elizabeth's equivocation with James that, as soon as the danger passed, her Ambassador was reproved for offering more than the Queen meant to give.[1] In the winter of 1587/8, with uncertainties both in the north and in the heart of the kingdom, the English government mustered its forces.

Bacon was only one of eight collaborators who wrote *Misfortunes of Arthur*. Five of these men were in the House of Commons and only one had not yet been called to the Bar at Gray's Inn.[2] The Induction offers this play for 'instant use'; five law students, captives of the tragic Muse, are led before Elizabeth. They praise her in her double capacity; they serve the goddess of justice, Astraea, but their Queen embodies for them, as for Spenser, 'both private and imperiall vertues all'. The implicit corollary of their compliment is that Elizabeth has only to view a tragedy on stage to prevent one in her kingdom:[3]

> To serue a Queene, for whom her purest gold
> Nature refind, that she might therein sette
> Both priuate and imperiall vertues all.
> Thus (Soueraigne Lady of our lawes and vs)
> Zeale may transforme vs into any shape....(105-9)

> How sutes a Tragedie for such a time?
> Thus. For that since your sacred Maiestie
> In gratious hands the regall Scepter held
> All Tragedies are fled from State, to stadge. (125-33)

A moment of dismal prophecy in Act IV (iii.13-38) suggests an exact congruence of Elizabethan present and tragic past and casts doubt on the power of the crown to preserve the realm. The ancient chronicler, Gildas, whose silence on the subject of King Arthur had been noted by sceptics, is brought on stage like a figure in the medieval *Ordo Prophetarum* to attest the legal importance of Arthur's imperilled empire. Arthur's cause is England, Ireland and Scotland united by allegiance to one sovereign, encircled by one crown, independent of European domination. If bodies politic remain unchanging this Arthurian empire lives on in Elizabeth herself. From the shifting sands of legend and legal theory Gildas inspires a proleptic prophecy.

In this legal tragedy Mordred and Gawain polarize the possible choice

1 Conyers Read, *Walsingham* (Oxford, 1925) III, 322-3.
2 See Appendix and also Jacques Ramel, 'Biographical Notices on the Authors of *Misfortunes of Arthur*', *N&Q*, CCXII (1967), 461-7.
3 Line references from *EECT*.

of James Stuart and Elizabeth's Catholic subjects. In Arthurian Britain, as in the Elizabethan situation it parallels, there is no true heir. Chronicle sources are altered to heighten the legal significance of Gawain's loyalty and Mordred's treachery.[1] They are brothers, born of one mother, Arthur's twin sister. Mordred, born in incest, is Arthur's bastard. Gawain is the legitimate son of that exemplary king of Albany who carried the sword before Arthur at Caerleon in sign of Scottish homage to his superior king; he is 'valiant Gawin Arthurs Nephew deare / and late by Augels death made Albane King' (IV.ii. 139-40). Gawain's support of the British king in his anti-Roman wars and in the civil war affirms a strong 'feudal' bond between the kingdoms and implies the historical subjection of Scotland to England.

Mordred, prepared to enforce his claim to the crown with foreign troops, is shown dividing the realm among foreign kings in return for their military support; in the narrative of the last battle Mordred goads the now familiar Gorgon, the personification of division; Arthur's bastard is described as 'the spurre of fiends/ And Gorgons all' (IV.ii.123-4).

With the Armada provisioned and ready to sail at any moment, the lawyers hope that Elizabeth will find latter-day Gawains and not Mordreds to defend the realm. But should James Stuart and the Catholics choose the course of Mordred they must be removed from all authority. The past is clear; the future in question.

Thomas Sackville, old Lord Buckhurst, who certainly sat in the audience for the *Gesta Grayorum* of 1594/5 and probably also in 1587/8, might feel some authorial responsibility for these Inns of Court tragedies of 'unhappy families'. Gorboduc had spawned popular offspring as well who make an appearance in Tarleton's (?) *Seven Deadly Sins* (c.1585, rev. 1590), a play in which professional and coterie traditions meet.[2] Only the descriptive plot survives but it shows well enough the mixture of morality play conventions and historical figurae which forms the basis of so many of the 'history' plays of the nineties. Political consequences of the sin Envy are shown simultaneously in two periods

---

1 Geoffrey of Monmouth and Malory agree that Gawain is son of Arthur's sister and Lot, king of Lothian. The lawyers, however, derive him from Augel, king of Albany whose ceremonial role at Caerleon is of legal significance. Geoffrey says that Arthur's sister is Anna married to Loth; both Gawain and Modredus are their legitimate sons. The lawyers follow Malory in making Mordred Arthur's bastard. Arthur's twin birth seems to be their invention. Geoffrey writes of two children born to Uther and Igerne; Malory calls Arthur's sister Morgawse; she is his half sister 'by the modre's side Igerne'.

2 W.W. Greg prints a facsimile and transcript of the plot in *English Dramatic Documents* (Oxford: Clarendon, 1932) II, 2.

of history: Henry VI, imprisoned, lies asleep on stage (Endimion-fashion); the poet Lydgate acts as expositor; Envy enters, struggles with six other sins and gains the playing place, whereupon this serpent of division brings in a pageant of the warring Ferrex and Porrex. Gorboduc, played by Richard Burbage, enacts Sackville and Norton's crucial addition to the chronicle story after he 'hath *Consulted with his Lords* he bringeth his 2 sonnes to seuerall seates'. The action is twice interrupted at moments of fatal conflict by a speech from Lydgate and again from Henry VI. In the absence of any script one may suppose that when both the poet and his king deliberately break into the ancient British action their audience is invited to see the power of Envy in at least two historical perspectives as well as their own. Heterogeneous exempla are bent to a common dramatic form and purpose when Sloth follows Envy as possessor of the playing place to bring on the story of Sardanapalus; this vice is in turn followed by Lechery with her Ovidian pageant of Tereus and Philomele. It is as if the dumbshows of Sackville's *Gorboduc* or Gascoigne's *Jocasta* had become playlets in their own right. There had been similar thematic links between the two independent plays *Misfortunes of Arthur* and a 'comedy' of Catiline's conspiracy (16 Jan. 1587/8) given at Gray's Inn during the first *Gesta Grayorum* revels.[1] Two references to Catiline in *Misfortunes* ask for a double historical perspective by drawing an analogy between Catiline's treachery and that of Mordred, Arthur's bastard. Again the script for this 'comical' history has not survived but it suggests that when 'a comedy of errors' was performed in 1594/5 we have good reason to look for thematic links with the other entertainments, as we did in 1561.

Ephesus, twins and aliens

When James, like Gawain, stood with Elizabeth against foreign invasion the English succession might have been settled. However, once immediate danger had passed, as I have said, Elizabeth repudiated her promise; James was not to have the assured native status of an English Duke. John Leslie's call to amity (on the 1584 title page of his succession treatise) went largely unheeded: 'an exhortation to the

---

1 The cast list for the Catiline play survives in BL MS Lansdowne 55, fol. 11; it is printed in Malone Society *Collections I.2*, pp.179-80. I see no reason to question the endorsement which labels this list the cast for 'a comedy', or to posit from this medley of characters a Plautine comedy followed by a history play. A comedy such as Edwards' *Damon and Pithias* mixes historical characters with Grim, Will and Snap, Plautine humour and a masque of the nine Muses. Pikeryng's *Horestes* has a similar mixture of characters and conventions. This cast list is discussed by Percival Vivian in *Campion's Works* (Oxford, 1909), pp. xxix-xxxi, and by Leslie Hotson in *Mr W.H.*, pp.227-8.

English and Scottish nations for vniting of them selues in a true
league of Amitie: All Britaine Yle (dissentions ouerpast) In peace & faith,
will growe to one at last'.

Uncertainty about James's religion had been a genuine cause of dis-
quiet; if, however, both rulers were Protestant what possible objections
could there be? John Hayward makes the religious foundation for political union quite explicit for a modern reader in his *Treatise of Vnion*
(1604) when he cites St Paul the chosen apostle of Protestantism:

> The first is, by incorporating the people into one politicke body;
> the second, by knitting their minds in one contentment and desire:
> euen according to that which Saint Paul saith: one body, and one
> spirit of these two parts of Vnion, the first may be termed of law
> and the second of loue.   (p.8)

The political meaning of St Paul's *Epistle to the Ephesians* was
presumed so that it might scuttle, once and for all, the troublesome
common law maxim against alien inheritance. Paul's language settled
easily over the king's mysterious second body - tailor made:

> at that tyme ye were without Christe, beyng aliantes from the
> common wealth of Israel and strangers from the testamentes
> of promise, hauyng no hope, and without God in this worlde.
> But nowe in Christe Jesus, ye whiche sometyme were farre of[f]
> are made nigh by the blood of Christe. For he is our peace, whiche
> hath made both one: and hath broken downe the midle wall that
> was a stop betweene vs.

> Takyng away in his fleshe the hatred (euen) the lawe of com-
> maundementes (conteynd) in ordinances, for to make of twayne
> one newe man in hym selfe, so makyng peace:

> And that he myght reconcile both vnto God in one body through
> (his) crosse, and slue hatred thereby. (*Bishops Bible, Ephes.* II.12-16)

The revels of 1594/5 and Shakespeare's *Comedy of Errors* manifest
their authors' awareness of the specific political implications of such
general moral and religious language.[1] As with *Horestes* and Pikeryng
in 1567, we cannot be certain that 'a comedy of errors' is Shakespeare's
play;[2] but we can be certain from the texts of his comedy and the *Gesta*

---

1 The *Comedy's* allusions to *Acts* and *Epistles* of Paul have been discussed by
R.A. Foakes in his excellent preface to the Arden edition (1967).

2 A balanced account supporting an Inns of Court performance for *Comedy
of Errors* is given by Sidney Thomas, 'The Date of The Comedy of Errors',   *SQ*,
VII, (1956), 377-84. This is only one of many essays which make the most
of meagre evidence to forge links between Shakespeare and the Inns: Frances
Yates, *A Study of 'Love's Labours Lost'* (Cambridge, 1936); Leslie Hotson,
Shakespeare's Sonnets Dated (London, 1949); *Mr. W.H.* (London, 1964);
Peter Alexander, 'Troilus and Cressida, 1609', *The Library*, IX (1928) 267-86;
J.M. Nosworthy, *Shakespeare's Occasional Plays* (London, 1965); the corres-
pondence of Neville Coghill and others in *TLS* (19 Jan. to 4 May 1967); Francis
Fergusson, 'Philosophy and Theatre in *Measure for Measure*', *Kenyon Review*,
XIV (1952), 103-20; E.A.J. Honigmann, 'Timon of Athens', *SQ*, XII (1961),

masques of *Amity* and *Proteus* that the lawyers and the poet recognized and used the same coinage. Shakespeare's play is a perpetual delight whereas the Gray's Inn masks are interesting chiefly for their period value. Yet a brief comparison brings out quite clearly the terms in which Shakespeare, at the very beginning of his dramatic career, was revolving and questioning in a comic mode the paradox of the ruler's two bodies.

But such a comparison will not *prove* that Shakespeare's play was written for a first performance at Gray's Inn. It is amply clear from a passage in the *Gesta* that inspiration might have flowed the other way.[1] The revels knights were urged to 'frequent the Theatre, and such like places of Experience. . .whereby they may not only become accomplished with Civil Conversations. . .but also sufficient, if need be, to make Epigrams, Emblems, and other Devises appertaining to His Honour's learned Revels' (pp.29-30).

Although this advice is a light jest, it is probably true to say that Marlowe and Shakespeare had few serious creative rivals among the amateur dramatists. The suggestion that theatrical language might prepare an Inns of Court man for his future at court and in law is an implication worth a pause. Revels kingdoms earlier in the century had been modelled on the court at Whitehall for obvious educative reasons. The tacit notion in 1594/5 is that the theatre will instruct for the future; the lawyer's prince and his knights might begin to model their behaviour on courtiers and player kings of the public stage. As we shall see in the following chapter, the London theatre of the late eighties and nineties was perhaps the freest forum for speculation about the future succession to the throne, and the player kings of the 'history' plays formed prefigurations of a possible 'saviour'.

The Gray's Inn knights of the helmet might well have seen Shakespeare's play and written a revels fiction with similar themes or they may have commissioned his play specially for the occasion. In either case we can assume an easy flow of themes, emblems and iconography between the two theatres. In his comedy Shakespeare draws on a fund of metaphor familiar to the authors of *Misfortunes of Arthur:* political brothers, ships of state foundering upon the Petrine rock, breaches of faith between husband and wife, servant and master of whose

---

3-20; M.C. Bradbrook, 'The Comedy of Timon', *Renaissance Drama,* IX (1966), 83-103.

1 Ed. W.W. Greg MSR (Oxford, 1914); all quotations are from this edition. Questions of influence are complicated by such Inns of Court men as Marston and Beaumont. See Philip Finkelpearl, *John Marston of the Middle Temple* (Cambridge, Mass., 1969); Mark Eccles, 'Francis Beaumont's Grammar Lecture' *RES,* XVI (1940) 402-14.

bond the Phoenix is both religious and political symbol. The new setting Shakespeare chose for Plautus's comedy of twin brothers had current religious and political connotations. Homely misunderstandings caused by the Ephesian and alien twins in the *Comedy* by their very absurdity minimize the gravity of legal conflict between two warring states and prepare for a comic resolution.

A rift in the 'old Amity' between the 'states' of Purpoole and Templaria was the revels theme in 1594/5. The outraged departure of the Templarian Ambassador on Innocents' night, the second evening of the revels, initiated a deft parody of language and manoeuvres then employed between the Scottish and English courts. Following this breach of amity 'a Comedy of Errors (like to Plautus his Menechmus) was played by the Players' (p.22). The following day a revels trial inquired whether the rift between the two 'states' was caused by an enchanter (a creator of theatrical illusions) or by misinterpretation of law (p.23). After trial the innocent enchanter was freed and the old law of misrule, impersonated by the revels Attorney and Solicitor, was stocked and 'sent to the Tower'.

A distinguished audience assembled to celebrate the return of concord in a masque of Amity on 3 January 1594/5 when the golden chain of the Knights of the Helmet was bestowed upon the newly reconciled Ambassador of the Inner Temple. Among the spectators were men who had had to bear the brunt of James's outrage when Elizabeth made him a Knight of the Garter and neglected to invest him with the order and its golden chain, possibly because he still resolutely refused to do homage.[1] Of these distinguished guests - the Lord Keeper (Sir John Puckering), the Earls of Shrewsbury, Cumberland, Northumberland, Southampton, Essex, the Lords Buckhurst, Windsor, Mountjoy, Sheffield, Compton, Rich, Burghley, Mounteagle, Lord Thomas Howard, Sir Thomas Heneage and Sir Robert Cecil - at least Buckhurst (Thomas Sackville) and Burghley, and probably Puckering and Heneage, could remember revels exactly thirty-three years before when the Templars under Dudley had conferred the order of Pallas to solve problems forcibly presented in *Gorboduc*. Closer amity with Scotland was a question which arose in their daily government work, though not all were then engaged as actively as was Essex, who (with the help of Anthony Bacon) was carrying on a cipher correspondence with James VI. Robert Cecil was present, the man who in Elizabeth's final year ensured James's peaceful accession. But in 1594 the Cecils had not tipped their hand.

1 See Helen G. Stafford, *James VI of Scotland and the throne of England* (New York, 1940), p.144; *CSP Scot. 1547-1603*, X (1936) 324 and XII (1952) 324.

The masque proceeded as four pairs of famous friends entered arm in arm (to avoid questions of precedence) and two by two offered incense at the Altar of the Goddess of Amity; after successful offerings by Theseus and Pirithous, Achilles and Patroclus, Pilades and Orestes, Scipio and Lelius, there followed Graius and Templarius; but 'troubled Smoak, and dark Vapour' choked the flame. Angry Amity was finally pacified by 'certain mystical Ceremonies and Invocations' which successfully obliterated the 'former Night of Errors' and 'uncivil Behaviour' (p.25). Templaria's Ambassador received his golden chain; amidst bawdy double-entendre describing the Order, three rules have serious overtones. The first draws attention to plays which criticize the monarch; the other two stress the essential subordination of a Christmas Prince's 'titles and pretences' to those of Elizabeth. These clauses suggest that Henry Helmes, as he learned the business of good government, illustrated in game the behaviour expected of the Queen's royal homager:

> no Knight of this Order shall take upon him the Person of a Male-content. . .making odd Notes of His Highness's Reign, and former Governments; or saying, that His Highness's Sports were well sorted with a Play of Errors; and such like pretty Speeches of Jest, to the end that he may more safely utter his Malice against his Excellency's Happiness.

> Every Knight of this honourable Order, whether he be a Natural Subject, or Stranger born, shall promise never to bear Arms against His Highness's Sacred Person, nor his State; but to assist him in all his lawful Wars, and maintain all his just Pretences and Titles; especially, His Highness's Title to the Land of the Amazons, and the Cape of Good Hope. (pp.27-8).

> Lastly, All the Knights of this honourable Order, and the renowned Sovereign of the same, shall yield all Homage, Loyalty, unaffected Admiration, and all humble Service, of what Name or Condition soever, to the incomparable Empress of the Fortunate Island. (p.31).

The counsellors' speeches which followed this masque are thought, on Spedding's authority, to have been written by Francis Bacon.[1] These revels games were played by and for some of the best statesmen in the kingdom.

Shakespeare encloses the plot of Plautus's comedy of twin brothers between his own opening and closing scenes. Beginning with a judgement scene, Shakespeare precipitates a potentially tragic conflict. Duke Solinus, ruler of Ephesus, decrees death for an alien merchant, Aegeon, who seeks his lost heirs in this enemy state. But even as he pronounces the death sentence the ruler expresses a conflict within himself which the rest of the play will humorously and irreverently

1 *The Works,* VIII, 325-43.

explore. Who sees truer in judging an alien, the law or the prince's compassion? There is a conflict, as we see from the shifting pronouns, between the ruler's two bodies:

> Now trust *me,* were it not against *our* laws,
> Against *my* crown, *my* oath, *my* dignity,
> Which princes, would they, may not disannul,
> *My* soul should sue as advocate for thee.
> But though thou art adjudged to death,
> And passed sentence may not be recall'd
> But to *our* honour's great disparagement,
> Yet will *I* favour thee in what *I* can. (I.i.143-50 my italics)

His is a problem peculiar to a king 'twin born with greatness'. This paradox is externalized in the manner of Lyly and physically embodied in the comic plot. Legal differences between Ephesians and Syracusians seem more and more absurd as all the characters fail to distinguish between the enemy alien and his Ephesian twin. The quarrel between Ephesus and Syracuse which must cost Aegeon his life is preposterous.

Duke Solinus's baffled inability to distinguish between an alien and a denizen when the twins stand before him (in Act V) undermines legal precedence so seriously argued by sixteenth-century lawyers:

> *Duke:* One of these men is genius to the other;
> And so of these. Which is the natural man
> And which the spirit? Who deciphers them? (V.i.332-4)

As he sets aside the death penalty or ransom decreed for aliens and joins a christening, precedence and primogeniture are comically resolved in the exchange of the twin servants, who exit hand in hand:

> *Dromio of Ephesus:* Methinks you are my glass, and not my brother;
> I see by you that I am a sweet-fac'd youth.
> Will you walk in to see their gossiping?
> *Dromio of Syracuse:* Not I, sir; you are my elder.
> *Dromio of Ephesus:* That's a question; how shall we try it?
> *Dromio of Syracuse:* We'll draw cuts for the senior; till then, lead thou first.
> *Dromio of Ephesus:* Nay then, thus:
> We came into the world like brother and brother,
> And now let's go hand in hand, not one before another. (V.i.416-24)

Reunited, after thirty-three years of separation and misunderstanding, the characters celebrate new identities at a 'gossips' feast - a christening or baptism. Solinus's participation in this festivity is figurally appropriate to Innocents' Day, celebrated in the Gray's Inn Christmas kingdom. The Old Law is put aside; in enlightened Ephesus there will be no slaughter of Innocents. The appropriateness of *The Comedy of Errors* to this occasion may be confirmed by the only certain performance of

Shakespeare's play which took place similarly on Innocents' Day 1604. On that night it was performed at court for the royal alien himself. James, living proof that there is 'a time for all things', comfortably seated upon the throne of Elizabeth, was then deeply engaged in his cherished plan for the union of his two Protestant kingdoms.

Proteus and homage

Henry Helmes followed Christopher Hatton's path to preferment. This Christmas Prince distinguished himself in the masque and tournament performed by the Grayans at court on the following Shrove Tuesday, and became one of Elizabeth's Gentlemen Pensioners.[1] The masque of Proteus in which Helmes danced faces a challenge to the Queen's supreme authority and demonstrates her lawyers' ability to deal effectively with such a threat. Blenerhasset's earlier exposition of England and her Queen as Neptune's crown helps us to see what would have been immediately apparent to the court audience. In Thomas Campion's opening song his sea gods have got their iconography and precedence wrong. Amphitrite, Thamesis and the Sea-Nymphs sing of homage and tribute 'to decke great Neptune's Diadem', praising the crown itself without demanding the source of its power. They herald the arrival of Proteus and his Adamantine rock. The shapeshifter has challenged the Prince of the Law to produce something more powerful than his Adamantine rock 'which claymes kindred of the Polar star,/Because it drawes the needle to the North' (lines 221-2). His fable of the rock delicately touches the question which turned all eyes to Scotland in the last decade of the Queen's reign:

> He told him then, how vnder Th'artik pole
> The Adamantine rock, The seas true star,
> was scituate, which by his power devine,
> Hee for his ransome would remoue and plant,
> whereas hee should appoint: assuring him,
> That the wide Empire of the Ocean,
> (If his fore telling spirit faild him not,)
> Should follow that, wheare ere it should be sett.   (148-55)[2]

[1] The Gentlemen Pensioners Rolls in the PRO are not complete. There is a gap between the years 1591 and 1597. Henry Helmes first appears as Gentleman Pensioner in a roll for 41 Eliz. (1598-99) E 407/41-5. He continued in this capacity to serve James I. Francis Bacon who tried in the same year through ordinary channels of patronage to become the Queen's Attorney General was not so successful. His bid, which began in 1592/3 and failed in Oct. 1595, and the suit to be Solicitor General are discussed by Spedding who prints the relevant letters in *Works,* VIII, 231, 288, 313-14, 320, 360, 369-70. See also Thomas Birch, *Memoirs of the Reign of Queen Elizabeth* (London, 1754) II, for letters on this subject and on the cipher correspondence of Anthony Bacon with James VI..

[2] Quotations and references for this masque from the text of BL MS Harley 541, printed in the introduction to MSR *Gesta.*

So confident was the Prince of victory that he entered the rock as hostage and directed Proteus to place it before the Queen of England.

This timely introduction re-interprets the familiar pageant rock and gains resonance from a well-known earlier spectacle when Truth or Troth came from a rock in 1558 to herald the accession of Elizabeth. In her presence the Adamantine rock splits open revealing the Gray's Inn prince and his knights who manifest a personal loyalty unshaken by the allurements of the 'northern star'. This Adamantine rock is only an impresa of power; like Neptune's crown of the opening hymn it is powerless without the personal bond between subject and prince which gives it its meaning. Readjusting the iconography, concluding speeches and songs correct these errors and reaffirm the bond between Elizabeth and her Fortunate Isle, to whom Neptune, Proteus and the northern star are subordinated. This affirmation of loyalty is couched in terms of the double person of the monarch:

> Excellent Queene, trew adamant of Hartes. . .
>
> Proteus stout Iron homager of your Rock,
> Impresa of force, and Instrument of warres,
> Hath praise in deed yet place your praises right,
> (for force to will, and warres to peace doth yeeld). . .
> what can your Iron doo without Armes of men,
> And armes of men from hartes of men doo move,
> The hartes of men, that's it thence motion springs
> Lo Proteus then Th'attractive Rock of hartes,
> Hartes which once truly touched with her beames
> *Inspiring purest zeale and reverence*
> *Aswell vnto the person as the Power*. . .
> Turne fortunes wheele, they euer keepe their course,
> And stand direct vpon the Loyall line.
>
> Your Rock claymes kindred of the Polar star,
> Because it drawes the needle to the North.
> Yet, euen that starr, giues place to Cynthias rayes,
> Whose drawing virtue gouernes and directs
> The flotes & reflotes of the Ocean. . .
> This Cynthia high doth rule those heavenly tydes,
> Whose Soveraigne grace, as it doth wax or wane
> Affections so and fortunes eb and flow.   (197-229 my italics)

It is Cynthia, not Neptune's crown or the northern star, who directs the waves of Ocean and commands the allegiance which is likened to those waves. With a shift of imagery the monarch is described (as was Arthur in the tragedy of 1587/8) as the land itself, a political refuge, both shrine and saint:

> In the protection of this mighty rock,
> Haue scepters straind recoverd wonted skope
> People oppressed have preserued breath.
> Vnder the shadow of this blessed rock
> In Britton land while tempests beat abroade,
> The lordly and the lowly Shepheard both

> In plenteous peace haue fedd their happy flockes.
> Vpon the forcce of this inviolate rock,
> The giant like attempts of power unjust,
> Haue suffred wreck: And Proteus for the seas,
> Whose Empire lardge your praised rock assures,
> Your guift is void, it is already heer. . .
>   well may your present bee,
> Impresa apt thereof, but sure no cause.   (243-57).

Proteus and the water gods enter the rock and discord is drowned in the harmony of the dancing lawyers.

This imagery used to compliment the Queen in the masque of Proteus can be found throughout Shakespeare's plays, but only once and with absolute decorum does he assemble and apply to Elizabeth Tudor herself images which together formed the ideal of the monarch, body natural and politic.   At Elizabeth's christening in *Henry VIII* Archbishop Cranmer invests her with her complex identity. She shall combine the princely and private virtues, her counsel shall be holy and heavenly. Because *Henry VIII* is a Jacobean play, Cranmer can speak of her successor with the complacent certainty of Isaiah in the medieval prophet plays   (V.v.14-62).

Distinctions between private and princely, natural and immortal aspects of the prince, are only lightly dealt with in *The Comedy of Errors* and in the *Masque of Proteus;* they were pondered more seriously in the lawyers' moots and cases and in Shakespeare's own histories and tragedies. Identical twins and a shapeshifter such as Proteus offer dramatic solutions for what are in reality baffling legal complexities. *The Comedy of Errors* which began tragically may end happily because its dramatic duke can overrule the demands of his old law and be baptised anew with the twins, dismissing with a wave of his hand a world where 'princes would they, may not disannul'   their oaths and laws.

7

TYPES OF SUCCESSION

History Plays and Polemics of the 1590s

Two, and in the final decade three, theories of sovereignty were in common currency; each supported possible claimants to the English throne, but Elizabeth would confirm none of them. Under such circumstances it is hard to talk of a Tudor political orthodoxy. The concept of the king's two bodies was very widely recognized but a dramatist who used its language and iconography did not thereby imply his firm belief in it. A dramatist who doubted the miracles of the body politic might still use a figural view of history because it offered an immediately recognizable political testing ground. If it is granted that Elizabeth's reign, however admirable, was not for these men the final and assured millennium then the celebratory element in their plays may be seen as prophetic of future events.

A good deal has been written in recent years to question E.M.W. Tillyard's view that the history play was an affirmation of Tudor historical myth and political orthodoxy.[1] I need not labour the point here but will try, positively, to show why celebratory episodes were speculative. Scenes of ceremonial homage, coronation, marriage and prophecy were intimately linked to the language and imagery of succession debate in Elizabeth's final years. My purpose is not narrowly antiquarian because the theories which made these scenes a focus of intense interest to Elizabethans raise abiding questions about the essence of political authority. If the *terms* of the contemporary sixteenth-century succession debate, which are sometimes recondite, are recognized, these stage actions and symbols release a fuller meaning and become available to modern readers, producers and actors. Speeches and scenes often 'cut' in twentieth-century performances might be meaningfully restored.

A politically engaged dramatist announced his entry into debate by his choice of character, not his mode of imitation. This is where I differ

1 E.M.W. Tillyard, *Shakespeare's History Plays* (1946) pp.55-63; Ribner *EHP*, pp.10, 105, 116-17, 128-9; Ernest Talbert shows the effect of two succession theories in the drama in *Problem of Order* pp.66-8; Maynard Mack Jr. discusses Shakespeare's use of the king's two bodies in *Killing the King*. Martha H. Fleischer in *The Iconography of the English History Play* (Salzburg, 1974) maintains that the popular Elizabethan history plays 'belong so distinctly to the realm of fiction that they are in the main unnecessary to the study of Tudor historiography' p.30. I disagree with her conclusion but welcome her approach to the importance of stage emblem and stage picture.

most sharply with Irving Ribner. It seems to me that 'romance' histories use the modes and conventions of court masque and pageantry whereas the plays he isolates as 'true' histories use an apparently reasoned language of political debate and chronicle event. I say apparently because these two modes were recognized as quite interchangeable in both sixteenth-century law and poetry, as we have seen in the work of both Plowden and Thomas Blenerhasset. Both Ribner and I would be on shaky ground if we were to insist that 'history' meant anything more than 'story'. I accept his test of relevant analogy to sixteenth century political issues and want to extend it to some of the plays he has dismissed.

The immortality of the realm might be evoked as an actual genealogy or as a crown-encircled isle or as two bodies — a woman-and-an-angel, as Blenerhasset has shown (ch. V p.68). Shakespeare in his history plays habitually spins off realistic sounding genealogy in prophetic speeches: in *2 Henry VI* 'Edward the III, my lord had seven sons', or the Archbishop's interminable disquisition on Salic law and French family trees in *Henry V* which usually raises a laugh when the prelate comes up for breath with:

> So that, as clear as is the summer's sun,
> King Pepin's title, and Hugh Capet's claim,
> King Lewis his satisfaction, all appear
> To hold in right and title of the female:
> So do the kings of France unto this day (I.ii.86-90).

Symbolic or iconographic prophecy is often recognizable in his comedies and romances. *Misfortunes of Arthur* might alert us to the potential seriousness of a mode in which chronicle 'begats' are replaced by an icon of the crown-encircled isle. The moss-covered stage Irishman as symbol of political rebellion (in the dumbshows of *Misfortunes*) needs no up-dating, but the Gorgon, Pallas, Diana and the crown-encircled island do. Shakespeare's comedies and romances have in common with the plays of Robert Greene and George Peele coherently linked iconographic textures; moments of prophecy reveal in them recognizable patterns of political engagement and threads which bind an imaginative poetic fabric to the century which inspired it.

I have suggested that the public stage of the 1590s was the freest open forum for political speculation. There was of course more safety in private conversation and anonymous publication but certainly the dramatists were freer than the burgesses and knights of the lower house of Parliament to initiate the forbidden subject of the succession.

The Janus-face of authority can be seen in the treatment meted out to the Protestant Parliamentarian Peter Wentworth by Christopher

Hatton and Thomas Sackville. All three men, as we know, were keenly interested in a succession settlement but Wentworth chose Parliament, the two Inns of Court men the stage. It was probably in 1587 that Wentworth composed a supplication urging the Queen to settle the succession. He tried in vain to present his petition to Elizabeth and finally allowed it to circulate in manuscript. For this he was imprisoned from August to November 1591 and confined for several more months. Hatton, then Lord Chancellor, accused him of writing a 'booke of the heyre apparante, affirmyng allso that yt came owte of coblers & taylors shoppes'.[1] During the Parliamentary meetings of 1592/3, in a friend's chambers at Lincoln's Inn, Wentworth made plans to gain support for his petition in the House. Wind of this reached the privy council who in February 1592/3 called Wentworth to appear (not without some irony) before Thomas Sackville, Lord Buckhurst. *Gorboduc* had been reprinted only two years before, together with a narrative on the same theme concerning the feud between Caesar and Pompey and called *The Serpent of Division*.[2] The author of *Gorboduc* examined Wentworth and committed him to prison. This stubborn Protestant supporter of James Stuart refused to acknowledge the illegality of his petition and consequently spent the rest of his life in prison. He died there in 1597.[3]

Wentworth saw a hope of uniting Catholic supporters of Mary Stuart and Protestant supporters of the Suffolk line in the common cause of James VI. If, as he believed, the barrier of a common law maxim against aliens had been erected against Stuart Catholicism rather than their Scottish ancestry then James's declaration of his Protestant faith had toppled the wall. He was no longer an alien in St Paul's religious sense of the word. With his customary courage Wentworth wrote a treatise supporting James, accepting the theory and miracles of the king's two bodies and retailing them for Protestant readers. The treatise was printed posthumously and, not surprisingly, in Edinburgh. Probably recalling Sackville's tragedy, Wentworth writes:

> O that your Maiestie would but remember the miserable state of this
> land after King Lucius, and after the death of King Gorbodug and
> his two sonnes, Ferrex and Porrex.[4]

1 Wentworth to Burghley, 27 Sept. 1591: SP 12/240 fol.21.

2 If the references in Henslowe's Diary and Dekker's *Satiromastix* may be trusted then Gorboduc and his sons were familiar stage figures in the 1590s. See *Henslowe's Diary*, ed. R.A. Foakes, R.T. Rickert (Cambridge, 1961), pp.132-4; *The Dramatic Works of Thomas Dekker*, ed. Fredson Bowers, I (Cambridge, 1953) I.ii.339-42 and 391-2.

3 J.E. Neale, 'Peter Wentworth', *English Historical Review*, XXXIX (1924), 184-205.

4 Peter Wentworth, *A Pithie exhortation to Her Maiestie for establishing her Svccessor to the Crowne. Wherevnto is added a Discourse containing the Authors*

Wentworth's words predicting a catastrophic interregnum are a simple paraphrase from the play which Leicester took to court (*Gorboduc* V.ii.264-70):

> who shall call this Parliament? Or at whose commandement will the states assemble? for after that her Maiest. breath is out of her bodie (as the Erle of Leicester did not stick to tell her) her Highnes privie councell, is then no more a councel. (Pt II, pp.86-7).

Since the succession could not be discussed in a free Parliament, Wentworth wrote his opinions, as Plowden had done, for some private friends. His belief in and staunch life-long support for Parliament as the central law-making body of the realm makes it the more remarkable that he should have accepted wholesale Plowden's argument that blood royal and not Parliament should determine Elizabeth's successor. He argues:

> If the crowne might be lawfully given at the pleasure of Parliament, what reason is there to call Rich 3 or any such others vsurpers: for they cannot deserue so odious a name, receiving the crowne no otherwise, then at the hand of parliament. (Pt II. p.55).

In all Wentworth's historical examples supporting the miracles of the body politic, to quote Erich Auerbach on biblical history, 'the fact is subordinated to an interpretation which is fully secured to begin with'. A similar technique is apparent on the public stage where 'the event is enacted according to an ideal model which is a prototype situated in the future and thus far only promised'.[1] Enactment, however, did not necessarily encourage belief; the finest plays ask more questions than they answer.

If James thought he could rally all his mother's Catholic supporters to his cause he was mistaken. Religious fissures ran deep; there were those who wanted a genuinely Catholic candidate, and consistency of theory be damned. In 1594 a book appeared to answer such a need. Robert Doleman's *Conference about the next succession to the Crowne of Ingland* brought together arguments for a Spanish successor which

---

opinion of the true and lawfull successor to her Maiestie, (1598), Pt I, p.30. The two tracts are separately paginated; for convenience called here Pt I and Pt II. Wentworth combats arguments about James's foreign birth with Plowden's historical examples of the power of the crown. He argues for the union of the two realms in one political body (Pt II, p.69) and re-interprets the statute 25 Edward III to show that James is not a foreigner. Interpretation of that statute had been complicated since Plowden's treatise. Elizabeth's judges had ruled that *Infants du Roy* applied to children of the first degree. Wentworth counters this decision with another reported in *Dyer's Cases,* in which a Scotsman on trial in England in 1571/2 was denied a jury of Scots by a judge who said 'that a Scot was not to be accompted in England for a stranger' - Wentworth adds scornfully, 'as the meanest student in the Inns of Court knoweth' (Pt II, p.11)

1 Erich Auerbach, *Scenes from the Drama of European Literature,* pp.59-60.

had been circulating since 1571.[1] To support the candidature of the Spanish Infanta, daughter of Philip II of Spain, Doleman (whom contemporaries identified as the Jesuit Robert Parsons) turned his back on the theory of the king's two bodies and consistent arguments about primogeniture in favour of a contractual theory of sovereignty. This efficient and pragmatic theory had found favour throughout the sixteenth century with whichever religious party was furthest from power. Protestants had played with it while Mary Tudor held the throne; it had a chequered, multi-party past.[2] Clearly Doleman could find no genealogical support for a Spanish princess in the immediate Tudor line. He therefore challenged those who believed in succession by blood royal to return with him to the Norman Conquest and ascend family trees from the prime root. Plowden and the Stuarts had been content with a diminutive family tree springing from Henry Tudor and an eclectic, wide-ranging series of legal analogies. Suffolks had been similarly content with that scope though they placed their faith in the power of Parliament and common law maxims to delimit a pure native line. Doleman wanted earlier kings as actual progenitors. He traced a dubious Spanish line from William through the Houses of Britany and Lancaster pausing to show the importance of Constance mother of Arthur of Britany, Dauphin Lewis of France and Blanche, niece of King John, Edward I and his Spanish bride Elinor and the Spanish descendants of John of Gaunt. The implications of this *ab ovo* approach for plays such as Shakespeare's *King John* and Peele's *Edward I* will be considered below, as will Doleman's insistence that the recent rivalry for the crown of Portugal (concluded in favour of Philip of Spain) 'includeth also the very same pretence and contention of the crown of England' (Pt II, p.186).

This Spanish genealogy, which is of the first importance in restoring the critical edge to such plays as *The Spanish Tragedy, Battle of Alcazar* and *Captain Stukeley,* would not have been altogether a surprise to the English. Pageants linking the English and Spanish royal houses had fallen out of fashion with the first rumblings of Henry VIII's conscience but were revived for Mary and Philip in 1554 and were recorded in Hall and the *Great Chronicle* of London for anyone who was interested.[3]

1   Doleman refers to arguments urged in 1571 by Highington one time secretary to Thomas Percy, Earl of Northumberland, *Conference* Pt II, pp.6-9.

2   C.H. McIlwain discusses Doleman's debt to *Vindiciae Contra Tyrannos* and the effect of his tract on seventeenth-century thinkers in Appendix D in *Political Works of James I* (Cambridge, Mass, 1918), pp.xcii-xciv.

3   Sydney Anglo, *Spectacle, Pageantry and Early Tudor Policy* (Oxford, 1969), pp.61, 194-5, 334-5. *The Great Chronicle of London* ed. A.H. Thomas and I.D. Thornley (London, 1938), p.298; Hall, *Chronicle,* p.638; Corpus Christi MS 298 no.8, fols 136-42; *The Chronicle of Queen Jane and . . . Queen Mary,* ed. J.G. Nichols, Camden Soc. (1850), pp.80, 149-50.

However, the speciousness of Doleman's Portuguese succession argument must have been apparent to any well informed Englishman, as an outrageous contradiction of both a primogeniture theory and a contractual one. Philip of Spain had become King of Portugal by ousting Don Antonio whose claims were preferred by the Portuguese people; he became king of Portugal, as he had hoped to become king of England, by force of arms.

As I have said, Doleman drew together arguments which had been in currency since Highington, secretary to the Earl of Northumberland, had first written them down in 1571 in anticipation of a Spanish invasion which never materialized; they suggest a further range of politically charged historical characters and an impudent appropriation to a contractual theory of Elizabeth's cherished metaphor of the marriage of monarch and realm.[1] Arguments for the primacy of the Spanish House of Lancaster seem to have affected Peele's interpretation of the character of the first Earl of that House, brother of Edward I. Peele portrays him as a veritable Iscariot. Doleman shows us why. A true estimation of the character of Edmund Crouchback,

> importeth very muche for deciding the controversie between the houses of Lancaster and yorke ... we read that this Lord Edmond was a goodly wise and discreet prince, notwithstanding that some authors cal him crokback and that he was highly in the favour both of his father King Henry, as also of his brother King Edward. (Pt. II, p.32).

Edmund receives his character from each writer's assessment of the claims of his descendant the Spanish Infanta. According to Doleman the pure Lancastrian line passed from Edmund to his grand-daughter Blanche who brought it to her husband John of Gaunt. Upon the death of Edward III not Richard II but Gaunt, the eldest living son, should have had the crown. Richard's motives are all explained as fear of that more legitimate claim. This is why (according to Doleman) Richard sent Gaunt to Spain hoping he would be killed seeking to win the kingdom of Castile; it is also why he appointed Roger Mortimer his heir and why he cravenly banished Gaunt's son Bolingbroke, hoping to extinguish Lancastrian claims altogether.[2] The same accusations are made in the ghost prophecy and masque of Cynthia in the anonymous play *Woodstock* and are apparently denied by Shakespeare in *Richard II.*

Doleman's view of the social contract affects his interpretation of the coronation ceremony and, by analogy, the marriage ceremony; he alerts

1   See above p.92 n 1.

2   Doleman's tract is discussed by L.B. Campbell, *Shakespeare's Histories* pp.176-81 and Talbert, *Problem of Order* pp.66-7.

one to the importance of contemporary stage directions. Coronation, he says, makes a king and not blood royal; in the crowning ceremony, and not before, subject and sovereign swear conditional oaths. If the sovereign breaks this oath he may be deposed. As he scans history for confirmation, Doleman finds only one exception; Henry V received the allegiance of his subjects *before* he had sworn his coronation oath. This exception was allowed (Doleman argues) because the English nobles knew that the son of Henry IV was in every way an admirable young man. Doleman's legal point about the nature of kingship turns upon a 'reading' of Henry V's character and reputation *before* he came to the throne. Shakespeare and the author of *The Famous Victories of Henry V* had in mind another theory of kingship and other versions of Hal's character to support it. Meditating on the marriage ring which bound Henry to his realm Doleman makes a hopeful leap into metaphor to persuade the English to reject the amorous advances of James Stuart.

Characteristically Doleman discusses the monarch's marriage to the realm as a contract, not, as Plowden had done, an affair of the heart. He was on uncertain legal ground (as investigations of the legality of the Grey-Hertford marriage have shown). There was serious confusion over the legal status of a marital pre-contract and the marriage ceremony itself (promise *de futuro* and marriage *de praesenti*). Doleman's view is clarified by his certainty about the social contract: claim by blood royal is only a marital pre-contract. Only coronation can confirm the legality of a succession claim; at the coronation the heir is *elected* by the people and this ceremony is the proper marriage *de praesenti* (Pt I, pp. 132-3). By metaphor Doleman persuades the reader to accept the social and marital contracts as identical. Then he argues that if marriage contracts can be broken because of difference in religion, so, too, can the claims of an heir presumptive to the throne. Invoking St Paul's decree that no Christian need remain married to a heathen, he assumes that non-Catholics are heathen. James is Protestant, and the English are urged to reject him before the legally binding ceremony of coronation. Doleman's reliance on the political marriage metaphor should confirm the political engagement of 'romantic' histories such as *Locrine* where wife and crown are bestowed simultaneously. These plays have over-arching metaphors which govern both gesture and juxtaposition of scenes.

Impassioned objections from loyal Catholics to whom a Spanish ruler was abhorrent register disgust at the reversal Doleman made in Plowden's original arguments. People had grown used to the Suffolk and Stuart cases, and Plowden's historical precedents for Scottish homage had even reached the Index of Holinshed's *Chronicle* (1587). One had only to turn to 'homage' to be directed to the relevant pages in the reigns of the Conqueror, Henry II, John, Henry III, Edward I, Edward III and Henry VI. Texts of the oaths were printed together with the description of John Baliol's ceremony.

Sometime between the appearance of Doleman's book in 1594 and Wentworth's tract of 1598 Sir Edmund Ashfield wrote to the King of Scots alerting him to the danger of Doleman's book and to the urgent need for a Protestant Stuart counterblast. Tracts which had been prepared for the King's Catholic mother had become 'dangerous' because they implied a consequent return to Catholicism and gave offense to Protestants. He urged James to woo the common lawyers who were 'mightie rich and pollitique' and held the greatest offices. They kept the key to his legal status; James must convince them that he was native born:

> They doe entertaine some feare of thaire owne particular estates yf there happen alteration of State, therfore may it please your Majestie to insert some inducements (into the said bookes) insinuating to the Lawers that you hould and esteeme them most necessarie members in well gouerned state as they would be taken to be and indeede are found[ation] for the support of regall power and authoritie. This course doutlesse will prepare their hartes and affections towardes your highnes, and make them willinge at all times to expound the Lawes and Statutes on your behalfe whereby you shall not be reputed nor excluded as a stranger borne.[1]

William Watson, a seminary priest, wrote from prison in April 1599, to Edward Coke, the Attorney General, offering to expose Doleman (whom he identified as Robert Parsons) for his theoretical volte-face. During Mary Stuart's lifetime, he believed, Parsons had written *Leycester's Commonwealth*, a scurrilous book arguing for the Stuart succession through the popularized theory of the king's two bodies. Watson said that many Catholics were disillusioned by the ease with which 'Doleman' now abandoned his earlier theories about the body politic. Watson would discredit Doleman by quoting his earlier tract against his later:

> So long as Doleman was Scotts and Leicesters common wealthe in Requeste: there were diuers Sem. [inary priests] dolemanists ... But after dolemans dryfte was oure descried I thinke there was not neyther is there anyone Sem. this day aliue that wisheth a Scotts gouernment, except Respectiuely rather then a Span: should haue yt and the Reason is for that all who fauoured the Scotts title before time were then dolemanists but therefore now bond either to Spaine with him or else finding at length what his drifte was first for Scotland and then for Spaine, they utterly haue abandoned abhorred, and detested all his practyses and bookes of state seeking to supresse them to the uttermost as tending to no end but raysing of slanders against prince and peeres.[2]

1   BL MS Cotton Julius F. VI fol. 139.
2   Inner Temple MS Petyt 47 fol. 103.

A fair test of the circulation of Doleman's arguments is the Common-place Book of Edmund Pudsey, a delightful index to the literary and political tastes of an educated gentleman. Pudsey saw the implications of the recent Portuguese conflict for the English succession controversy; he realized that the character of Edmund Crouchback might determine the legitimacy of Spanish Lancastrian claims. His notebook (best known for its transcriptions of lines from the plays of Shakespeare, Jonson, Dekker and Marston, and from the Middle Temple *Prince d'Amour*) has a long section on the 'Genealogies of Kings' which is transparently Pudsey's eclectic gleanings from succession literature current at the turn of the century.[1] His jottings on Edward I and his brother Edmund (fol. 5) have a direct quotation from Doleman (Pt II, fol. 32), showing that the founder of the House of Lancaster was 'wise, goodly and discreet high in favour both with his father and his brother'. Pudsey follows the Lancaster line from Edmund to 'the now king of Portugal', he brands the Suffolks with bastardy but traces Catherine's line to her son 'Ld Bewchame' (fols. 6,8). He had no doubt that Mary Stuart ordered Darnley's murder, but he carefully draws the genealogy from James IV to James VI, 'married to the king of Denmarkes daughter' (fols. 7v,8). Margaret Tudor's second family is traced to Arbella Stuart, daughter of Darnley's younger brother Charles Stuart.

Henry Hooke, a Stuart supporter, writing as he says 'Anno 43 Eliz' (1600-1) has nothing but scorn for Doleman whose pseudonym was well chosen: 'He giueth himself not vnfittingly the name of Doleman, that hath sowne the seede of dissention ... a man of woe and sorrowe.'[2] Hooke deplores this reopening of the York-Lancaster dissension. 'There is no more reason nowe to craue the voyce and consent of old John of Gawnt in the succession to come, then in the dayes of the twoe last Henries of England, lawfull kings of famous memorie' (fol. 12v). Hooke is certain that the crown will follow the eldest female and descend by Margaret Tudor to James Stuart.

Thomas Wilson, nephew to Elizabeth's principal secretary of that name, had no sympathy with Doleman's arguments either but felt it necessary to refute them as well as the older arguments for the Suffolks in his 'State of England', written in 1600. He begins by listing the '12 Competitors that gape for the death of that good olde Princesse the now Qu: the Eldest Pr; in yeares and raygne through out Europe or our Knowne World'.[3] He is clearly in favour of James VI although he recognizes that Arbella Stuart, his English-born cousin, may

1 Bodley MS Eng. Poet. d. 3.
2 Of the Succession of England: BL MS Royal 17 B XI fol. 12v.
3 SP 12/280 p.2.

better satisfy the requirements of the common law against aliens: 'she is english borne (the want whereof if our Lawyers opinions be corant is the Cause of his exclusion)' (p.3). However he dismisses Arbella and the rival house of Suffolk, both on grounds of bastardy. It is indicative of the turn which Protestant polemic had taken that Wilson does not list James Stuart with the 'foreign claimants'. These he considers to be the King of Portugal, the Duke of Parma, the King of Spain and the Infanta of Spain. He unmasks Doleman, 'a father fryar called Robt Parsons in Spayne,' who has lately made a book for the Infanta fetching her title '480 years since from Henry 2' and further off '540 yeares agoe from Constance daughter to Wm the Conqueror'. He cannot see how Doleman can trace a genealogy through the House of Britany since that line ended with Arthur and his mother (another) Constance. When Wilson presents his own arguments for James Stuart they prove to be those originally put forward by Plowden and published by Leslie: the crown is a corporation; Henry VII prophesied the union of the kingdoms through the marriage of James IV and Margaret Tudor; Henry VIII's signature on his notorious will was forged. One section of Wilson's argument against the validity of Henry VIII's will shows his familiarity with the attack as it appeared in *Leycester's Commonwealth* (p.191); Wilson recounts the testimony of William Herbert, Earl of Pembroke, at an early meeting of Elizabeth's council; the episode pictures counsellors about to rush to Cheapside to proclaim the Scots Queen heir presumptive but restrained at the last minute by the Earl of Leicester.

Watson, Ashfield, Hooke, Pudsey and Wilson spoke out against Doleman and accused him of re-opening the war of the roses. It may be that the rage of historical re-assessment he created worked in the end for James Stuart whose most illustrious progenitor had after all, and to everyone's relief, ended that conflict.

Miracles of the body politic?

Though characters in Elizabethan history plays and 'romance' histories sometimes advance a theory of contractual kingship they are almost always contradicted, defeated or discredited. In the kingship controversy of the 1590s the anonymous author of *Woodstock* therefore stands out, unconventional and audacious. He bases his play on the proposition that a king must protect his realm or lose his right to govern; he posed situations which questioned axioms of the theory of the king's two bodies: that the king's body politic protects the realm, never errs, is never under-age, is never senile, transforms to English a foreign wife, or foreign-born heir.

98

The author of *Woodstock,* using morality play techniques, created a dramatic character, separate from King Richard II, who embodies the first vital aspect of kingship; Thomas of Woodstock is Protector of the realm during the king's nonage. When Richard comes of age and turns against his uncle the dramatist exploits for all it is worth this dramatic separation of the kingly figure from the kingly function.

According to English chronicle sources Richard II came lawfully to the throne with the consent of Edward III. During Richard's reign his uncle, Thomas of Woodstock, one of Edward's sons, was killed. Both *Woodstock* (the anonymous play) and Shakespeare's tragedy *Richard II* ask covertly, 'What did Richard have to do with the death of Woodstock?' Both plays raise basic issues about the nature of kingship. A theory of the king's two bodies would absolve Richard of guilt. Doleman's contractual theory, on the contrary, suggested that by destroying Woodstock, Richard destroyed his only sound claim to the throne; his deposition would thus be justified.

The anonymous dramatist's audacity is apparent in the prophecy of the ghost of Edward III and the deadly masque of Cynthia in which Woodstock is carried to his death. It was a master-stroke of dramatic economy to make Woodstock the Protector of England; for thus when Richard persecutes his uncle and condemns him to death he strikes down both a man and a legal ideal. Woodstock himself utters pious homilies of non-resistance to tyranny but as he patiently awaits his end in prison a more authoritative voice reveals his folly. The ghost of Edward III throws doubt on Richard II's title, reminds Woodstock of Richard's foreign birth and urges the Protector to arms:

> behould me heere. sometymes faire Englands lord
> (7) warlicke sonnes I left, yett being gone
> no one succeeded In my kingly throne
> Richard of burdex, my accussed grand child
> Cutt of yor titles to the kingly state
> & now yor liues and all, would ruinate
> murders his grand siers sonns: his fathers brothers
> becomes a landlord to my kingly tytles . . .
> thy brothers Yorke & Gaunt are vp in Armes
> goe Ioyne wth them. preuent thy further harmes [1] (2466-85).

England's hero-king expresses an argument which Elizabeth's government considered treasonous. Multiple voices of drama made it possible for the author of *Woodstock* to make this denunciation while at the same time explicitly denying it. Immediately after the appearance of the ghost, Woodstock muses:

[1] *The First Part of the Reign of King Richard the Second or Thomas of Woodstock,* ed. Wilhelmina P. Frijlinck, MSR (1929). I have called the play *Woodstock* following its modern editor A.P. Rossiter (*Woodstock, A Moral History,* 1946) to avoid confusion with Shakespeare's play; the MS is untitled.

twas but my fancye
alls whist & still, & nothing heere appeeres (2496-7).

Simple statement denies but cannot cancel the more vivid visual reality of the ghost of Edward III. One voice contradicts another, yet the evidence of our eyes and the swift destruction of Woodstock confirm the ghost's prophecy.

But perhaps the most powerful visual effect is one which immediately precedes Woodstock's imprisonment. King Richard appears in a masque of the goddess Cynthia and her attendants. Not Richard but one of his flatterers impersonates Cynthia, giving wordless support to the Duke of Lancaster's earlier accusation that the king no longer rules the realm; the vizarded figure of the immortal body politic is a base sham. Though the audience knows Richard to be among the murderous dancers and recognizes the king's voice, all the dancers are vizarded and the king cannot be identified until the very last line of the scene, when, tellingly, he uses the royal 'we'. This grim parody of the masques presented to Elizabeth questions the theory of the immortal body politic. Cynthia and her attendants disappear carrying the Protector to imprisonment and death, but the user of the royal pronoun is still visored. There is no man who can accuse the king and thus no man who can condemn the dramatist of treason.

This analysis of *Woodstock* is not meant to identify its author as a rebellious Catholic or an advocate of the Spanish succession; for, if we could, so certainly could the more alert government of Elizabeth. It should, rather, underline what is meant by the freedom of the stage. The manuscript of *Woodstock* shows signs of long use as a prompt copy in a playhouse; its revisions and deletions could themselves be the subject of an entire essay on censorship and conditions of public performance. No one has been anxious to tie the play to a particular date. It might have been written and performed at any time between 1590 and 1625. I believe it belongs in the 1590s and should be considered as the most daring and outspoken of all the Elizabethan history plays. I have considered it first because as one of Ribner's unquestionable canon it illustrates the extraordinary protection and interchangeable advantages of both modes of imitation - the powerfully reasoned genealogical argument and the telling denunciation of masque iconography.

In its broadest outline the action of Kyd's *Spanish Tragedy* shows the destruction of all successors to the crowns of Portugal and Spain who have unjustly tried to possess Bel-Imperia. By means of Hieronymo's pageants for the King of Spain and the Portuguese Ambassador at the end of Act I, the enemies of Bel-Imperia are identified as enemies of England. John of Gaunt, essential to the Spanish Lancastrian claims, appears in the last pageant, not as the genial progenitor who sat amiably beside Alphonso the Wise of Castile in London pageants for Catherine of Aragon (1501) or Charles V (1522) or Philip and Mary (1554), but as the English conqueror of Spain.

Spanish King and Portuguese Ambassador appreciate the 'misterie' of the old judge's pageant, admitting that both their countries have submitted in the past:

> Since English warriours likewise conquered Spaine,
> And made them bow their knees to Albion. (I.v.55-6)[1]

In the final act Hieronymo, denied all lawful justice, achieves his revenge against Portugal and Spain by means of a play. *Soliman and Perseda* accomplishes, in deadly miniature, the larger topical purpose of Kyd's whole *Spanish Tragedy*. The entire Spanish Lancastrian House is wiped out and as the King of Spain surveys the dead bodies of the royal actors he mourns the extinction of his entire line:

> What age hath euer heard such monstrous deeds?
> My brother, and the whole succeeding hope
> That Spain expected after my discease.
> Go, beare his body hence, that we may mourne
> The losse of our beloued brothers death;
> That he may bee entom'd what ere befall.
> I am the next, the neerest, last of all. (IV.iv.201-7)

Without so much as a legal argument Kyd showed that no Spanish blood claim could be *directly* traced from the sixteenth century back to John of Gaunt. The historicity of his events is of no importance; he does not even name his Spanish king; it is quite sufficient for his purposes that this nameless Spanish monarch came *after* John of Gaunt. The pageants, like the dumbshows of the Inns of Court, provide the necessary historical perspective and the events of the play release an important part of their meaning.

Bel-Imperia, as her name suggests, has a theatrical ancestry which stretches back to Widow England and Lady Respublica. We have seen this personification in classical dress and in ancient British weeds at the Inns of Court where both Jocasta and Videna had allegorical overtones. The metaphor of the monarch's marriage to his realm, as well as the legal proposition about foreign wives transformed by the king's body politic, bring some of the 'romantic' histories Ribner left beyond the pale firmly within the genre. The lively native strain of the wooing play enriches the following plays but its comedy is in no way incompatible with the scepticism I have emphasized.

---

1 *The Works of Thomas Kyd,* ed. F.S. Boas (Oxford, 1901).

Bastardy and the Prince's foreign wife

Peele's *Edward I* and Greene's *Friar Bacon and Friar Bungay* are two apparently episodic plays which Ribner dismisses because they do not use the past for its analogy to present problems. He seems to have been decidedly uneasy in the company of juggling friars and didn't respond to the techniques by which the analogy was drawn. Both plays revolve the question of the crown's power to transform Edward I's Spanish wife into an English Queen. Both authors face squarely the English nightmare: a Spanish Infanta seated upon the throne of Elizabeth. Plowden had insisted that in law the crown made a king's foreign wife English; it would therefore make a *foreign claimant* English. Peele and Greene test the first part of this legal analogy in the historical past for the light it may shed upon the second, untested part of the analogy. Both use a figural framework but within it use different dramatic techniques to reveal and contain the Spanish threat.

Peele sees sixteenth-century Spanish claims to the English throne as illegitimate. He therefore takes this political metaphor and draws the portrait of a lustful fourteenth-century Spanish princess whose shameless incontinence before and after her marriage to Edward I leaves the entire genealogy (by which the sixteenth-century Infanta claimed) illegitimate. Queen Elinor in this play is neither an historical portrait nor a psychological study; she is more like Eve of the mystery plays, and Peele's hope of political redemption demands her guilt. Each episode of this play seems to me to illustrate a different branch of the genealogical tree. Peele suggests that all are rotten, and asks the audience to snap them off, to recognize the one sound branch of legitimate succession which will pass precariously through the weak Edward II. This freedom of selection and interpretation was fully sanctioned by a figural view of history. Why should characters live on (as historically they did) when for the purposes of the Elizabethan succession their lines were finished? Edward I and his 'adulterous' brother, Edmund first earl of Lancaster, disguised as friars stand by Elinor's bedside and hear her confession which is also a prophecy:

> In pride of youth when I was yong and faire,
> And gracious in the king of Englands sight,
> The daie before that night his Highnes should,
> Possess the pleasure of my wedlockes bed,
> Caitife accursed monster as I was,
> His brother Edmund beautifull and young,
> Vppon my bridall couch by my concent,
> Enioies the flowre and fauour of my loue.
> > *The King beholdeth his brother wofully*
> And I becam a Traitresse to my Lord...
> For Ione of Acon the supposed child,
> And daughter of my Lord the English King:

> Is baselie borne begotten of a Frier...
> His onelie true and lawfull sonne my frendes,
> He is my hope, his sonne that should succeed.
> Is Edward of Carnaruan latelie borne...
>
> *King.* Vnhappie King dishonored in thy stocke,
> Hence faigned weedes, vnfaigned is my griefe. (2747-2800)[1]

Elinor dies, the King is estranged from the treasonous earl of Lancaster; another Scottish rebellion is announced; Elinor's illegitimate daughter dies of grief. Why should Joan live on (as she historically did), why should Lancaster remain loyal to strengthen an illegitimate Spanish claim? For purposes of the succession their lines are exterminated with a sexual pun. Bastardy, incest, death are to be seen as dramatic metaphors in a figural view of history. And yet the play is not really didactic because though Peele is clear about who shall not succeed to the English throne, he is not so sure who shall. His play is profoundly sceptical: the crown is unable to control the foreign queen's lust, and the king is driven into shifty disguise to obtain that knowledge which the law presumed him *always* to possess.

Greene, too, dramatized Edward I's Spanish marriage and took an ostensibly more cheerful view of the power of the crown to alter a Spanish princess to a good English breeder. He keeps his prescient Friar and his wayward Edward as separate characters. Each, according to his ability, attempts to protect England from the threat posed by the political power of Elinor's foreign relatives, the King of Castile and the Emperor of Germany. During the first half of the play Bacon's magic assures the supremacy of England over these continental powers. Greene does not argue the issues theoretically, instead he makes pageant-like equivalents suggesting at least three versions (as Blenerhasset had done) for the monarch's body politic: the focal images are the perpetual crown as a wall of *gold* protecting the island from its foes, the tree of succession, and the contrast between friar and prince.

Edward's deliberations on matrimony in *Friar Bacon* concern the nature of the prince's metaphorical marriage with the crown. The 'hey-presto' language of Plowden's treatise is certainly susceptible to comic treatment, which is what Greene gives it: but treatment and tone should not blind us to the fact that important topical issues are being dealt with. Edward is in love with Peggy the faire mayde of Fresingfield, 'Suffolks faire Hellen, and rich Englands star' (line 1424).[2] His plight begins to take shape as a temptation of Paris. Marriage with Elinor, Princess of Castile, proposed by his father Henry III, would assure

1 W.W. Greg, ed, MSR (1911).
2 *The Honorable Historie of frier Bacon and frier Bongay,* ed. W.W. Greg, MSR (1926).

Edward all the qualities of the rival goddesses in Peele's *Araygnement:* love, policy and empire. Edward's dereliction of duty as heir apparent is counterpointed by the Fool's masquerade as Prince in Oxford. During these early scenes Friar Bacon serves to remind the audience of a higher purpose symbolized by his ambition to protect England with a wall of brass. Wider vision offered by Bacon's magic glass enables Prince Edward to discover how unsuitable is his passion for an English commoner. Edward renounces his love and marries her off to the Earl of Lincoln, thus securing England from the danger of a native claimant of inferior blood.

> *Lacie:* Humbly I take her of my soueraigne,
> As if that Edward gaue me Englands right,
> And richt me with the Albion diadem. (1075-7)

Troublesome questions of homage and subjection to foreign powers which a foreign bride might bring with her are imaginatively handled in a scene preparatory to the meeting of Elinor and Edward. The German Emperor, the King of Castile and Elinor arrive with Henry III to meet the famous Friar Bacon. At Oxford the Friar holds his 'consistorie court,/ Wherin the diuels plead homage to his words' (lines 636-7). Here a three cornered dispute between the German divine Vandermast, the Suffolk Friar Bungay (who has been trying all along to marry the milk-maid to the Earl of Lincoln) and Bacon, is staged as a conjuring contest. Its subject is the power of 'spirits'; the visual object of dispute is a royal family tree conjured by Bungay. In response the foreign magician conjures up Hercules 'Alcmenas basterd' (line 1203) to strip the branches from Bungay's tree. Bacon steps in to prevent this bastardly attack on the native tree, forcing the foreign challenger off stage on the back of his own devil. European monarchs (unflatteringly likened to devils) are made to acknowledge English superiority. This achieved, the meeting of Edward and Elinor of Castile takes place, and he loves her at first sight. Juxtaposition of scenes assuring England's continued supremacy is important. From this point in the play power lies in Prince Edward. Bacon, who had vowed,

> And I will strengthen England by my skill,
> That if ten Caesars livd and raignd in Rome,
> With all the legions Europe doth containe,
> They should not touch a grasse of English ground (232-5).

fails to build his wall of brass. England will be walled not with brass but with gold. The ideal end of his magic is seen as a metaphor and symbolized by the golden circlet carried in the marriage procession in the play's final scene.

This legal 'truth' dictates the concluding heraldry. In ceremonial action the Emperor of Germany and King of Castile acknowledge

English supremacy, which, in another mode, the earlier conjuring scene had assured; they carry swords before the English Prince. Suffolk Peggy safely married to an English Earl is properly subordinated in procession to Edward's bride:

> Enter the Emperour with a pointles sword, next the King of Castile, carrying the sword with a point, Lacie carying the globe Ed. Warr, carrying the rod of gold with a doue on it, Ermsby with a crowne and Scepter, The queene with the faire maide of Frisingfield on her left hand, Henry, Bacon with other Lords attending. (2074-9)

Inspired by this stately show Friar Bacon renounces his magic and prophesies that a greater successor shall spring from the royal union. But Greene does not altogether deny the strife and misery depicted in Peele's *Edward I;* according to Bacon the offspring of Edward and Elinor, like the sons of Adam and Eve, will initially bring discord; but within the historical figura he sketches the promised redemption, hailing Queen Elizabeth as the matchless flower of the rose tree of state and the peace of heaven which shall harbour in these leaves. His language, expanding conventions of compliment used in Peele's *Araygnement of Paris* and in pageant moral heraldry, is integral to the mode of imitation Greene has chosen:

> I find by deepe praescience of mine art,
> Which once I tempred in my secreat cell,
> That here where Brute did build his Troynouant,
> From forth the royall garden of a King,
> Shall flowrish out, so rich and faire a bud,
> Whose brightnesse shall deface proude Phoebus flowre,
> And ouer-shadow Albion with her leaues.
> Til then, Mars shall be Maister of the field,
> But then the stormie threats of wars shall cease. . .
>   plentie shall enrich,
> The strond that gladded wandring Brute to see,
> And peace from heauen shall harbour in these leaues,
> That gorgous beautifies this matchles flower,
> Appollos Hellitropian then shall stoope,
> And Venus hyacinth shall vaile her top,
> Iuno shall shut her Gilliflowers vp,
> And Pallace bay shall bash her brightest greene,
> Ceres carnation in consort with those,
> Shall stoope and wonder at Dianas rose.

> *Henrie.* This Prophesie is mysticall,
> But glorious commaunders of Europas loue,
> That makes faire England like that wealthy Ile,
> Circled with Gihen, and first Euphrates,
> In royallising Henries Albion,
> With presence of your princelie mightines. . .
> Thus glories England ouer all the west. (2121-55)

Yet even this is not naive wish-fulfilment. Earlier in the play we have seen Bacon's magic fail; the brazen head spoke of past, present and future, and no-one was able to interpret its meaning. Now Bacon himself speaks a prophecy which ends not in Diana's rose but 'peace from heaven' which 'shall harbour in these leaves'. What, one may ask, is the power of this emblem? Is it a remnant of the Friar's now discredited magic? or the promise of a more powerful reality?

Spenser too, had made imaginative links between chronicle history and romance. He paused in the two genealogies offered to Prince Arthur to paint a political emblem which we recognize as a visual equivalent for his faerie genealogy: a city encircled with a wall of gold (II.x.79). This, as I have tried to show, is the political medium of Greene's plays. Greene's conjuring Friar Bacon discerns the power of this crown. In *The Scottish History of James the fourth, slaine at Flodden* (pr. 1598) this erring progenitor of James VI is reclaimed from tragedy by the faerie king, Oberon. Why Oberon? If one remembers his romance origin in *Huon of Bordeaux* (printed at least three times between 1534 and 1601) it becomes apparent why this faerie king lent himself so readily as a figure for the monarch's second body. He was sired by Julius Caesar, the first Roman to aspire to empire; his mother was a faerie; he was conceived as she predicted Caesar's triumph over Pompey. In the romance, Oberon is the god in the machine; he provides a living link between the glories of the Roman empire and the world of Charlemagne in which the romance is set. He has remained alive in a fustian-sounding Castle of Mummery to recall the erring Charlemagne to just rule. Oberon's last act in the romance is to settle a rivalry between Huon (the French claimant) and King Arthur for the sovereignty of faerie land. Oberon possesses, quite simply, all those powers attributed in legal argument to the body politic, but his medium is magic drinking horns and adamantine rocks, not legal formulae or chronicle genealogies. He offers visual equivalents for the powers of empire.

When Spenser chose Oberon as progenitor of his Faerie Queene, and Greene allowed Oberon to intervene in a war between the Scottish and English kings, they were lightly, but deliberately suggesting England as a third world empire, and the Tudor monarch as successor in glory to Caesar, Charlemagne and Arthur, in the medium of court masque. The happy denouement of Greene's *Scottish History* is only possible at the cost of Scots independence. The lustful James IV who had tried to kill his English wife to make room for a Scottish paramour is brought to his knees by his wife's father, the English king. Scots subjects recognize superior force when they see it and 'they descend downe, open the gates, and humble them' (line 2128).[1] But the Scots king remains defiant. As the historic battle is about to begin his English wife appears, pleads with the king of England in the name of the union of the two realms which her marriage symbolizes:

1   A.E.H. Swaen, ed. MSR (1921).

> Ah mightie Prince, this king and I am one,
> Spoyle thou his subiects, thou despoylest me:
> Touch thou his brest, thou doest attaint this heart,
> Oh bee my father then in louing him. (2518-21)

Tragedy is averted and the Scots king finally humbles himself to his English overlord,

> first I submit
> And humble craue a pardon of your grace. (2555-6).

Thus the unhappy massacre of Flodden field is obliterated from the chronicles of Anglo-Scottish relations, and set down in its place is a clear pictorial record of submission, a ceremony of homage for the realm of Scotland. The rewritten episode looks to the future. Greene has brought the rose of English policy to full bloom despite the canker worm lurking in the Scottish garden.

The Tragedy of Locrine (pr. 1595) has been attributed to Robert Greene on the grounds that it is a sentimental love affair whose historical significance seems perfunctory.[1] I can shed no new light on authorship but suggest the play's political iconography is worth notice. Its first scene as well as the dumb show to Act II provide a recognizable political perspective for the tragedy of Brute's eldest son who, after becoming supreme ruler of the British Isles, defeats a Scythian invasion only to fall in love with the invaders' foreign queen. Brute's division of the kingdom opens the play, a scene common to arguments about the succession. If we attend to the staging we see that Locrine is given first a wife and then a crown; he must cherish the one to keep the other:

> *Brute.*   *Puts the crowne on his head*
>   Locrine stand vp, and weare the regall Crowne,
>   And thinke vpon the state of Maiestie,
>   That thou with honor well maist weare the crown,
>   And if thou tendrest these my latest words,
>   As thou requirst my soule to be at rest,
>   As thou desirest thine owne securitie,
>   Cherish and loue thy new betrothed wife.
> *Locrine.* No longer let me wel enjoy the crowne,
>   Then I do peerlesse Guendoline. (227-36)[2]

A metaphorical reading of this scene clears up subsequent problems posed by literal interpretation of what happens to Locrine and his wife, and accounts happily for the double plot which continually contrasts the parallel marital and extramarital difficulties of King Locrine and one of his subjects.

1   Ribner, *EHP*, p.237.
2   R.B. McKerrow, ed, MSR (1908).

The Scythian invasion of Britain is foreshadowed in a dumb show to Act II where Ate explains an analogy between Locrine's marriage and the pageant abduction of Andromeda:

When Perseus married faire Andromeda,
The onlie daughter of king Cepheus,
He thought he had establisht well his Crowne,
And that his kingdome should for aie endure.
But loe proud Phineus with a band of men,
Contriu'd of sun-burnt Aethiopians:
By force of armes the bride he tooke from him,
And turnd their ioy into a floud of teares.
So fares it with yoong Locrine and his loue,
He thinkes this marriage tendeth to his weale,
But this foule day, this foule accursed day,
Is the beginning of his miseries.
Behold where Humber and his Scithians
Approcheth nigh with all his warlike traine   (440-55).

But Scythian Humber has no designs on Guendoline's person. It is a political rape he plans. The danger is complex; though Locrine defeats the Scythians in battle he falls in love with their Queen Estrilde. The ghost of Brute's faithful old warrior Corineus (an ancient British worthy who figured in London coronation pageantry) denounces him as traitor to the realm and to his daughter Guendoline. Locrine prefers love to rule and finally, like the Scythian Humber, kills himself. Guendoline is left to rule. She and the crown have clearly been unable to protect the king from the dangers of foreign wives. The cobbler's comic wooing, marriage, separation, battle and second marriage closely parallel the life of the King. Life is simple for a cobbler; his adventures end happily - not so for a king.

Shakespeare had a fundamentally tragic view of kingship; it permeates his history plays, early and late, and its imagery is scattered throughout his comedies and romances. That he expressed this view in the language of the king's two bodies is perhaps only an accident of history. Critics content to find legal language in his works are nevertheless reluctant to allow Shakespeare an active political engagement which might suggest that he wrote for his age and not for 'all time'. The kingship debate which racked England during Shakespeare's life-time surely has abiding interest because it raised and faced deep questions. Shakespeare's audience understood both the fundamental conflicts, which are with us still, and the particular detail of such debate which time and fashion have now obscured. If they could see that his play of *King John* had for its ground plot a radically different theory of kingship than the *Troublesome Raigne,* should we ignore this and continue

108

to speculate about whether he wrote both? Is it better that he should seem a hack-writer employable by either faction than a man of some conviction of his own? Similar questions may be asked about *Henry V* and his other histories. I shall confine myself to these two plays for they may amply demonstrate my point that rival succession theories help to solve problems about Shakespeare's 'sources' and his selection of character and episode.

Although the anonymous *Troublesome Raigne of King John* (pr.1591) is generally accepted as Shakespeare's most obvious source, critics from time to time reverse the order of composition or suggest the anonymous history as early wood-notes and *King John* as its subsequent revision. [1] To me Shakespeare's *King John* (with all its other excellence) seems more in the nature of a searching and sceptical reply to the anonymous author's jingoistic play which excluded all foreign claimants to the English crown. The essential differences between the two plays are as interesting as their more often remarked similarities.

Princely characters in *The Troublesome Raigne* featured in the claims of Mary and James Stuart and Philip and the Infanta of Spain. Very roughly, the two parts of the play deal respectively with the claims of Arthur Plantagenet and of Lewis of France in right of his wife Blanche of Castile. As we have seen, Arthur's claim by blood had been used as precedent for Mary Stuart. [2] Of equal importance in the succession controversy was Constance, Arthur's mother (the Ate of Part I). Doleman supposed that she re-married after Arthur's death and produced more children, vessels of Britany, through whom the blood of William the Conqueror wafted to the Infanta of Spain. In the anonymous play the behaviour of Constance as well as that of Lewis of France and Blanche of Castile seems partly governed by the dramatist's desire to discredit any claims made through them.

Richard I had an impeccable right to the English throne but died without having married. His spirit is invoked in *Troublesome Raigne* to guide the audience in the maze of claim and counterclaim that followed his death; not as a ghost, but as a 'lively counterfet/ Of Richard Cordelion', his illegitimate son, Falconbridge, enters the story. This visual image of England's hero king, alive in his bastard (a shrewd swipe at the theory that the blood royal could reproduce its image perfectly

1 Geoffrey Bullough gives a balanced account of the relationship of the two plays in *Narrative and Dramatic Sources of Shakespeare IV* (1962); this may be supplemented by the introduction to the Arden edition of the play, ed. E.A. Honigmann. See also Michael Manheim, *The Weak King Dilemma* (Syracuse, 1973). Quotations from *Troublesome Raigne* and *Famous Victories of Henry V* are taken from Bullough, IV.

2 This is noted by both Campbell (*Shakespeare's Histories*, pp.142-3) and Ribner *EHP*, p.80.

only under legitimate circumstances) always sides with the English born John. The Bastard's valour and loyalty testify to the power of a mixture of common and *native* blood royal - his actions contrast favourably with the self-seeking 'foreign' claimants Constance, Lewis and Blanche, who to gain a crown, will even ally themselves with the murderer of King Richard. Alone the Bastard ignores self-interest for honour and revenges Richard's death. In this context the title, Duke of Normandy, conferred on him by John had special point. Dolemanists had dragged the controversy back to the Conquest. The play's strategy proposes, 'let the Duke of Normandy guide the audience but let them also remember that the founder of all these lines was himself illegitimate'. The Bastard's protest against Blanche's marriage to French Lewis makes sense in terms of the claim which will derive from this match (his promise to cuckold Lewis is a further jibe at the 'illegitimate' Spanish claim). If, as we must, we continue to endorse the Bastard's sympathies, Arthur's claim, however good in theory, is weakened by the support he accepts from foreign powers and from the Pope; there is no conjuring to disguise this unpleasant fact as there was in Greene's *Friar Bacon.* Although Arthur is treated with sympathy, the Bastard fights against Arthur's party to maintain English independence from foreign powers and later to assert independence from Rome.

Ceremonial tableaux in Part II force the audience to witness the treason of the Barons' revolt against John - a revolt directly motivated by succession claims (Magna Carta is not even a gleam in their rebellious eyes). Their disloyalty is visualized as they kneel to John and immediately afterwards to King Lewis. Only the Bastard remains true; his loyalty, hard to understand in terms of character, will be justified in the revealed course of history: the sinful John prophesies a successor who will defeat Rome, and Lewis of France, forced to witness the accession of Henry III, is firmly subordinated to the vital line. The anonymous author's choice of scenes and characters combats historical arguments for Catholic Stuart and Catholic Spanish claims to Elizabeth's throne. Can the same be said of Shakespeare's play?

Although the crown passes in pageant from the tyrant John to his son Henry at the end of Shakespeare's play all the major characters testify to Arthur's rightful claim to that crown. No one speaks of Arthur's right more eloquently than the Bastard son of Coeur de Lion and he speaks in the imagery of the two bodies catastrophically disjoined by Arthur's death, an event, which, in legal theory should never happen:

> Go bear him in thine arms.
> I am amaz'd, methinks, and lose my way

> Among the thorns and dangers of this world.
> How easy dost thou take all England up!
> From forth this morsel of dead royalty
> The life, the right, and truth of all this realm
> Is fled to heaven; and England now is left
> To tug and scamble, and to part by th'teeth
> The unowed interest of proud-swelling state.
> Now for the bare-pick'd bone of majesty
> Doth dogged war bristle his angry crest
> And snarleth in the gentle eyes of peace   (IV.iii.139-50).

What sympathy one feels for Constance is dependent upon her care for Arthur, 'the life, the right, and truth of all this realm'. In Act IV her death is reported. This, with the pitiful behaviour in her last scene, tearing her silvered hair and reiterating a wish for death, lends credence to the report. We are certainly not left with the impression that she will recover, remarry and produce offspring for the Infanta of Spain.

Shakespeare's Barons rebel because they are outraged at the treatment of Arthur; this motive is treated with sympathy; we hear their reasoned grievances and regrets; there are no pageants to perjure them and thus the effect of their broken allegiance is softened. However, the marriage of Blanche and Lewis (forebears of the Infanta) is treated as an unmitigated disaster - human and political; John is the cause and bears the full brunt of its consequence; without that marriage the Barons would have had no alternative allegiance and there would have been no legal claim to cloak invasion. It is consistent with Shakespeare's presentation of John as villain that the king should die believing his kingdom lost. By metaphor the evils, conflicts and dissensions of the reign are concentrated in the figure of the wicked king who describes both his land and his mortal self:

> in the body of this fleshly land
> This kingdom, this confine of blood and breath,
> Hostility and civil tumult reigns
> Between my conscience and my cousin's death.   (IV.i.245-8).

During John's troubled reign the two bodies of the monarch had been disjoined; with the death of Arthur one fled like Astraea to heaven. The crown was clearly unable to protect the vulnerable child to whom it should have miraculously descended. Who, then, is England? We are a long way from the comfortable assurance of characters like Imperial Majesty, Respublica or Widow England. The cipher-like crown passes in pageant before the audience. When the Bastard delivers his brave speech at the end of the play he leaves this question unanswered:

> Come the three corners of the world in arms,
> And we shall shock them. Nought shall make us rue,
> If England to itself do rest but true.   (V.vii.116-18)

The final rhetoric neatly avoids the crucial question: who is England?

There had been no such doubt in the *Troublesome Raigne* where the crown had defined the king.

Intense interest in Henry V produced a spate of plays in the final decade of Elizabeth's reign.[1] Anne Barton has suggested that there was a group of 'king as common man' plays in which the ills of the realm are solved when king and subject meet. She finds these plays based on a ballad and folk notion of the 'king disguised' and suggests that Shakespeare used Henry V's disguise on the eve of Agincourt 'to summon up memories of a wistful, naive attitude toward history and the relationship of subject to king which this play rejects as attractive but untrue, a nostalgic but false romanticism'.[2] 'Naive' and 'romantic' may well describe their theatrical conventions but the levelling of the king belongs, too, to a pragmatic, hard-headed theory of sovereignty wholly hostile to Stuart discriminations. It is probably unfair to imply that ballad kingship is necessarily naive in intention or that its dramatic techniques are exclusively so. Plowden's sophisticated legal miracles were susceptible, too, of naive treatments. The climate of succession debate does not blur Anne Barton's perceptive basic division but rather suggests that these 'common man' plays may deliberately challenge the special differences between princes and commons on which the Stuarts relied. Both Suffolks and Dolemanists insisted that the crown could not change the man; he remained himself; Suffolks insisted upon one law for king and commoner, Doleman upon a mutual contract.

Doleman rested a case for contractual sovereignty upon the excellent character of Henry V before he came to the throne. Stuarts had used Henry's Agincourt victory as a precedent for their claim to England; 'No king of England if not king of France' rang with a prophetic note at the turn of the sixteenth century. These arguments may be recognized in the little group of 'biographical' history plays.

The author of the *Famous Victories of Henry V* gives inept but emphatic endorsement to the miracles of the body politic. Early scenes present a most unpromising young prince, the companion of thieves. Prince Henry's vehement destruction of his own reputation in this crude play is more consonant with polemic than art. He seems to be speaking directly to disprove Doleman and his sect as he says:

1   *The Famous Victories of Henry the Fifth,* played by 'the Queenes Maiesties Players', was registered on 14 May 1594 and printed in 1598 by Thomas Creede. *Henslowe's Diary* records a new play 'harey the v.' performed by the Admiral's Men during 1595 and 1596; Shakespeare's 1 *Henry IV* was printed in 1598 and 2 *Henry IV* in 1600. *1 Sir John Oldcastle* was performed in 1599. A pirated version of *Henry V* was printed in 1600.
2   'The King Disguised: Shakespeare's *Henry V* and the Comical History', *The Triple Bond,* ed. Joseph Price (1975), p.99.

> but thers some wil say the yoong Prince will be a well toward
> yoong man and all this geare, that I had as leeve they would breake
> my head with a pot, as to say any such thing. (492-4)

The Prince wilfully blackens his reputation with the Chief Justice. Even
cobblers and pewterers of London know that their Prince is a thief. This
dramatist shows the crown passing from the hands of Henry IV directly
to his son (no contract or subjects intervene) while thieves and ruffians
testify to the miraculous transformation of their old companion.

It is enough for the anonymous author to state Henry's just claim to
France via the female issue of the French king; another miracle assures
his military success. Each episode and ceremony illustrate in very plain
terms a view of history and legal theory which would bring James
Stuart safely to the throne of England. This dramatist is content to
show miracles; he does not use the legal language which might express
or support them.

Shakespeare allows the two miracles to be proposed, uses the
language of Plowden's legal arguments and probes with characteristic
sensitivity that scarcely credible transformation on which the future
of England seemed to turn. Can Hal's change from Eastcheap rake to
hero-king be attributed to the crown as it is in the *Famous Victories?*
And thus, tacitly, can the crown change a Scot from enemy to protector?
Could an Agincourt victory bring a Stuart to the throne?

Critics divide and Hal is seen gradually ripening, or rotting, beneath
the nettle leaves of Eastcheap in the earlier plays of the tetralogy. But
whichever character one sees emerging, one *is* prepared; one *sees* no
miracle. This uncertainty which has caused critical discussion in the
twentieth century is surely intensified by the five prologues and the
epilogue which provide a figural perspective for the history. Like the
Inns of Court dramatists Shakespeare continually breaks into the past
with reminders of Henry's evanescent glory, the disasters which
followed, the tense situation as Essex sets off for Ireland to re-establish
the unity of England, Scotland and Ireland precariously achieved by
Henry's captains. Through these choruses one historical event is seen
through another; Shakespeare's scepticism about the future darkens the
past.

Henry's cry 'No king of England, if not king of France' has an
ambiguity elucidated by the analogy drawn between the English
common law maxim against alien inheritance and the French Salic law.
If Henry's claim to France was valid, then so too is the Stuart claim to
England.[1] Leslie had argued:

---

1 Campbell, *Shakespeare's Histories,* p.261 draws attention to this parallel without coming to the same conclusions. The argument quoted in my text comes from

> For whereby do or haue the Frenchmen hither to excluded the Kings of this Realme, claiming the Croune of France by the Title of Edward the third, falling vpon him by the right of his mother, other then by a politike and ciuil law of their owne, that barreth the female from the right of the Croune? [an English common law barring the Stuart claim] ouerthroweth the foundation and bulworks, wherby we mainteine our foresaid Title and claime. If we may by our municipal law exclude the said Queene of Scotland, being called to the Croune by the Title of general heritage: then is their municipal law [Salic law] likewise good and effectual, and consequently we do and haue made al this while an vniust and wrongful claime to the Croune of France. (fol. 40v)

Shakespeare devotes 114 (frequently cut) lines at the beginning of the play to an exposition of Henry's claim to France and French objections to it. Politic prelates have outlined the disputed points of the succession before the king enters. It is they who discuss the sudden transformation of a Gadshill thief into the mirror of all Christian kings, a power of the crown urged by the Stuart polemicists to explain how an ancient Scots enemy could upon the accession of the crown be altered to England's firm protector.

> The courses of his youth promis'd it not.
> The breath no sooner left his father's body
> But that his wildness, mortified in him,
> Seem'd to die too. Yea, at that very moment
> Consideration like an angel came
> And whipp'd th'offending Adam out of him,
> Leaving his body as a paradise
> T'invelop and contain celestial spirits. . .
> Never came reformation in a flood. . .
> Nor never hydra-headed wilfulness
> So soon did lose his seat, and all at once,
> As in this king. (I.i.24-37)

Rationalizing the change with their moral of the strawberry and the nettle, they insist that Englishmen believed, with the Dauphin of France, that Henry before his accession was as unpromising as his Gadshill followers, given to 'riots, banquets and sports'.

Henry inquires of the prelates whether the Scots, his ancient enemies, will take military advantage during his absence. Here, Shakespeare begins to draw a parallel between the incursions of the Scots king against England, and Henry's own Gadshill thieveries, a similarity which, when

Leslie's *Treatise* (1571); this and the argument quoted below appear in all editions of his *Treatise*. The following version comes from *Leycester's Commonwealth* (ed. F.J. Burgoyne, London 1904): 'Seeing God hath given no better successe that way in two Women one after the other: it were not convenient (say they) that an other of that sexe should ensue: with high commendation of the Law Salick in France, whereby women are forbidden to succeed. Which speech though in shew, it bee delivered against the Queene of Scots and other of King Henry the seventh his line, that discend of Sisters: yet all men see that it toucheth as well the disabling of her Majesty, that is present' (p.145).

perceived, illuminates the behaviour of the remaining Gadshill companions in the French campaign. Henry hears that he may safely embark
for France:

> Since we have locks to safeguard necessaries
> And pretty traps to catch the petty thieves.
> While that the armed hand doth fight abroad,
> Th'advised head defends itself at home   (I.ii.176-9).

In the past, even while Edward III fought for the crown of France,
England subdued the invading Scot and made him prisoner when he
'Came pouring, like the tide into a breach' (I.ii.149).

Yet how can the body politic resolve the paradox of a just claim
prosecuted by soldiers who have not had the offending Adam whipped
out of them? Is Henry's French war different in kind from his Gadshill
robbery or the familiar forays of the Scots into England? Is there a
magic in the body politic which distinguishes Henry from Pistol with
his hollow rhetoric and shameful petty thieveries, or Bardolph who so
obviously mimics his cry of 'Once more unto the breach'? Ambiguity
and verbal echoes linking Henry and Pistol and Bardolph are testimony,
not, I think, to Shakespeare's doubts about Henry V *as a person* but to
doubts about the soundness of an historical figura as basis for a Scottish
claim in 1600. An honourable cause, a just title, but a history and
supporters so unsavoury that only a miracle could transform the enemy
of the realm to its protector. Pistol, if you like, corresponds to the
Dauphin's scornful view of the entire claim: a fustian, thieving alien
play-king, extorting crowns from people who cannot even understand
his language. It is a matter of theatrical interpretation just how far the
parallel between the king and his old companion is to be drawn. But no
matter how much sympathy one wishes to elicit for Pistol, he is
inevitably subjected to the Welsh leek in a scene which illustrates the
precarious unity of the British realm, a unity which has been temporarily
achieved in the prosecution of the French claim. The four parts of the
kingdom, with their caricatures, Gower, MacMorris, Fluellen and Jamy,
are held in an uneasy unity, fighting for a theoretical claim which, in
Shakespeare's time, might unite them for good. The continuing necessity
for this British unity is emphasized in the choric allusion to the Earl of
Essex in Ireland and the hope that he will return with 'rebellion
broached on his sword'.

Thus far one might illuminate the design of the play. But the eloquent
disagreements of critics over its tone seem to me to underline the very
real ambiguity which is the essence of figural history. A performance of
this play will depend upon faith, not so much in the historical person of
Henry V as in the body politic. That Shakespeare did not find the
demands of political theory conguent with the greatness of the human

spirit is everywhere apparent in the tragedies. However, one may be misled by reading back from them to this history play. *Henry V* was written in anticipation of a miracle. Shakespeare's questioning is correspondingly circumscribed. Hal, on the eve of Agincourt thoughtfully addresses his second body which, in theory, must assure this future stability.

> What kind of god art thou?   (IV.i.237)

An entire stage history of personification lies behind that apostrophe: Bale's Imperial Majesty, the Inns of Court goddesses, the magicians, the faerie kings. The Prince concludes his searching speech with, 'No, thou proud dream'. Although Henry questions the reality of his double persona, a good actor will have no difficulty demonstrating the charismatic quality of the king's language, his essential difference from Pistol. Shakespeare allows the miracle of Agincourt, but firmly contains it by his last gloomy chorus. Henry wins a wife and a crown but these famous victories 'lasted but small time'. They are prototypes of another victory situated in the future whose advent is awaited. The epilogue recalls the disaster which followed in the reign of Henry VI, 'which oft our stage hath shown'. The fifth Henry's golden reign is not tarnished for being short lived. Simply it is as evanescent as the entertainment at the Globe. To achieve a better, one must look beyond the wooden O to find,

> A kingdom for a stage, princes to act,
> And monarchs to behold the swelling scene.

8

MIRACULOUS SUCCESSION
The Phoenix and the Turtle (1601)

> as when
> The bird of wonder dies, the maiden phoenix,
> Her ashes new create another heir
> As great in admiration as herself,
> So shall she leave her blessedness to one -
> When heaven shall call her from this cloud of darkness -
> Who from the sacred ashes of her honour
> Shall star-like rise, as great in fame as she was,
> And so stand fix'd. Peace, plenty, love, truth, terror,
> That were the servants of this chosen infant,
> Shall then be his, and like a vine grow to him;
> Wherever the bright sun of heaven shall shine,
> His honour and the greatness of his name
> Shall be and make new nations.   (*Henry VIII*, V.v.39-52)

In *Henry VIII* (1613) Cranmer's confident 'prophecy' of the phoenix describes the peaceful transition of power from Elizabeth to James. Comfortable tones of assured hindsight distinguish this Jacobean history play from the strident tones of *Henry V*. In 1601, however, there was neither comfort nor assurance. Elizabeth was sixty-seven, the succession as uncertain as ever. In that year Shakespeare wrote his most enigmatic prophecy, the poem commonly known as *The Phoenix and the Turtle,* in a book permeated by this sense of crisis, looking to the future, gathering up and reviewing the iconography and myths of Elizabethan succession drama and pageantry. Whatever else it may be, Shakespeare's poem is politically engaged. To deny this one must ignore the context of the poem's first appearance and its integral place in Shakespeare's work. I have little sympathy with those who prefer it as 'ravishing nonsense'. It was a politically philosophical occasional poem, a distillation and continuation of thoughts about kingship, love and duty which appear in the histories and tragedies and, less eloquently, in the speeches and writings of his contemporaries.

Shakespeare's better known collaborators in *Love's Martyr* were Marston (MT c.1595), Jonson and Chapman; the book was planned by Robert Chester, an obscure patriot variously identified as a Hertfordshire justice of the peace or a Middle Templar.[1] There were two

---

1 The identity of Robert Chester is disputed and is tied in some measure to evidence of friendship with Sir John Salusbury to whom the book is dedicated. A.B. Grosart (*Robert Chester's 'Loves Martyr'*, [London, 1878], pp.vii-x) believed him to be identical with the JP for Hertfordshire, resident of Royston, knighted by King James in 1603. Carleton Brown (*Poems by Sir John Salusbury and Robert Chester,* EETS [London, 1914], pp.xlvii-liv) points out that Robert Chester of Royston was admitted to the Middle Temple on 14

editions of this book, one published in 1601, two years before Elizabeth's death, the other in 1611, eight years after the accession of James. The contents of the two editions are identical, the titles are different. This is not puzzling if one remembers the age's continuing pre-occupation with the theory of the monarch's two bodies, single nature's double name. The theme of this book is the search for perpetuity; its two titles reflect personal and public aspects of a common theme. In 1601 it was entitled:

> *Love's Martyr: or Rosalins Complaint* Allegorically shadowing the truth of Loue, in the constant Fate of the Phoenix and the Turtle.

In 1611,

> *The Anuals [Annals] of great Brittaine,* or A Most Excellent Monument, wherein may be seene all the antiquities of this Kingdome, to the satisfaction both of the Vniversities, or any other place stirred with Emulation of long continuance. Excellently figured out in a worthy Poem.

In 1601 England's future seemed to depend on the miracle of the Phoenix. Elizabeth claimed that love of her subjects and marriage to her realm justified her virginity, and that she would somehow provide a successor. Viability of this policy depended on her subjects' trust. Love for an individual would have to be transcended, for only by loving an ideal could Elizabeth's subjects accept a new monarch as the offspring of their Queen. The 1601 title, *Love's Martyr,* stresses the inevitable sacrifice. In 1611 the miracle had, nominally, occurred; that particular love so often expressed as a passionate and erotic devotion had apparently been consumed by the ideal. The story of Phoenix and Turtle Dove became what its authors had predicted, a remarkable chapter in a book of Britain's Monuments. That perpetuity which Queen Elizabeth had embodied and which the peaceful succession seemed to assure, gives its name to the second edition: *The Anuals of Great Britain.*

This Phoenix myth is an artistic offshoot of firmly rooted political theory; the currency of its terms may be seen in a succession treatise dedicated to James in 1603:

> In Succession there is no occasion for an Interrex or an Interregnum. But according to the French proverb, *The dead King gives life to the next Successor,* that is puts him in Possession of the Kingdom,

---

Feb. 1600 and might there have met Sir John Salusbury (MT 19 Mar. 1594/5). He prefers, however, a humbler Robert Chester, native of Denbighshire. On the basis of Christ Church MSS 183 and 184, containing poems by Chester, Salusbury and Ben Jonson, Brown conjectures that the Denbigh Chester served the Salusbury family, perhaps as chaplain.

and when the body of the dead King is deposited into his Sepulchre, and the Funeral Song (*the King is Dead*) is sung, with a mournful accent, joyful acclamations are return'd by way of response, *Let the King live.* [1]

Yet in 1601 there was no agreement about *who* that successor should be; without unanimity Elizabeth's demise would produce no second Phoenix.

Rosalin's Complaint voices a monarch's reproach to her subjects, and her poet's reassurance that the transcendent power of love will preserve the body politic. The heroine, Rosalin, laments, as Prospero was to do, the brittleness of faith and allegiance. In 1601, *Love's Martyr* was intended to foster belief in the power of allegiance. These poets hoped (as Prospero would) that art might alter nature, that they might convert Elizabethan Sebastians by the music of their verse to exclaim:

> Now will I believe
> That there are unicorns; that in Arabia
> There is one tree, the phoenix' throne; one phoenix
> At this hour reigning there.   (*Tempest* III.iii.21-4)

They were not alone in wishing to influence their countrymen, to impress upon them a personal responsibility for the peaceful transfer of authority. Henry Hooke, in the same troubled year 1601, writes 'Of the Succession of England' and, although prose is his medium, his language is that of *Love's Martyr.* [2] Love and joy greeted Elizabeth in 1558 when she ascended the throne of England and from her a 'bewtyful order of government followeth' (fol. 9v). Intimate, even erotic language expresses the relationships between Queen Elizabeth and her subjects, and its idiom has often led students into unfortunate literal interpretations, hypothetical liaisons between individual courtiers and the ageing Queen. Hooke explains why the sixty-seven year old Queen was to him 'perfect beauty' and in what terms we must understand his 'love and desire' to be united to her:

> The glory which then she gayned, she hath not lost, but increased it by her growing in graces and giftes euen in this her age meete for a Queene: so should we giue case vnto her, to testifie vnto vs, that the loue & desire we had vnto her in her youth, is not dead nor decayed in vs towards her in her age; but as the blessedness of her government doth still deserue our loue, so we should loue her, as long as she gouerneth. . .For if it were a benefitt at first to be united with so peereles a prince into our body, of a most peaceable, most honorable, most religious comon weale, let vs acknowledge the goodnes of god in continuinge that benefitt. . .which our harts desired, and thereby admonysh ourselues that this ought to be the continuall desire of our harts.   (fol. 7v, 8)

1 Thomas Craig, *Concerning the Right of Succession to the Kingdom of England,* trans. James Gatherer (London, 1703), pp.71-2.

2 BL MS Royal 17 B XI, fols. 1-19.

He interprets the Queen's behaviour over the succession (as it turns out, correctly) to imply her preference for James Stuart. Controversy is a reproach to her careful provision for the future. All that is required of her subjects is love and faith. In the following passage transfer of authority is described in language remarkably close to Cranmer's prophecy in Shakespeare's *Henry VIII*:

> When Elizabeth hath chaunged mortalytie for imortalyte. . .so at her departure, she will bequeath vnto her people a legacye aboue all estimation, as namely herself dyeing revived in one of her owne blood, her age renued in his younger yeeres; her aged infirmities repaired in the perfection of his strength, her vertues both of christianytye, and princlyke qualytie, doubled vpon him, who shall arise and stand vp, a man, in steede of a woeman, retayninge in his lyfe, the memory of her never dying honor: expressing in his lyfe patterne of her clemency & iustice, and preserving to his owne glory, & his peoples comforte, the state of his kingdome as he found it. . .(fol. 6)
>
> Religion & iustice with many peaceable fruites thereof, which Elizabeth leaveth established to his handes, shall through the faithfullness of his ministry be reviewed and polished, to florish in perfect bewtie.   (fol. 19v)

In *Love's Martyr* Shakespeare and his fellow poets were writing about a mystery, but they wrote coherently and in terms readily intelligible to any of their contemporaries. One major source of confusion in reading *Love's Martyr* is the pronouns - the curious shifts of person, identity and gender. These make sense if we recall that the Phoenix is at the same time a figure for Elizabeth and for the monarch's body politic in which the poets see their own political identity as subjects. The Dove is at once a symbol for the love and fidelity of the monarch in her capacity as a natural woman, and for the love and fidelity of her subjects. As Bacon argued, quoting Plowden, 'There is in the king not a body natural alone, nor a body politic alone, but a body natural and politic together'. [1]

Critics who insist that the dove is simply male misread the poems. In the very first description of Phoenix in Chester's book *she* is described as both a Phoenix and an earthly dove:

> One rare rich *Phoenix* of exceeding beautie,
> One none-like Lillie in the earth I placed;
> One faire *Helena,* to whom men owe dutie:
> One countrey with a milke-white Doue I graced:
> One and none such, since the wide world was found
> Hath euer Nature placed on the ground. [2]

1 Bacon, *Works,* VII, 667-8.

2 Grosart, ed., *Loves Martyr,* p.10. References to the pagination at the bottom of this edition.

120

The royal bird is both Phoenix and dove; it can only perpetuate itself by finding the reciprocal love of another dove prepared to sacrifice itself in kindling the regenerative flame. This, unorthodox as it may seem in terms of bestiary tradition, is the myth of the Phoenix which Shakespeare (as even his Arden editor admits) adopted from the pages of *Love's Martyr*.[1]

In bestiary tradition the Phoenix traditionally lives five hundred years, grows old, flies into a fire and is rejuvenated from its own ashes; it is not a simple chastity symbol like Diana or Belphoebe since its essence includes the mortal process of decay and rebirth. The Turtle is the intrusion of the Elizabethan political paradigm into the myth: only a Turtle Dove can kindle flame for the rebirth of Chester's Phoenix because Chester writes of kingdoms where monarchs die and loyalty falls in question. Thus the human heart, the Turtle Dove, symbol of troth, enters the Elizabethan myth and is essential to the regenerative process. The purity of the Dove's devotion assures the creative heat of the flame.

The structure of *Love's Martyr* is loose; the book is most often seen as a miscellany.[2] Chester's story of the Phoenix who fears extinction is interrupted at intervals by material which does not seem to further the narrative. However, unity emerges through theme and analogue, as each section reveals to the reader aspects of perpetuity in a mutable world.

Chester begins in a manner reminiscent of Blenerhasset's *Revelation* with a parliament of the gods, entitled:

> Rosalins Complaint, metaphorically applied to Dame Nature at a Parliament held (in the high Star-chamber) by the Gods, for the preseruation and increase of Earths beauteous Phoenix. (p.9)

Nature refers to the earthly home of the Phoenix as both Arabia and Brytania; conventional geography is best forgotten for Nature sees two aspects of the single earthly kingdom, corresponding to the twin-personed Phoenix-Dove. Nature fears the fires of this kingdom are too 'dull and base' to renew the Phoenix.

> This *Phoenix* I do feare me will decay,
> And from her ashes neuer will arise

1 F.T. Prince, ed., *Shakespeare's Poems* (London, 1960), p.xxxix. An excellent essay on the poem is by Walter J. Ong, 'Metaphor and the twinned vision' *Sewanee Review* LXIII (1955) 193-201.

2 Irma Reed White in a letter to the *TLS,* 21 July 1932, p.532, gives a useful account of Chester's source material. William H. Matchett, *The Phoenix and the Turtle* (The Hague, 1965), sees Chester as a 'poetic pack rat'; his interpretation of Chester's intentions rests upon the view that Essex is the Turtle.

An other Bird her wings for to display,
And her rich beauty for to equalize:
The *Arabian* fiers are too dull and base,
To make another spring within her place.   (p.15)

Jove reassures Nature and prescribes a journey; Nature and Phoenix leave Arabia-Brytania in the chariot of the sun, journeying to Paphos Isle, where they find 'a second Phoenix loue'. Jove describes Blener-hasset's iconographic isle, Lyly's Utopia inhabited by elves, angels, Diana and Venus, the island of the poets where magic and supernatural forces can resolve all personal and political evils. Apollo's chariot is clearly the only possible vehicle for such a destination. There Brytania's Phoenix will find the Paphian Dove, 'True Honors louely Squire', symbolizing the nobility of the human heart, the 'troth' or loyalty of 'true faithfull seruice and desart' (p.19). This Paphian Dove, rekindling the Arabian fires, will assure perpetuity for Phoenix and her triumph over enemies in Arabia-Brytania. But who are these enemies of Phoenix? They are various imperfections of the heart, symbolized in the poems by the serpent (sometimes called tyrant), Envy, the serpent who caused disloyalty in Eden, lack of faith and broken troth, the failure of love between servant and lord. It is Envy, or scepticism, within the human heart which dims the fires of the kingdom.

Moving on, Chester next identifies Dove and Phoenix in an Elizabethan context. The poet prays for himself, his fellow subjects and for his Queen; they are all earthly doves, mortal, subject to imperfections of heart, and he calls for divine grace to free them from the serpent Envy, to transform them to the Paphian Dove, that they may share 'perfect troth'. Neoplatonic ideas of earthly and heavenly love elucidate this prayer, but the bond of allegiance best explains why subject and monarch are first doves and then, *together,* Phoenix. Chester prays that he may lead a poetic journey to a land where Envy has no power. Poetry will give eyes of faith to both disheartened monarch and disbelieving subject. Each will discern the monarch as not only an earthly Dove who will perish, but as the perpetual Phoenix. If poetry has power the Paphian Dove will appear; the union of the two birds will occur; such a union will be a marriage because it is a vow of mutual love and creative responsibility; it will be chaste because entered into without regard to the perishable bodies of the two birds. It will thus be 'married chastity'. Its offspring, seen with the eyes of faith, will be another Phoenix, ensuring the political blessing 'Peace':

Let her not wither Lord without increase,
But blesse her with ioyes offspring of sweet peace. (p.23)

Next, follows the imaginative journey called 'A meeting Dialogue-wise

122

betweene Nature, the Phoenix and the Turtle Doue'. It includes Phoenix's complaint, the actual journey to Paphos, a section of 'Britain monuments', the story of King Arthur, hymns to earthly and heavenly love, a herbal, a bestiary and a description of the final sacrifice of the two birds.

After Phoenix's lament,

> I am no *Phoenix* I,
> And if I be that bird, I am defaced,
> Vpon the *Arabian* mountaines I must die,
> And neuer with a poore yong Turtle graced   (p.24)

and Nature's reassurance that

> All Birdes for vertue and excelling beautie,
> Sing at thy reuerend feet in Loue and Dutie.   (p.25)

Nature assures Phoenix of Jove's promise and conveys the doubting bird to Paphos Isle, passing not through space but through time. Phoenix and Nature simply rise higher and higher above Brytania to view all of Europe in an historical perspective revealing the operation of God's grace in history for the exorcism of Envy and preservation of Britain. In this section, as in historical pageantry, unity is provided by thematically relevant figurae. Nature identifies the ancient founders of noble civilizations by giving an account of 'Britain Monuments' reminiscent of the *Faerie Queene,* Book II canto 10. In this eclectic statesman's paradise English monarchs are numbered among the Nine Worthies.[1]

The allegory of the fall and redemption of civilizations plays behind each episode as in so many Elizabethan 'history' plays. The story of Arthur has a special place here. As we have seen, the lawyers had found the first British oath of fealty sworn in his reign. Chester tells the story of Arthur, centring on his coronation to describe countless subjects kneeling and four vassal kings bearing swords before him. His theme is the power of *troth* - the bond of homage and allegiance - and its iconography:

> These foure attired in rich ornaments,
> Four golden Swords before the King did beare,
> Betokening foure royall Gouerments,
> And foure true Noble harts not dreading feare,
> That *Enuie* from their breasts can neuer teare:
> Before them playd such well-tun'd melodie,
> That birds did sing to make it heauenly.   (p.58)

Arthur's Queen follows in procession:

[1] King Arthur and, among the nine women worthies, Matilda, the mother of Henry II.

> Foure Queenes before her bore foure siluer Doues,
> Expressing their true Faith and husbands Loues.   (p.59)

In pre-conquest Britain, as in the Olympian Parliament, envy is a foe
of love or troth. In Arthur's court Mordred is contrasted with Gawen.
Like Envy and Satan, Mordred is described as a tyrant: 'that monster
Mordred. . .A cruell Tyrant, horrible, mightie, full of strife' (p.84).
He is the baseborn haggard who threatens Arthur the royal bird:

> Mordred, thou deceitfull kinsman,
> (Begot of Treasons heyre) thus to rebell. . .
>   thou some base-born Haggard mak'st a wing,
> Against the Princely Eagle in his flight,
> And like a hissing Serpent seek'st to sting.   (pp.75-6)

Here stands the historical epitome of Phoenix's enemies. By contrast
the poet sees in Gawen, who gave his life to defend monarch
and country, an Arthurian portrait of the Paphian Dove, whom Jove
had called 'true Honor's louely Squire'.

This historical excursion ends with Phoenix admiring London as the
centre of law and government. Nature calls it Troynouant where the
descendants of Aeneas redeemed the disaster which lust had brought
to Troy; she recalls that Aeneas sacrificed his personal love for Dido
to 'reare the Pillars of a Common-weale'. The royal throne had
power 'For to reuiue his Honor-splitted Name,/ And raise againe the
cinders of his Fame' (p.86).

A Spenserian contrast between kinds of love is taken up in song.
Nature laments Cupid who beguiles men's senses, while Phoenix sings
of perfect love which is pure beauty 'Loue is a holy, holy, holy thing'
(p.88); it is a power of divine majesty,

> She builds her Bower in none but noble minds,
> And there due adoration still she finds.   (p.88)

Apollo's chariot has served its purpose; Phoenix knows that Envy can
be overcome. With her hymn to heavenly love the chariot arrives in
Paphos Isle. The following section, which critics have called a lapidary,
herbal and bestiary, is a fulfilment of the poet's promise to 'those
of light beleefe' that they shall see with new eyes, discovering 'herbs and
trees true nomination'. Mutability is still found on the isle but, after her
historical journey, Phoenix is able to see in each of the creatures and
plants that principle which makes earthly things 'eterne in mutability'.
Her vision is similar to the crown of Pallas in Blenerhasset's book.
Phoenix can exclaim, 'Blest be our mother Earth that nourisheth,/ In
her rich womb the seede of Times increase' (p.103). Nature now
regales her royal bird with Ovid's tales of metamorphoses, of maidens
threatened by lust transformed into flowers, and with stories of herbs,

124

trees and flowers whose medicinal properties remedy human ills.

Both Pelican and Swan of this 'bestiary' section are important for the book's climax. Sacrificing herself for her brood, the Pelican had been a timeworn figure of Christ and been adapted to honour Elizabeth.[1] The Swan, sacred to Apollo, shadows the poets themselves who, in *Love's Martyr*, sing at the approach of death to tell of the sadness of mortality yet prophesying 'prosperity and perfect ease'. Pelican, Swan and Dove are each seen as embodiments of a single transcendent truth, constancy until and through death. Phoenix is touched by her first glimpse of the drooping Paphian Dove, 'the perfect picture of hart pining woes'. She asks,

> Is this the true example of the Heart?
> Is this the Tutor of faire *Constancy?*
> Is this Loues treasure, and Loues pining smart?
> Is this the substance of all honesty?
> > And comes he thus attir'd, alas poore soule.
> > That Destinies foule wrath should thee controule. (pp.131-2)

The Phoenix and her new-found love have now been brought together. Nature leaves, suggesting by her departure the transcendence of what is about to happen, yet each bird recognizes the other to be a child of Nature. *Both* are doves. They anticipate the pain of personal loss as the Paphian Dove says:

> My teares are for my Turtle that is dead,
> My sorrow springs from her want that is gone (p.133)

and Phoenix responds:

> Come poore lamenting soule, come sit by me,
> We are all one, thy sorrow shall be mine,
> Fall thou a teare, and thou shalt plainlie see,
> Mine eyes shall answer teare for teare of thine. . . .
> > I will beare
> Halfe of the burdenous yoke thou dost sustaine,
> Two bodies may with greater ease outweare
> A troublesome labour. . .
> But tell me gentle Turtle, tell me truly
> The difference betwixt false Loue and true Sinceritie. (pp.133-4)

Simply the Turtle gives an answer proposed by every section of *Love's Martyr:*

> False loue is full of Enuie and Deceit. . .
> > Alwayes inconstant, false and variable,
> > Delighting in fond change and mutable. . . .
>
> True loue, is louing pure, not to be broken. . . .
> True loue is Troths sweete emperizing Queene:

1   Roy Strong, *Portraits of Queen Elizabeth I* (Oxford, 1963) p.60.

Troth or true love cannot, of course, be illustrated without two beings; this English Pheonix can only be self-immolating in a very special sense. When the lovers find and recognize one another, their identities merge. As she contemplates their union and sacrifice, Phoenix recognizes that 'Thou shalt be my selfe, my perfect Loue' (p.135).

Resolved for death, the birds call upon Apollo to kindle a mutual flame by the power of poetry itself:

> O sweet perfumed flame, made of those trees,
> Vnder the which the Muses nine haue sung
> The praise of vertuous maids in misteries. . .
>   Accept my body as a Sacrifice
>   Into your flame, of whom one name may rise. (p.139)

The Dove plunges first into the rekindled fire: Phoenix divines the creation of empires:

> O holy, sacred, and pure perfect fire,
> More pure than that ore which faire Dido mones,
> More sacred in my louing kind desire,
> Then that which burnt old Esons aged bones,
>   Accept into your euer hallowed flame,
>   Two bodies, from the which may spring one name. . . .
>
> I come sweet Turtle, and with my bright wings,
> I will embrace thy burnt bones as they lye,
> I hope of these another Creature springs,
> That shall possesse both our authority. (pp.138-9)

The Pelican as sole witness of the 'happy tragedy' vows to report it to posterity.

After the burning comes a series of cantos which have been cited as proof of Chester's superficial concern with the theme of chastity.[1] Dismal as they are, these cantos illustrate the main theme and are designed to be read in two ways so that conventional love verses can be seen, through the use of acrostic, as something transcendent.

It is unfair to look in *Love's Martyr* for the simple celebration either of chastity or physical love between man and woman for, although the work contains elements of both, it is only coherent so long as it is read as neither one nor the other. This is one reason why in his contribution Shakespeare's language is so finely strained. The mythic pattern which orders Shakespeare's poem is the same as that of Chester's cruder work. Phoenix and her re-birth constitute perfect beauty; but beauty can only 'be', the miracle can only occur, in conjunction with perfect 'troth'. Since the proof of beauty is the response it evokes in the beholder,

1 *Shakespeare's Poems,* p.xl.

re-birth can only occur for a chorus of faithful who sing the requiem; the believers' chant assures their miracle. Shakespeare's poem follows the splendid ritual 'The King is dead, long live the King!'

These important lines precede Shakespeare's poem, and set the scene by asking the reader to *suppose* that the burning has occurred:

> Svppose here burnes the wonder of a breath,
> In righteous flames, and holy-heated fires. . .
> The flame that eates her, feedes the others life:
> Her rare-dead ashes, fill a rare liue vrne:
> One Phoenix borne, another Phoenix burne. (p.181)

Shakespeare, like all the poets of *Love's Martyr*, was writing in anticipation of an historical moment of transition. His poem is, first, a confession of personal faith; at the same time it invites the reader to 'assist at' the miracle by joining the procession and the song, and it celebrates that miracle.

The first word of Shakespeare's poem is double-voiced and sets the tone for his prophetic celebration. Because the poem itself is both proposition and exhortation, 'Let' must be taken to mean both *suppose* and *allow*.

> Let the bird of lowdest lay,
> On the sole *Arabian* tree,
> Herauld sad and trumpet be:
> To whose sound chaste wings obay. (p.182)

In Chester's myth (as in Shakespeare's *Tempest*) there is only one bird who sits upon the sole Arabian tree: the Phoenix. Critics protest that the bestiary phoenix is not usually remarkable for its powers of song. [1] More to the point is Chester's identification of the loyal poet as Dove, Swan and Phoenix. At the opening of Shakespeare's poem the Phoenix sitting upon the sole Arabian tree is a symbol of union and uniqueness: its properties are those of the powers which created it, including the power of song. It is fitting that the royal bird should not be named, because only when it receives the recognition of perfect love and duty can it be acknowledged as Phoenix. The summons issued from the sole Arabian tree is an announcement of the end and the beginning; an unnamed miracle is proposed and will be accomplished only if the summons is heard and obeyed. Shakespeare's poem, like Chester's

---

1 Peter Dronke, ('The Phoenix and the Turtle', *Orbis Litterarum*, XXII [1968], 208), however, points out that Phoenix is described as 'the bird of greatest lay' in Lactantius's *De Ave Phoenice* (lines 45-50). The power of the Phoenix's song is mentioned, too, in the Anglo Saxon *Phoenix* (line 128) in a phrase which means literally 'louder raised' (*beorhtan reorde*) (*The Exeter Book Part I,* ed. Israel Gollancz, EETS London, 1895, p.208).

whole story, celebrates three aspects of a single miracle: the bird sitting upon the sole Arabian tree, the act of sacrifice, and the 'rare-live urne' itself. *Each* of these must be acknowledged and only a reverent, loving response will sustain the miracle. Phoenix is created by the vow of *troth* and will 'live' as long as the fires of love sustain it. Troth is exemplified in the *actions* of Phoenix and loyal Dove, in command and obedience, in mutual vows and in mutual sacrifice. But to continue it must also be present in the bystanders, who obey the royal summons and whose hearts must be kindled. *Troth* is audible in the sigh of those 'true and fair' who come to mourn and wonder at the urn. In the long story of Phoenix and Dove leading up to Shakespeare's requiem Chester has shown that this flame will burn only before believing eyes; the ideal can be seen only by those who will perpetuate it by being themselves 'true and fair'. The next four stanzas of Shakespeare's poem summon the necessary actors (troth, fidelity, selflessness, chastity, prophecy, qualities which the story has identified with particular birds: Dove, Pelican, Swan etc.) and exclude Phoenix's enemies, disbelief and disloyalty.

The loyal birds are summoned to a 'session', the oddly legal word indicating here that the assembly is a trial, testing the power of the Phoenix, recalling Chester's earlier parliament of the gods in the high Star-chamber, 'for the preservation and increase of Earth's beauteous Phoenix'. The summons to 'chaste wings' is issued for the same purpose. The shrieking harbinger, a bird who announces death, must, like Chester's fiend Envy, be banished from this 'demise':

> But thou shriking harbinger,
> Foule precurrer of the fiend,
> Augour of the feuers end,
> To this troup come thou not neere.   (p.182)

Birds of 'tyrant wing', too, must be excluded in order to preserve the royal bird (Chester had seen King Arthur as the royal eagle to be saved from the disloyal haggard Mordred, a bird of tyrant wing).[1] Shakespeare's stanza thus means equivocally, 'the obsequy must be kept strict in order to save or preserve the feathered King', and also, simply, 'Let only the royal bird be present',

> From this Session interdict
> Euery foule of tyrant wing,
> Saue the Eagle feath'red King,
> Keep the obsequie so strict.   (p.182)

---

1 'false *Mordred,* thou deceitfull Kinsman. . ./ But thou some baseborne Haggard mak'st a wing,/ Against the Princely *Eagle* in his flight' (pp.75-6). On p.84 Mordred is described as 'monster' and 'a cruell Tyrant, horrible, mightie, full of strife'.

128

Shakespeare follows Chester in making the Swan figure the poet's
own *troth;* Apollo's bird, unlike the shrieking harbinger, prophesies at
death 'prosperity and perfect ease'. The swan-poet *divines* death,
perceives and foretells it, but his immortal song also makes death
itself divine, revealing it as the cause of new life, so he is essential to
the miracle:

> Let the Priest in Surples white,
> That defunctiue Musicke can,
> Be the death-deuining Swan,
> Lest the *Requiem* lacke his right. (p.182)

The Crow which, in bestiary fashion, creates its young by the breath
it gives and takes shadows another aspect of the miracle: the new
Phoenix is created simply by the breath of a mutual vow:

> And thou treble dated Crow,
> That thy sable gender mak'st.
> With the breath thou giu'st and tak'st,
> Mongst our mourners shalt thou go. (p.182)

That breath of troth creates the Phoenix from the 'rare dead ashes' in
the 'rare live urn'. Only a naive scepticism will ask whether the bird
on the Arabian tree is the old or new Phoenix. The creative vow insists
they are the same.

The birds who sing the Anthem evoke troth in its second aspect,
sacrifice, the destruction of two bodies to create one flame. Now the
love between the Turtle and his Queen is described in language used by
lawyers and poets for their phenomenon of the king's two bodies:

> Though there be in the king two bodies, and that those two bodies
> are conjoined, yet are they by no means confounded the one by
> the other. [1]

This vision altered common distinctions of number, property, in-
dividuality and enabled a subject to see himself and his 'right' as part
of the 'body' of his Queen:

> So they loued as loue in twaine,
> Had the essence but in one,
> Two distincts, Diuision none,
> Number there in loue was slaine.
>
> Hearts remote, yet not asunder;
> Distance and no space was seene,
> Twixt this *Turtle* and his Queene;
> But in them it were a wonder.
>
> So betweene them Loue did shine,
> That the *Turtle* saw his right,
> Flaming in the *Phoenix* sight;
> Either was the others mine.

1 Bacon, *Works* VII, 668.

> Propertie was thus appalled,
> That the selfe was not the same:
> Single Natures double name,
> Neither two nor one was called.
>
> Reason in itselfe confounded,
> Saw Diuision grow together,
> To themselues yet either neither,
> Simple were so well compounded.   (p.183)

Here in the Anthem, the sacrifice is described *as if it had occurred.* But the key words in the next stanza, spoken by Reason, are *if* and *seemeth*; the poet is still writing as prophet. Sacrifice, thus described, will ensure the identity of the bird upon the Arabian tree only *if* what parts (is fled, is sacrificed) can so *remain,* if that love and constancy can survive as a flame after the destruction of individuals. Love has reason, reason none, *if* the mourning birds can, with the loyal Turtle, see their right flaming in the Phoenix sight:

> That it cried, how true a twaine,
> Seemeth this concordant one,
> Loue hath Reason, Reason none,
> If what parts, can so remaine.
>
> Whereupon it made this *Threne,*
> To the *Phoenix* and the *Doue,*
> Co-supremes and starres of Loue,
> As *Chorus* to their Tragique Scene.   (p.183)

The urn which encloses the cinders of Beautie, Truth and Raritie is, of course, the Phoenix: ('Her rare-dead ashes, fill a rare liue vrne:/ One *Phoenix* borne, another *Phoenix* burne' p.181). Shakespeare expresses this exquisitely:

> Beautie, Truth and Raritie,
> Grace in all simplicitie,
> Here enclosde in cinders lie.   (p.184)

Death is a nest; something is born. The next lines appear to say that the Turtle is dead, but in fact affirm that his loyal heart is eternal:

> Death is now the *Phoenix* nest,
> And the *Turtles* loyall brest,
> To eternitie doth rest.   (p.184)

They have left no posterity because, if what parts can so remain, there is only one perpetual and unchanging ideal. The bond of 'married chastity' is the creating fire which will burn unchanged *if* the 'chaste wings' obey this summons from the Arabian tree. If the miracle occurs the birds who burned in mutual flame *are* the true and fair who come to the urn; there is never a moment when there is not a fire or a Phoenix:

> Leauing no posteritie,
> Twas not their infirmitie,
> It was married Chastitie.   (p.184)

The tone of this poem is elegiac; in 1601 there can be no assurance that any true or fair will answer a poetic summons. The only troth of which the poet can be assured is his own. His final verses reaffirm that beauty and truth can only exist in conjunction, by beholding each other and, like the sable gender of the crow, live by breath given and taken. Phoenix and Dove are a vow, a song, a prayer, an ideal cherished against mutability. With the authority of a long dramatic tradition behind him, Shakespeare celebrates this ideal, in spite of death and disaster, as chorus to a tragic scene.

> Truth may seeme, but cannot be,
> Beautie bragge, but tis not she,
> Truth and Beautie buried be.

> To this vrne let those repaire,
> That are either true or faire,
> For these dead Birds, sigh a prayer.   (p.184)

9

THE PROBLEM OF UNION:
King James I and 'King Lear'

Queen Elizabeth died on 24 March 1602/3. There had been policy in her silence about the succession (as Henry Hooke pointed out). She had taken care that nothing should prejudice the Stuart claim, and her counsellors acted accordingly.[1] James Stuart rode in progress from Scotland and was received with acquiescence, even joy, by his English subjects. In those first months of the new reign the transition of authority defined by Plowden, predicted and celebrated by the poets of *Love's Martyr,* seemed to have occurred. Had dissension over the succession followed Elizabeth to her grave, leaving the realm her child, 'Joy's offspring of sweet peace'?

James Stuart's peaceful accession seemed to confirm the theory of kingship which Plowden first urged in Mary's cause and which drew the Puritan Wentworth's support once Mary's son declared his Protestantism; blood royal carried the crown and the day. Plowden's son prepared a manuscript of the old lawyer's succession treatise for presentation to the new King. Poets and dramatists worked up pageants for James's coronation, translating into icons the legal theory which had supported the new King. Their pageant iconography declared that it was not the land, or the estates of Parliament, but the King who represented the power of government and the perpetuity of the realm. Plowden's theory provides a ground plot for several of the pageants. Since I cannot agree with those modern critics who, with James, accept pageant 'compliment' at face value, a little recapitulation will be necessary.[2]

Thomas Middleton's triumphal arch, the descent of Astraea, showed a separation and reunion of bodies politic and natural as the poets of *Love's Martyr* had done. Queen Elizabeth's heavenly body, Astraea, goddess of laws and justice, ascended to heaven and returned like the Holy Ghost to be locked in the breast of the new King. Middleton affirmed this perpetuation of the state by the breath of allegiance whose 'immaculate fires' were painted on the actors' robes.[3]

---

1 Her policy is well described in Neale, *Eliz.,* pp.385-6 and Stafford, *James VI* pp.123, 197.

2 Wickham, *Early English Stages,* I, pp.78, 80, 82 and 'From Tragedy to Tragi-Comedy *King Lear* as Prologue', *SS* XXVI, 33-48; Bergeron, *Civic Pageantry,* pp.71-90.

3 The King's formal entry from the Tower through the city took place on 15 March 1603/4. His public arrival in London was delayed for almost a year after

James was hailed as the new Phoenix at Soper Lane by the pageant of *Nova Faelix Arabia.*[1] The chief actor on the scaffold was called Arabia Britannica (p.355). Refurbished iconography from Elizabethan plays hailed the Queen's successor: James was the new Phoenix, the stem whose flower supports the diadem, a second Brute sent to redeem political sin committed when the first king divided Britain (pp.357-8). This Phoenix show concluded with birdsong and a refrain which celebrated the transformation of Troynovant into a summer arbor, a nest for an eagle, fairyland, a paradise where the lion and unicorn sport, a wedding hall for the marriage of four kingdoms, a bridal chamber for James and his realm (pp.358-9).

Ben Jonson, too, was busy pageant making; putting aside his celebrated classical learning, he took up the myth of Brute's foundation of the realm. Edward Alleyn, idol of the Elizabethan stage, dressed as an ancient Briton, clarified the 'dumb mysterie' of Jonson's first pageant. British history was a figural prelude for the union of Britannia and James Stuart. Alleyn spoke of London:

> When Brutus' plough first gave thee infant bounds,
> And I, thy Genius, walk'd auspicious rounds
> In every furrow; then did I forelook,
> And saw this day mark'd white in Clotho's book.
> The several circles, both of change and sway,
> Within this isle, there also figur'd lay;
> Of which the greatest, perfectest, and last
> Was this, whose present happiness we taste. (p.384)

These pageants were based on legal *theory.* James (followed recently by several literary critics) did not distinguish clearly between Stuart propaganda and English law. Plowden's theory hatched in the Inns, widely (if clandestinely) propagated, simply would not stand up to the pressures of the English House of Commons' scepticism - as Elizabeth seems to have known when she kept the entire succession debate out of Parliament.

England received James Stuart as king probably because there was no other single, strong competitor, not because the country as a whole accepted his succession arguments. In the glow of welcome it may have seemed that the English had forgotten their traditional enmity with Scotland, that they agreed that the Scots were not foreigners. James

his accession because of plague. References for the Middleton pageant and subsequent details from this entry from Nichols, *The Progresses of King James I* (London, 1828), I, 371-2.

1 The political theory which informs this pageant is the more evident when one compares it to the different use of Phoenix as a Seymour heraldic device in the coronation pageants for Edward VI analysed by Sydney Anglo, *Spectacle, Pageantry,* pp.289-90.

clearly believed this to be the case when, on 19 May 1603, he declared by royal proclamation the union of his kingdoms and the naturalization of all Scotsmen born after his accession to the English throne. When he addressed his first Parliament on 22 March 1603/4 he expected immediate ratification of his proclamation and a Parliamentary declaration that Scotsmen born *before* as well as after the accession were naturalized English subjects. He proposed the union of his kingdoms under the ancient name of Great Britain, in a speech whose metaphors spring from the old and fertile notion of the king's two bodies. In James's argument king and realm are indistinguishable: as there was one king there should be one not two kingdoms and one law for Scotland and England. Only if his audience believed that a union of two countries could be made in the blood of a king could they agree with James that the separation of Scotland and England made him a monster with a divided body and that to refuse James his wish was to cleave the king asunder:

> The second great blessing that God hath with my Person sent vnto you, is Peace within, and that in a double forme. First, by my descent lineally out of the loynes of Henry the seventh, is reunited and confirmed in mee the Vnion of the two Princely Roses of the two Houses of LANCASTER and YORKE, whereof that King of happy memorie was the first Vniter, as he was also the first ground-layer of the other Peace. . . .But the Vnion of these two princely Houses, is nothing comparable to the Vnion of two ancient and famous Kingdomes, which is the other inward Peace annexed to my Person. . . .Giue me leaue to discourse more particularly of the benefits that doe arise of that Vnion which is made in my blood. . . . But what shoulde we sticke vpon any naturall appearance when it is manifest that God by his Almightie prouidence hath preordained it so to be. . . . What God hath conioyned then, let no man separate. I am the Husband, and all the whole Isle is my lawful Wife; I am the Head, and it is my Body; I am the Shepherd, and it is my flocke: I hope therfore no man will be so vnreasonable as to thinke that I that am a Christian King vnder the Gospel, should be a Polygamist and husband to two wiues; that I being the Head, should haue a deuided and monstrous Body. . . . How much greater reason haue wee to expect a happie issue of this greater Vnion which is only fastened and bound vp by the wedding ring of Astrea. . .And as God hath made Scotland the one halfe of this Isle to enioy my Birth, and the first and most vnperfect halfe of my life, and you heere to enioy the perfect and last halfe thereof; so can I not thinke that any would be so iniurious to me, no not in their thoughts and wishes, as to cut me asunder the one halfe of me from the other.[1]

James completely misjudged the feelings of his subjects. While the plan for Union received enthusiastic support from his judges and most of the House of Lords, the Commons baulked. Apparently James did not realize that he was re-opening the familiar arguments which had caused such heated, though clandestine, debate during the succession contro-

---

[1] *The Political Works of James I,* ed. Charles H. McIlwain (Cambridge, Mass., 1918), pp.271-3.

versy. At the King's request, then, the Commons debated all the issues which Elizabeth had kept out of Parliament. With her sensitivity to metaphor she must have seen that the Stuart mystique of blood royal could not stand the harsh reality of the lower House. James hoped for a speedy ratification of his plan; but the Commons, once launched on the long forbidden topics, debated Union for five years. Both Houses met and appointed English commissioners who discussed unification of the two legal systems with the Scots; among the commissioners sat Inns of Court men. Christopher Yelverton, Francis Bacon, Thomas Sackville (Lord Buckhurst) and Richard Martin were key figures in the Union debates.[1] Between 1604 and 1608 the House argued the vexed questions of England's supremacy over Scotland, of subjects born out of the allegiance of the English King, and most momentous of all: was the object of allegiance King or soil?

The parliamentary commission achieved only one notable piece of legislation, a repeal of the hostile Border Laws. Further action was impossible because the Commons objected on two main points. They did not want to make the Scots equal in rights with native born Englishmen, and they objected to the alteration of the 'ancient and honourable name England'. They anatomized the concept of Union, delayed action on the *ante-nati* and even questioned the legality of the King's proclamation for the *post-nati*.

Many reasons urged in the House against the name Britain and against the King's plan for uniting the two crowns were precisely those raised by the Suffolk faction when they had first protested that the Scots crown ought not to take precedence over the English. The Commons' reluctance to naturalize the Scots was simply a new expression of the arguments Hales hurled against the Stuart claim, barring aliens from property inheritance in England.

James sent message after message to Parliament urging them to a decision. He addressed them personally three times during the five years of debate. All that remains of the King's messages are the fragmentary jottings in the *Journals of the House of Commons* but these trace clearly enough the familiar figures and images which he sought to impress upon his plan.[2] James as 'father' of his 'children' gives them one name 'Britons'; 'let there be no Cause of Strife, for we are Brethran' (p.176). Two days later on 20 April 1604 the Commons were invited to be 'like Astrologers, look to the Stars of our State: see their Motion,

1 The Union question is discussed in detail by Wallace Notestein *The House of Commons 1604-1610* (New Haven, 1971), pp.78-84, 211-54.

2 *Journals of the House of Commons*, I (London, 1803). References and quotations from this volume unless otherwise stated.

their Influence' (p.179). They were urged to think their king worthy of the greatest name – Britain: 'the name will beget love, unity in diadem, in name and in government' (p.182). In a message of 1 May 1604 urging union, he talked of the political fall of Adam:

> I hoape, that God, in his Choice, and free Will of youris, will not suffer you, with olde Adame, to choose the worste, and so to procure the Defacing of this earthlie Paradise; but, by the contraire, that he shall inspyre you so, as with the seconde Adame, ye shall produce Peace; and so beutifie this our Kingdom. (p.194)

Impatient with the wrangling Commons, James enlisted sympathetic polemicists. In the same May the House was outraged by the publication of a book on Union by the Bishop of Bristol. It was printed *cum privilegio,* dedicated to the King, and met the Commons' objections. When he published the substance of these Commons debates the Bishop infringed their ancient privileges, and Richard Martin was sent to the House of Lords to express grief that the King had consented to the publication of this offensive book. The Bishop unwillingly altered his text, and his second edition, bristling with veiled animosity, makes no mention of the Commons and their debates. This second edition praises the Union and (echoing James) likens the division of the realm to the first sin committed in Paradise. With lyrical fervour the prelate conjures Union as the goddess Pallas:

> If I could express the image of this vnion in lively colours, I would surely make her a Goddes, faire, and beautiful, having a garland, & crowne of al blessings upon her head, & sitting in a Chaire of State, with al good fortunes, vertues and graces attending her, and as a Goddes in triumphant chariot going into the capitol, or temple of mighty Jupiter: where also the Poets have found her, but called by another name, even Pallas, who is also named Monas, that is Vnitie: because having only one parent, shee resideth in Jupiters braine, even in the chiefe seate of his wisedome; where al the Muses are her companions. . .[1]

Polemicists demanded Union in the name of Henry VII, Henry VIII, in the name of Aeneas, Christ and the pagan gods, but the Commons saw the projected Union simply as the policy of a Scotsman called James.

During the Christmas recess of Parliament in 1606, on St Stephen's Night, Shakespeare's *King Lear* was performed before King James at Whitehall by 'his Majesty's servants playing usually at the Globe on the Banksyde'. James and his court saw the tragedy against the backcloth of a struggle for Union. I have not re-woven that old fabric to account for their attendance; what was essential for *Gorboduc* is patently gratuitous for *Lear.* Shakespeare's tragedy of age and filial ingratitude is timeless in

[1] John Thornborough, *The Joiefvll and Blessed Revniting the two. . .kingdomes England & Scotland into their ancient name of great Brittaine* (Oxford, n.d.), p.19.

136

its appeal. But the crown, the heavens, stars, thunder, gods, even the double plot have a meaning within a political tradition current in the decade of the play's first performances. That meaning is worth pondering.

A small controversy has rumbled in the last few years between 'pure' critics and those anxious to use historical material to elucidate the tragedy. If I find myself more often in agreement with the readings of Maynard Mack and Sigurd Burckhardt it is because their use of Shakespeare's literary antecedents has seemed to me to offer a fuller appreciation of the design of the entire play than the social and political material marshalled by Rosalie Colie and Glynne Wickham.[1] Professor Wickham has used the pageantry of accession and Union to suggest that *King Lear* is a prologue heralding the Jacobean regenerative tragi-comedy, a form which he derives from the political consciousness of the British people saved by the accession of James and fostered by 'final ratification of the Union of the two Crowns by Act of Parliament in 1608' (pp.36-42). This ratification simply did not occur. James was defeated by his Commons and, despite the propaganda celebrating Union, his recourse to the Exchequer Chamber and high court judges in 1608 was a retreat. I would stress the flat contradiction of iconographic propaganda by the hard facts of the continuing debate.[2] Yes, there was in 1606 a man who claimed to be King of Britain; yes, he had a son who was Duke of Albany and a son who was Duke of Cornwall; undoubtedly his reign was less cataclysmic than Lear's. It does not, however, follow that Shakespeare prefers or is even consoled by the prospect of Union. Union or the undivided crown is the pitiless ideal on which the old king is broken. We care very much about Lear; this could never be said of Gorboduc. Using a freedom which the lawyers had been first to develop and a currency of political imagery which had once affirmed the supremacy of the state, Shakespeare wrote his deeply speculative tragedy.

Some of the figures assembled in Shakespeare's scene of the division of the kingdom would certainly have been familiar to the Whitehall audience from Anthony Munday's pageant *The Triumphs of Re-United Britannia* presented to James on 29 October 1605. Munday's pattern like that of *Locrine* depicts the division of Britain

1 Maynard Mack, *King Lear in our Time* (London, 1966); Sigurd Burckhardt 'The Quality of Nothing' in *Shakespearean Meanings* (Princeton, 1968); Rosalie Colie 'Reason and Need: King Lear and the Crisis of the Aristocracy' in *Some Facets of King Lear,* ed. Colie (London, 1974); Wickham, 'From Tragedy. . .', *SS;* Ribner, *English History Play* pp.248-52.

2 A stark contrast between the British tragedy and Jonson's masque *Hymenaei* may be seen. D.J. Gordon gives a telling analysis of the iconography in that masque, 'Hymenaei Ben Jonson's Masque of Union' in *The Renaissance Imagination,* ed. Stephen Orgel (California, 1976).

by King Brute, as three female figures representing England, Scotland and Wales reprove Brute for his 'over-much fond love to his sons' and consequent division of the kingdom. Brute replies that his sin is now redeemed, despite his sons' tragedies, by royal James and justifies his *felix culpa* by pointing to the resurrected figure of the imperial lady Britannia.[1] James's polemicists had tirelessly repeated that upon the accession of their sovereign 'this Ilande is happily come within the circle of one diadem'.[2] The lawyers said, 'a King's Crown is an hieroglyphic of the laws'.[3] The Bishop of Bristol in the first version of his Union polemic likened the unity of one empire to the firmament of heaven:

> An Empire of many kingdomes thus reduced into one, is not vnlike the firmament of heauen, which God hath adorned with two great lights, the Sunne and Moone, and other Starres, euen the whole army and harmonie of the heauens in one firmament.

He warned the ungodly who might threaten the heavenly Union:

> Who so throweth a stone against heauen, saith the Wise man, it will fall vpon his own head. And if any one standing alone from the rest, speaketh against and oppugneth this Vnion, better it were (sauing my charitie) that *unus ille periret quam Unitas.*[4]

Shakespeare was familiar with that political body which Bristol likened to heaven, but with a charity greater than the Bishop's (or Sackville's) he saw the tragedy of the one man who must perish. *King Lear* is a sensitive study of the disintegration of an inhuman political ideal.

When Lear sunders the crown in the first scene of Shakespeare's tragedy, he unleashes a chain of events which is politically absolutely coherent. The old King's banishment, the storm, thunder, war, and death of Cordelia all stem from this act which divides the realm and places power in the hands of Lear's two evil daughters. Lear never understands the cause of these subsequent disasters, and this is part of his tragedy. If, as Lear himself believes, the disasters were caused simply by the rejection of Cordelia, the play should end with the reconciliation of IV.vii. One has only to compare (as Ribner does)

1 See Nichols *Progresses of James I,* I, 564-76. Bergeron discusses this pageant in *English Civic Pageantry* pp.141-5.

2 [Anon], *The Miracvlovs and Happie Vnion of England and Scotland* (London, 1604), D3v. For an exhaustive study of *King Lear* with particular reference to the contemporary philosophical background see William Elton, *King Lear and the Gods* (San Marino, Calif., 1966).

3 Edward Coke, 'Calvin's Case', *The English Reports: King's Division VI,* LXXVII (London, 1907), p.390.

4 John Thornborough, *A Discovrse plainely proving the. . .necessitie of the. . . Vnion of. . .England and Scotland* (London, 1604), p.11.

138

Shakespeare's tragedy with the 'source' play *King Leir* to see that
Shakespeare's is a tragedy of kingship.[1] The very absence of political
elements in the earlier play points up their force and coherence in
Shakespeare's. In the 'source' play Leir is an erring father who wrongs
his daughter Cordella, perceives his error and is happily reconciled.
His brief period of punishment ended, the whole play may be summed
up in the words of the Duke of Cambria: 'The heauens are just, and
hate impiety'.[2] In Shakespeare's play these words are echoed by
Edgar, but he speaks not of King Lear, but of the Earl of Gloucester's
private sin:

> The gods are just, and of our pleasant vices
> Make instruments to plague us:
> The dark and vicious place where thee he got
> Cost him his eyes.   (V.iii.170-3)

In Shakespeare's tragedy Lear both rejects Cordelia and sunders his
kingdom; there are two errors and two plots; the story of the Earl
of Gloucester who misjudges his children and the story of a king - the
parallels are clear but the contrasts are perhaps more significant. It has
been pointed out that in treating his kingdom as his property Lear
acts like an early seventeenth-century aristocrat and shows a mis-
apprehension about kingship.[3] Bishop Leslie, as we have seen,
suspected that Henry VIII had perpetrated such an error; but for
forty years opponents of the Stuart claim had insisted that there
was no difference in law between a king and a subject. Clearly
Shakespeare's tragedy rests on a legal structure which suggests a
terrible difference.

Maynard Mack and critics influenced by him have shown that
Gloucester's error is evoked and justified in romance and morality play
terms and traditions which emphasize Lear's suffering precisely
because these literary forms which avoid tragedy are so clearly
inadequate to express what the King goes through.[4] I agree and
would simply add that the very traditions of the morality play which
alternatively saw the king as everyman or the king as God's unique
vicar, had become politically charged by succession debate. Both
literary and political traditions enrich the contrast between the two
plots. The relative optimism of the subplot (Edgar after all survives,
perhaps to reign) has suggested to several critics a *felix culpa*

1 *English History Play*, p.248.

2 *King Leir* MSR (Oxford, 1907) line 1909.

3 Rosalie Colie 'Reason and Need', p.198.

4 Bridgett G. Lyons, 'Subplot as simplification in *King Lear*' in *Some Facets*, p.37.

interpretation.[1] And yet the tragedy eludes its historical and literary commentators and probably will continue to do so. Perhaps brevity will be the only merit but I should like to offer one or two ideas suggested by the legal traditions which Shakespeare acknowledges in the play.

King Lear is an old, fallible man in an office which demands that the king shall not err. His offence against Cordelia can be, and is, forgiven in Act IV.vii; but there is no remedy for his offence against his body politic, the Bishop of Bristol's 'heaven'. Politically, Lear commits the original sin. Shakespeare, writing of it in the darkest hours of the Union debate, holds out no hope of forgiveness and no palliative for the inexorable punishment.

Lear's political error is more heinous than any committed by a comparable Elizabethan player king. Gorboduc or Brute simply divided the kingdom. Lear makes an utter travesty of kingship by not only dividing the realm, giving away the power of his office and sundering the crown, but by retaining the name of king and thus the responsibility for all the ensuing disasters. He announces,

> I do invest you jointly with my power,
> Pre-eminence, and all the large effects
> That troop with majesty. Ourself, by monthly course,
> With reservation of an hundred knights,
> By you to be sustain'd, shall our abode
> Make with you by due turn. Only we shall retain
> The name, and all th'addition to a king:
> The sway, revenue, execution of the rest,
> Beloved sons, be yours; which to confirm,
> This coronet part between you.   (I.i.129-38)

It is after this appalling statement that Kent forcefully breaks into the scene. He had protested 'Good my liege. . .' at Cordelia's banishment, but at the sundering of the Crown he intervenes to remind Lear of the discrepancy between King and father, the fallible 'old man'.

> Royal Lear,
> Whom I have ever honour'd as my king,
> Lov'd as my father, as my master follow'd. . .
>   What wouldst thou do, old man?
> Think'st thou that duty shall have dread to speak
> When power to flattery bows? To plainness honour's bound
> When majesty falls to folly. Reserve thy state;
> And in thy best consideration check
> This hideous rashness.   (I.i.138-50)

Kent defends Cordelia but reserves his most forceful word of condemnation for the King's irresponsible gift, the sundered Crown:

1 F.T. Flahiff, 'Edgar' Once and Future King' in *Some Facets* pp.228 and 233.

> Revoke thy gift,
> Or, whilst I can vent clamour from my throat,
> I'll tell thee thou dost evil.   (I.i.164-6)

Through the eyes of Kent and the Fool we glimpse the implications of Lear's folly. Lear's abuse of his office, alone, enables Goneril and Regan to use power against him, as the Fool points out:

> When thou clovest thy crown i' the' middle, and gav'st
> away both parts, thou bor'st thine ass on thy back
> o'er the dirt. Thou hadst little wit in thy bald crown
> when thou gav'st thy golden one away.   (I.iv.159-62)

But Lear himself is unable to make this connection. Like Plowden's Agamemnon, he sees himself as a wronged father, not an erring king. He does not see that Goneril and Regan become deadly because of his own abuse of power. He sees them only as his 'unnatural' daughters and searches blindly within his personal, familial relationship for understanding.

The Gloucester plot is precisely circumscribed: the story of a purely familial relationship; in the differences of its scale and intensity it seems constantly to point out how much greater is Lear's punishment. As Lear gropes among the symbols of sex and lust which are so pertinent to Gloucester's case, it is apparent that they cannot, except as political metaphors, compass his errors or his daughters. Gloucester's story is one of physical error physically punished; at its source lies the act of adultery. There is no physical cause to explain Lear's unnatural daughters.

The audience's vision is always wider than Lear's. Yet it is essential to the movement of the tragedy that Kent, who has helped to establish this wider perspective, is himself changed by contact with Lear's suffering. Kent condemned Lear's gift and the banishment of Cordelia as offences against a just heaven:

> Now, by Apollo, King,
> Thou swear'st thy gods in vain.   (I.i.158-9)

> [to Cordelia] The gods to their dear shelter take thee, maid,
> That justly think'st, and hast most rightly said!   (I.i.182-3)

Yet Kent is instrumental in bringing the audience to a final sense of outrage; his certainty is shaken by Lear's ordeal, which in Edgar's account he seems to share:

> He fastened on my neck and bellowed out
> As he'd burst heaven. . .
> Told the most piteous tale of Lear and him
> That ever ear receiv'd; which in recounting

> His grief grew puissant, and the strings of life
> Began to crack.   (V.iii.212-17)

It is Kent who most clearly understands the cause of Lear's suffering
but who finally protests against heaven's justice.

> Vex not his ghost. O, let him pass! He hates him
> That would upon the rack of this tough world
> Stretch him out longer.   (V.iii.313-15)

When Lear is turned out into the storm he recognizes in the thunder
and lightning the force of divine punishment,

> Let the great gods,
> That keep this dreadful pudder o'er our heads,
> Find out their enemies now. Tremble, thou wretch,
> That hast within thee undivulged crimes
> Unwhipp'd of justice.   (III.ii.49-53)

and wrestles to understand the cause of his suffering. But before this
vast impersonal instrument of divine justice, he sees himself not as the
king who hurled the stone against the heaven of Union, but as 'a man,/
More sinn'd against than sinning' (III.ii.59-60). For one moment in
III.iv Lear's vision widens and he comes as close to full understanding as
he ever will. In his last fully lucid moments he recognizes that, as
king, in some measure he has failed. Lear's question, 'What is the cause
of thunder?' and the prayer in which he recognizes his responsibility for
the poor, mark his greatest understanding of the implications of his
failure as king; beyond this he cannot penetrate:

> O, I have ta'en
> Too little care of this! Take physic pomp;
> Expose thyself to feel what wretches feel,
> That thou mayst shake the superflux to them,
> And show the heavens more just.   (III.iv.32-6)

The 'trial' scene (III.vi) marks the turning away from an attempt to
understand heavenly justice. When Lear asks, 'Is there any cause in
nature that makes these hard hearts?' he asks essentially the same
question as, 'What is the cause of thunder?' but he has now turned his
eyes from the heavens to humanity.

After III.iv Shakespeare never allows his characters to mention
Lear's *responsibility* as king. The framework has been established by
the early speeches of Kent and the Fool, and once the original causal
factor has been understood we are asked to focus on Lear the man.
Lear's fatherhood means more to him than kingly power. As Burckhardt
has said, 'In Lear the tragic error is "made good"...by a determination

to live by it',[1] It is natural that he should ransack this area of his greatest grief searching for the cause of suffering; it is this misdirected search which reveals his human greatness. The qualities of the splendid old man gradually vitiate the relevance of the kingly ideal, and pity sweeps before it one's assurance that the King's punishment is just.

Lear fails to see the nature of the powers of evil he has unleashed in the kingdom. When he is reconciled with Cordelia he believes his punishment to be at an end. Sure that the heavens at last support him, Lear pronounces the terrible words which will ultimately explain (though they can never justify) Cordelia's death:

> He that parts us shall bring a brand from heaven   (V.iii.22)

The death of innocence decreed by Edmund for reasons of state is explicable in terms of Lear's first offence against 'heaven'. For us, recollection of the Gorgon-Fury who brought the firebrand from heaven to punish Gorboduc may elucidate Lear's metaphor.[2] Nevertheless, understanding cannot abate one's sense of outrage. Any sense of justice has been overwhelmed by compassion for Lear's suffering even before the old King enters with Cordelia dead in his arms crying,

> Howl, howl, howl, howl! O you are men of stones!
> Had I your tongues and eyes, I'd use them so
> That heaven's vault should crack.   (V.iii.257-9)

Lear's greatness is not the perfection demanded of a king; the heavens demand qualities quite other than his own. He is broken upon the rack of an impossible ideal.

Yet Lear is a powerful man; he has held his little band by their love; this is the bond that should unite empires but Shakespeare offers little hope that it will. By the end of the tragedy empires seem irrelevant. Despite its figural affinities with *Gorboduc* this is, politically, a dark tragedy. If Lear is finally in Act V a great king it is because kingship itself has been gradually re-defined. The concluding words 'Speak what we feel not what we ought to say' mark the deep gulf between Sackville and Shakespeare. Shakespeare is closer to the Greek dramatists, though the gods Lear invokes are not the classical pantheon and would have been more readily recognized at the Inns of Court than in Athens.

If the preceding essays have any value they will have suggested a more precise context for the heaven Lear defies: not to prescribe

1 Burckhardt, *Shakespearean Meanings*, p.241.

2 Maynard Mack draws attention to the earlier use of the fire from heaven in Bale's *Three Laws* and in *Darius*, p.59.

Shakespeare's own belief but to suggest a political tradition he both needed and transcended. Plowden's theory, for which he had found classical precedents, had all the pitiless inflexibility of the Greek gods, if little of their elegance. The old lawyer must bear a certain responsibility and a little reflected lustre, if only that of grit to pearl.

Epilogue

It is hard to exaggerate the publicity the Union controversy gave to the theory of the king's two bodies in the years immediately preceding and the year following the royal performance of *King Lear.* In 1606 for example Edward Forset published his full length book, *Comparative Discovrse of Bodies Natvral and Politqve,* in which he told his contemporaries:

> [the monarch] in his personall respects. . .is as one man, single and indiuiduall, yet as in the right of Soveraigntie, he gayneth the appellation and capacities of a corporation. . .the resplendence and power of soueraigntie in the royall person of a Soueraigne, shewing itselfe both in so great maiestie, as dazleth the eyes of all beholders, and in so admirable effects, as to transforme sauagenesse into ciuilitie, repugnances into concords, vices into vertues. . .[and] doeth in like sort (by such the conuersion of the body naturall, into a body politicall) beget thereunto a more admired glory, and a more deere esteeme. [1]

In the Commons in November 1606 the Instrument of Union was read; during February and March 1606/7 the well-worn cases of the succession controversy were re-opened to determine whether allegiance had been due to a monarch before he was crowned or after; whether a subject swore allegiance to the body politic symbolized by the diadem, or to the man who wore the diadem.

On 17 February 1606/7 Francis Bacon addressed the Commons and put the judges' argument for Union of the realms; he interpreted Plowden for merchants, burgesses and knights of the shire who had no legal training. He pleaded with them to abandon a narrow and personal point of view and to see the ideal figured in the natural body of their monarch:

> So in this cause, if an honest English merchant. . .should say, Surely I would proceed not further in the Union, were I as the King; it mought be reasonably answered, No more would the King, were he as an English merchant.[2]

If the Commons could abandon their personal identity and see

1 *A Comparative Discovrse of the Bodies Natvral and Politiqve* (London, 1606), p.34.

2 'Speech for General Naturalization', *Works,* X, 307-8.

themselves and their interests guaranteed and preserved in the welfare of the greater realm, Union would be assured; they would act with the King, they would 'see their right flaming in the Phoenix sight'. But they could not. Bacon's speech failed to impress the 'merchants', who held to their position. Next day, 18 February, the Commons decided not to consult the King's judges but to ask lawyers who were themselves of the lower House to judge the legality of Union, to 'deliver their Opinion, to rectify and direct the Consciences of the rest'.[1]

On 2 March Bacon tried to demolish the adverse verdict of the Commons lawyers with the most basic argument of all. He argued that the bond of allegiance, on which the Union would be based, had existed before all written laws and in situations when law enforcement was impossible. He postulated precisely the situation which Shakespeare dramatized in Act III of *King Lear*:

> A Case put: A King expulsed, yet a faithful Troop. . .the Laws are gone. Allegiance remains.[2]

But the Commons, like the Edmunds and the Sebastians of Shakespeare's plays, were unconvinced.

In vain the King and the House of Lords sent messages to the Commons pressing for a favourable decision. Finally, at the end of March, James addressed the Commons in person. Although his tone was conciliatory he spoke of harsh consequences if he were defied. Shakespeare, in *The Comedy of Errors* and in *Henry V,* had analyzed the mystery of kings 'twin born with greatness' and the errors which could result from double identity. Whereas James acknowledged the difficulties of the concept, he had no intention in the hard reality of Jacobean politics of following Duke Solinus or Henry V and dropping, even for a moment, the dignity which made him different from a London merchant:

> When I first propounded Vnion, I then thought there could haue bene no more question of it, then of your declaration and acknowledgement of my right vnto this Crowne, and that as two Twinnes, they would haue growne vp together. The errour was my mistaking; I knew mine owne ende, but not others feares. . . I protest before GOD who knowes my heart, and to you my people before whom it were a shame to lie, that I claim nothing but with the acknowledgement of my Bond to you; that as yee owe to me subiection and obedience: So my Soueraigntie obligeth mee to yeeld to you loue, gouernment and protection. . .I desire a perfect Vnion of Lawes and persons, and such Naturalizing as may make one body of both Kingdomes vnder mee your King. For no more possible is it for one King to gouerne two Countreys

1 *Journals of the House of Commons,* I, 1015, 1016.
2 *Journals of the House of Commons,* I, 1024.

> Contiguous. . .then for one head to gouerne two bodies, or one man
> to be husband of two wiues,. . .But remember also it is as possible
> and likely your owne Lawyers may erre as the Iudges. . .So would I
> haue you on the other part to beware to disgrace either my
> Proclamations or the Iudges, who when the Parliament is done,
> haue power to trie your lands and liues, for so you may disgrace
> both your King and your Lawes.[1]

But the royal threat failed. Once this had occurred the concept of the king's two bodies (although it remained a current idea) gradually lost that power which had depended quite simply on its being believed.

James turned from his intractable Commons back again to the judges who in 1608 considered a test case which might establish a legal precedent for the Union of the kingdoms and naturalization of the *post-nati* of Scotland. Francis Bacon presented to all the judges of England precisely the same legal arguments the Commons had refused. Here in the Exchequer Chamber Bacon spoke of the king's two bodies to the converted and was reported for posterity by Coke.   Political and historical differences between Scotland and England were argued away in *Calvin's Case* by the 'fact' that both realms were embodied in the person of one man. Allegiance was due to the king not to the inanimate land; it was a bond between man and man:

> no man will affirm, that England itself, taking it for the continent
> thereof doth owe any ligeance or faith, or that any faith or ligeance
> should be due to it. [2]

Finally citing the Bible, the *Aeneid* and the usual bewildering assortment of 'legal' authorities, the judges showed that allegiance had existed before those legal systems and institutions which nominally divided England and Scotland. The Scots owed allegiance to King James; the English owed allegiance to King James, therefore the Scots could not be considered aliens in England; if they were not aliens, they must be subjects; therefore the two realms were united.[3]

Despite the appearance of judicial unanimity, James's victory was hollow; Scotland and England had been 'united' without the consent of Parliament. It was a foretaste of bitter dissensions to come.

It would be hard to find a period in which the language of poetry was more closely linked with that of law and politics. During Elizabeth's reign both the Queen and her advisers made full use of an ideology which consisted of technical concepts, myth and metaphysics,

1 *Political Works,* ed. McIlwain, pp.291, 292, 296.
2 Coke, *English Reports K.B. VI,* LXXVII, 390-1.
3 Coke, *Ibid,* pp.392, 407.

suggestion, surmise, flattery and subtle coercion, to maintain a precarious balance of power. James did not really understand the complexity of the role he was asked to play when Englishmen hailed him as Elizabeth's successor. He did not really understand that he had been *asked,* but mistook veiled warning and criticism for compliment. Those pageants which greeted his entry into London were an expression of expectant hope and faith which demanded justification; they were not a celebration of James's actual achievements and personal virtues as King of Scotland. Only an obstinate inability to distinguish the two can account for the persistence with which he drew attention in his parliamentary addresses and messages to his second, invisible body, which looked, to a sceptical House of Commons, like a suit of the Emperor's new clothes.

Under Elizabeth the theory of the two bodies had been used to criticize and coerce the Queen. Elizabeth had suffered humiliations, had changed tactics without ever permitting Parliament a full and open debate on the succession. Outside Parliament she tolerated the fictions by which men of law pointed out discrepancy between her two bodies and made artful criticisms of her policy. James was now insisting in Parliament that there was no discrepancy; the millennium had arrived, perfection was achieved. His vision of union within his body natural did not correspond to political realities as the Commons saw them; worse, he had pre-empted the very theory by which they might have criticized him. On these terms opposition was driven to more explicit channels, and a workable consensus about the balance in the state broke down.

James and his son continued to enjoy plays and masques but by the second decade of the new century something indefinable had been lost from the drama. This phenomenon has often been noted; it can never perhaps be fully explained. One says the plays lacked structure, or simply that Shakespeare died. Perhaps the story of the king's two bodies in some measure accounts for the diminished importance of a play. During Elizabeth's reign and in the first few years of the new century there seem to have been tacit assumptions about the vital relation between the stage and the state. As long as men could accept as politically viable a vision of the monarch's two bodies, dramatists were perhaps best equipped to express its subtle complexity, to 'show. . .the very age and body of the time his form and pressure'. A dramatist could simultaneously express the ideal and the realities of political power at a time when not many men dared to do so.

By 1608 the Commons had publicly censured their monarch on an issue which had been the staple of the political drama; there was comparably less need for dramatic ghosts come from the grave to diagnose evil in the body politic, less expectancy that a play might be skilfully designed to catch the conscience of a king.

APPENDIX

The careers of some Inns of Court men

Name	Revels Activity 1561/2	Admission to Inner Temple	Post at Inn	House of Commons	Other Distinctions
Bashe [Edward]	Steward of the Household	15 Nov. 1556		Rochester City 1554, " 1558/9, " 1562/3	
Blaston [Marmaduke Blakston]	One of the Masters of the Revels	18 June 1556			
Broke, Arthur	'set forth certain plays & shows' Xmas 1561/2	18 Dec. 1561			trans. *Romeus & Juliet* pr. 1562
Copley, [Thomas]	Marshal of the Household	2 Nov. 1547		Galton Borough 1554, " 1557/8, " 1562/3	
Dudley, Robert	Lord Governor	22 Dec. 1561	'governor of this house'		Master of the Queen's Horse
Fuller, John	Chief Justice of the King's Bench	1532			
Hatton, Christopher	Master of the Game	26 May 1560		[begins in 1572]	Gentleman Pensioner [1564?]
Hare, Nicholas	Constable Marshal	5 Feb. 1547/8			
Jervise [Richard Jerves]	One of the Masters of the Revels	21 Oct. 15–			
Kelway, Robert	Lord Privy Seal	1525	IT Parliament	Bristol City 1547	
Kendall	Carver	26 Feb. 1559/60			
Lee, Garrett [Gerard Legh]		7 Feb. 1562/3			*Accedens of Armory* pr. 1562

Name	Revels Activity 1561/2	Admission to Inner Temple	Post at Inn	House of Commons	Other Distinctions
Manwood, Roger	Chief Baron of the Exchequer	10 Feb. 1547/8	IT Parliament	Cinque Ports, Hastings 1555 Cinque Ports, Sandwich 1557/8 Cinque Ports, " 1558/9 Cinque Ports, " 1562/3	
Martyn, [John]	Ranger of the Forests	June 1530		Plympton Borough 1529 " " 1554	
Norton, Thomas	co-author of *Gorboduc*	28 June 1555		Galton Borough 1557/8 Berwick 1562/3	
Onslow, [Richard]	Lord Chancellor	28 Jan. 1544/5	IT Parliament	Steyning Borough 1557/8 " " 1562/3	
Parker, [Bryan]	Lieutenant of the Tower	8 Feb. 1550/1			
Paten, ?	Chief Butler	1543			
Penston [Anthony Panyston] or [Thomas Pennyston)	One of the Masters of the Revels	3 July 1537 or 19 May 1560			
Pole, William	Chief Justice of the Common Pleas	1539	IT Parliament		
Sackville, Thomas	co-author of *Gorboduc*	1554		East Grinstead 1558/9 Aylesbury Borough 1562/3	

Name	Revels Activity 1561/2	Admission to Inner Temple	Post at Inn	House of Commons	Other Distinctions
Stapleton, Anthony	Lord Treasurer	1522	IT Parliament	East Grinstead 1553/4	
Stradling, [Edward]	Sewer	8 May 1552		Steyning Borough 1554 Arundel ” 1557/8	
Yorke [Peter]	One of the Masters of the Revels	27 Feb. 1557			

Name	Revels Activity 1587/8	Admission to Gray's Inn	Post at Inn	House of Commons	Other Distinctions
Bacon, Francis	Dumb shows: *Misfortunes*	1576	Utter barrister 1583 Assistant to Reader 1588	Taunton Borough 1586 Liverpool ” 1588	

Flower, Frauncis	directed *Misfortunes* at Court. wrote Choruses: Acts I & II			Huntington Borough 1584
				  ” ” 1586
				  ” ” 1588
					Gentleman Pensioner 1586

Fulbecke, William	Rewrote prologue & epilogue: *Misfortunes*	1584			*A Book of Christian Ethicks* 1587
Hughes, Thomas	author of *Misfortunes*	1579	Utter barrister 1585	Lyme Regis 1586	
Lancaster, John	Dumb shows: directed *Misfortunes* at Court	1564	Utter barrister 1577 Ancient 1587 Pensioner 1588		

Name	Revels Activity 1587/8	Admission to Gray's Inn	Post at Inn	House of Commons	Other Distinctions
Penruddoke, John	directed *Misfortunes*	1562	Utter barrister 1564 Pensioner 1582 Reader 1584	Wilton Borough 1584 Southampton Borough 1586	
Trotte, Nicholas	wrote pageant of muses for *Misfortunes*	1573	Utter barrister 1584		
Yelverton, Christopher	Dumb shows: *Misfortunes*	1552	Utter barrister 1553 Treasurer 1579 Treasurer 1585 Reader 1574 Reader 1583	Brackley Borough 1562/3 Northampton Borough 1572	Epilogue to *Jocasta* 1566/7

List of Primary Sources

1. Manuscript

Ashfield, Edmund, [Letter to James VI] BL Cotton Julius F VI, fol. 139.

Browne, Anthony, The Argument and Answere of Sir Anthony Browne knyght vnto the Matters of Sir Nicholas Bacon knyght. BL Lansdowne 254, fols. 185-98v.

—— The Argument and Aunswere of Sir Nicholas Bacon. BL Harley 555, fols. 11-47

Cecil, William, [Memorandum on Spanish Invasion] 25 February 1587. BL Cotton Vespasian C VIII, fol. 12.

—— Memoryall to the Queen at the end of the Parliament 1566. SP 12/41, fol. 75

Dyer, Edward, [Letter to Christopher Hatton] 9 October 1572. BL Harley 787, fol. 88.

Edwards, Richard, The songe of Emely. BL Additional 26737, fol. 106v.

Elizabeth I, [letter on friendship] BL Additional 46367, fol. 103.

—— Wordes spoken by the Queene to the Lords. SP 12/7.

Gentlemen Pensioners, [Rolls of Payment: Elizabeth I] E(xchequer) 407/41-5.

Grey, Catherine, Trial and Examinations relating to the marriage of the Earl of Hertford with the Lady Catherine Grey. BL Harley 6286, fols. 1-119.

Hales, John, A Discovrs Uppon certen pointes towching the Enheritaunce of the Crowne. BL Harley 537 fols. 50-5 and Harley 555 fols. 1-10v.

Hatton, Christopher, [Letter to Queen Elizabeth I] 3 April 1584. BL Additional 15891, fol. 127v.

Hooke, Henry, Of the Succession of England [1600/1] BL Royal 17 B XI, fols. 1-19.

Inner Temple, Acts of Parliament 1505-89.

—— Admissions to the Inner Temple to 1659, I, 1954.

Message of the damsell of the Q. of fayries, BL Ditchley, fol. 2.

Plowden, Edmund, A Treatice proving that. . .the Quene of Scotts. . .is not disabled by the Lawe of England, to receive the Crowne of Inglande by discent. BL Harley 849, fols. 1-38.

—— A treatise proveing that. . .the Quene of Scotts. . .is not disabled by the lawe of England to receave the crowne of England by discent. Bodleian Rawlinson A 124, fols. 1-47.

—— The treatise of the two bodies of the king. BL Cotton Caligula B IV, fols. 1-94.

Pound, Thomas, [Letter to Christopher Hatton] 18 September 1580. SP 12/142.

—— [Lincoln's Inn masques] Bodleian Rawlinson Poet. 108, fols. 24-37.

Pudsey, Edmund, [Commonplace Book] Bodleian Eng. Poet. d. 3.

Ramsey, John, De vita mea. Bodleian Douce 280, fols. 193v, 194.

Rawlinson, English Poems and prophecies. Bodleian Rawlinson C. 813.

Rudyerd, Benjamin, Noctes Templariae. BL Harley 1576, fols. 556-62.

Watson, William, [Letter to the Attorney General] April 1599. Inner Temple Petyt 47, fol. 103.

Wentworth, Peter, [Letter to Lord Burghley] 27 September 1591. SP 12/240, fol. 21.

Wilson, Thomas, State of England. [c.1600] SP 12/280.

2. Printed

Allen, William (Cardinal), *Letters and Memorials,* ed. Thomas F. Knox. London, 1882.

Anderson, James, *Collections Relating to Mary, Queen of Scots,* 4 vols. Edinburgh, 1727-8.

Bacon, Francis, *The Works of Francis Bacon,* ed. James Spedding, Robert Leslie Ellis, Douglas Denon Heath, 14 vols. London, 1857-74.

Beaumont, Francis, *Grammar Lecture,* ed. Mark Eccles. *RES,* XVI (1940), 402-14.

Baldwin, William, *Beware the Cat,* ed. William P. Holden. New London, 1963.

Birch, Thomas, *Memoirs of the Reign of Queen Elizabeth,* 2 vols. London, 1754.

Bland, Desmond S., ed., *Early Records of Furnival's Inn.* Newcastle upon Tyne, 1957.

Blenerhasset, Thomas, *A Revelation of the True Minerva,* ed. Josephine Waters Bennett. New York: Scholars' facsimiles and reprints, 1941.

Bond, Richard Warwick, ed., *Early Plays from the Italian,* Oxford, 1911.

Broke, Arthur, *Romeus and Juliet,* ed. J.J. Munro. London, 1907.

Buc(k), George, 'The Third University of England' (printed in) John Stow's *Annales or A Generall Chronicle of England.* London, 1631.

Bullough, Geoffrey, *Narrative and Dramatic Sources of Shakespeare.* 8 vols. London: Routledge and Kegan Paul, 1957-75.

Calendar of State Papers, Domestic 1547-80, ed. Robert Lemon. London, 1856.

Calendar of State Papers, Rome 1558-71, ed. J.M. Rigg. London, 1916.

Calendar of State Papers relating to Scotland 1547-1603, ed. Joseph Bain, W.K. Boyd, H.W. Meikle, A.I. Cameron, M.S. Giuseppi, 13 vols. Edinburgh, 1898-1969.

Calendar of State Papers Spanish: Elizabeth, ed. Martin S. Hume, 4 vols. London, 1892-9.

156

Camden, William, *Annales: The True and Royall History of Elizabethan Queen of England,* trans. Abraham Darcy & T. Browne.
London, 1625.

Campion, Thomas, *Campion's Works,* ed. Percival Vivian. Oxford,
1909.

Cecil, William, *A Collection of state papers. . .left by William Cecil,
Lord Burghley,* ed. Samuel Haynes and William Murdin, 2 vols.
London, 1740-59.

Chester, Robert, *Poems by Sir John Salusbury and Robert Chester,*
ed. Carleton Brown. London: EETS, 1914.
———— *Robert Chester's Love's Martyr: or Rosalin's Complaint,* ed.
Alexander B. Grosart, London, 1878.

Cobbett, William, *A Complete Collection of State Trials,* I. London,
1809.

Coke, Edward, *English Reports: King's Bench Division VI,* LXXVII.
London, 1907.

Collier, J. Payne, ed., *The Egerton Papers,* London: Camden Society,
1840.

Craig, Thomas, *The Right of Succession to the Kingdom of England,*
trans. James Gatherer. London, 1703.

Cunliffe, John W., *Early English Classical Tragedies,* Oxford: Clarendon
Press, 1912.

Dekker, Thomas, *The Non Dramatic Works of Thomas Dekker,* ed.
Alexander B. Grosart. 3 vols. re-issue New York, 1963.
———— *The Dramatic Works of Thomas Dekker,* ed. Fredson Bowers,
4 vols. Cambridge: University Press, 1953-61.

D'Ewes, (Sir) Simonds, ed., *A Compleat Journal of the House of Lords
and. . .Commons.* London, 1603.

Dodd, Charles, *The Church History of England,* ed. M.A. Tierney,
5 vols. London, 1839-43.

Doleman (*see* Parsons, R.)

Drayton, Michael, *Works,* ed. J. William Hebel, 5 vols. Oxford, 1961.

Dugdale, William, *Origines Juridiciales.* London, 1666.

Edwards, Richard, *Damon and Pithias,* ed. Arthur Brown and
F.P. Wilson. Oxford: Malone Society, 1957.

Egerton Papers (*see* Collier J.P.)

Exeter Book (*see* Gollancz, I.)

Feuillerat, Albert, *Documents Relating to the Revels at Court in the
Times of King Edward VI and Queen Mary.* Louvain, 1914.
———— *Documents Relating to the Office of Revels in the Time of
Queen Elizabeth.* Louvain, 1908.

Fletcher, R.J., ed., *The Pension Book of Gray's Inn,* 2 vols. London
1891, 1910.

Forset, Edward, *A Comparative discovrse of the bodies natvral and politiqve.* London, 1606.

Fortescue, (Sir) John, *A learned commendation of the politique lawes of England,* trans. Robert Mulcaster. London, 1567.

Foster, Joseph, *The Register of Admissions to Gray's Inn 1521-1889.* London, 1889.

Foxe, John, *The Acts and Monuments,* ed. Josiah Pratt, 8 vols. London, 1877.

Gascoigne, George, *The Complete Works of George Gascoigne,* ed. J.W. Cunliffe, 2 vols. Cambridge: University Press, 1907-10.

Gesta Grayorum, ed. W.W. Greg. Oxford: Malone Society, 1914.

Gollancz, Israel, ed., *The Exeter Book Part I.* Oxford: EETS, 1895.

Gray's Inn: Register of Admissions (*see* Foster, J.)
——— Pension Books (*see* Fletcher R.J.)

Greene, Robert, *The Life and Complete Works in Prose and Verse of Robert Greene,* ed. Alexander B. Grosart, 15 vols. London, 1881-6.

——— *The Plays and Poems of Robert Greene,* ed. J. Churton Collins, 2 vols. Oxford, 1905.

——— *Friar Bacon and Friar Bungay,* ed. W.W. Greg. Oxford: Malone Society, 1926.

——— *The Scottish History of James the Fourth,* ed. A.E.H. Swaen. Oxford: Malone Society, 1921.

Greg, W.W., ed., *Collections I:2.* Oxford: Malone Society, 1908.

Greg, W.W. (*et al.*), *Collections II:2.* Oxford: Malone Society, 1923.

Hale, (Sir) Matthew, *Pleas of the Crown,* 2 vols. London, 1736.

Hales, John (*see* Harbin, G.).

Hall, Edward, *The union of the two noble and illustre famelies York and Lancaster,* ed. Henry Ellis. London, 1809.

Harbin, George, *The Hereditary Right of the Crown of England Asserted.* London, 1713.

Harington, (Sir) John, *A tract on the succession to the crown A.D. 1602,* ed. C.R. Markham. Roxburghe Club, 1880.

——— *Nugae Antiquae,* ed. Henry Harington, 3 vols. London, 1779.

Hayward, John, *A Treatise of Vnion of the two realmes of England and Scotland.* London, 1604.

Henslowe's Diary, ed. R.A. Foakes and R.J. Rickert. Cambridge: University Press, 1961.

Heywood, Thomas, *The Dramatic Works of Thomas Heywood,* 6 vols. London, 1874.

Holinshed, Raphael, *Chronicles of England, Scotland and Ireland,* ed. Henry Ellis, 6 vols. London, 1807-8.

158

Hough, Graham, ed., *The First Commentary on 'The Faerie Queene'.*
n.p. 1964.

Huth, Henry, ed., *Ancient Ballads and Broadsides.* London, 1867.

Inderwick, F.A., *A Calendar of Inner Temple Records,* 5 vols. London,
1896-1937.

James I, *The Political Works of James I,* ed. Charles Howard McIlwain.
Cambridge, Mass: Harvard University Press, 1918.

Journals of the House of Commons, I. London, 1803.

King Leir, ed. W.W. Greg. Oxford: Malone Society, 1907.

Kyd, Thomas, *The Works of Thomas Kyd,* ed. Frederick S. Boas.
Oxford, 1901.

Lambarde, William, *Apxaionomia.* London, 1568.

Legh, Gerard, *Accedens of Armory.* London, 1562.

Leland, John, *J. Lelandi antiquarii de rebus Britannicis Collectanea*
6 vols. London, 1770.

Leslie, John, *Defense of the Honor of. . .Mary Queen of Scotland
with. . .declaration. . .of her. . .title. . .to the succession of the
crowne of Englande.* London, 1569.

—— *A Treatise Touching the Right, Title and Interest of. . .Marie,
Queene of Scotland, to the succession of the croune of England.*
Louvain, 1571.

—— *A treatise towching the right of Marie of Scotland.* Rouen,
1584.

Leycester's Commonwealth, ed. Frank J. Burgoyne. London, 1904.

Lincoln's Inn: Admissions (*see* Records of the Hon. Soc. of Lincoln's Inn)
          Black Books (*see*   "   " "   "   "   "   "   ")

Locrine, The Tragedy of Locrine, ed. Ronald B. McKerrow. Oxford:
Malone Society, 1908.

Lyly, John, *The Complete Works of John Lyly,* ed. Richard Warwick
Bond, 3 vols. Oxford, 1902.

Machyn, Henry, *The Diary of Henry Machyn,* ed. J.G. Nichols. Camden
Soc. XLII, 1848.

Marston, John, *The Plays of John Marston,* ed. H. Harvey Wood,
3 vols. London, 1934-9.

Martin, C.T, *Middle Temple Records,* 4 vols. London, 1904-5.

Middle Temple Admissions (*see* Sturgess, H.)

(The) Miracvlovs and Happie Union of England and Scotland. London.
1604.

Nichols, John, *The Progresses of King James I,* 4 vols. London, 1828.

—— *The Progresses of Queen Elizabeth,* 3 vols. London,
1823.

Parliaments of England 1213-1702. London, 1878.

Parsons, Robert, *A Conference Abovt the next svcession to the Crowne
of Ingland.* n.p. 1594.

159

Peele, George, *The Araygnement of Paris*. ed. Harold H. Child. Oxford: Malone Society, 1910.

—— *King Edward the First*, ed. W.W. Greg, Oxford: Malone Society, 1911.

—— *The Works of George Peele*, ed. A.H. Bullen, 2 vols. London, 1888.

Pikeryng, John, *Horestes*, ed. Daniel Seltzer, Oxford: Malone Society, 1962.

Plowden, Edmund, *Les Commentaries ou Reports de Edmund Plowden*. London, 1588.

—— *The Commentaries and Reports of Edmund Plowden*. London, 1779.

(Le) Prince d'Amour. London, 1660.

(The) *Records of the Honourable Society of Lincoln's Inn, I: Admissions 1420-1799*. Lincoln's Inn, 1896.

(The) *Records of the Honourable Society of Lincoln's Inn: The Black Books 1422-1845*, ed. J.D. Walker and W.D. Baildon. London, 1897-1902.

(The) Roxburghe Ballads, ed. Charles Hindley, 2 vols. London, 1873.

Salusbury, (Sir) John, (*see* Chester, R.).

Semphill, Robert *The Semphill Ballates 1567-83*, ed. Thomas George Stevenson, Edinburgh, 1872.

Shakespeare, William, *The Comedy of Errors*, ed. R.A. Foakes. London: New Arden, 1962.

—— *The Complete Works*, ed. Peter Alexander. New York: Random House, 1952.

—— *The Poems*, ed. Frank Templeton Prince. London: New Arden, 1960.

Spenser, Edmund, *Minor Poems*, ed. Ernest de Selincourt. Oxford: Clarendon Press, 1910.

Stow, John, *Annales or A Generall Chronicle of England*, London, 1631.

Sturgess, H.A.C., *Register of Admissions to the Honourable Society of the Middle Temple*, 3 vols. London, 1949.

Thornborough, John, *A Discovrse plainely proving the. . .necessitie of the. . .Vnion of. . .England and Scotland.* London, 1604.

—— *The Joiefvll and Blessed Revniting the two. . .kingdomes England & Scotland into their ancient name of great Brittaine.* n.d. Oxford.

Waterhouse, E., *A Commentary upon Fortescue*. London, 1663.

Wentworth, Peter, *A Pithie exhortation to Her Maiestie for establishing her Svccessor to the Crowne. Wherevnto is added a Discourse containing the Authors opinion of the true and lawfull successor to Her Maiestie.* n.p., 1598.

160

Wilmot, Robert *(et al.)*, *Tancred and Gismund*, ed. W.W. Greg. Oxford: Malone Society, 1914.

Woodstock, The First Part of the Reign of King Richard the Second or Thomas of Woodstock, ed. Wilhelmina P. Frijlinck. Oxford: Malone Society, 1929.

Woodstock: A Moral History, ed. A.P. Rossiter. London, 1946.

INDEX

(A date in parentheses indicates that the entry refers to an entertainment whose date of performance is known, with the single exception of the entry for Parliament, where the bracketed dates indicate sittings.)

Sussex, Earl of,   *see* Radcliffe

Talbot, Gilbert, seventh Earl of Shrewsbury,   82
Taming of the Shrew, The (Shakespeare),   55
Tarleton, Richard,   78-9
Tempest, The (Shakespeare),   118
Thomas of Woodstock (son of Edward III),   97-9
Thornborough, John, Bishop of Bristol,   135, 137, 139
Tillyard, E.M.W.,   88
Tilt,   (1561/2) 40, 42; (1564/5) 49
Tottel, Richard,   44, 55
Tourney,   67; (1561/2) 40, 42; (Bermondsey 1566) 50; (Oxford 1566) 50
Treason,   28, 30-1, 42, 50
Triumphs of Re-United Britania, The (Munday),   136
Trotte, Nicholas (GI),   153
Troublesome Raigne of King John, The,   107-9
Truth (troth),   44, 60, 86; 122-3, 127-30
Tyler, Wat,   7

Union of Great Britain,   Scotland and England: 21-2, 79-80, 131-47 *passim,* English precedence: 48, 75, 85, marriage of James IV, 36, 97; Bacon argues for 143-4, 145; border laws 134; Commons debate, 134-6, 143-7; Instrument of, 143; James addresses Parliament 133, 134, 144-5; treatises, 54, 80, 135, 137; in drama: *Gorboduc,* 47; *Horestes,* 59; *Misfortunes,* 77-8; *Gesta,* 83; *James IV,* 105-6; *Locrine,* 106-7; *Henry V,* 112-14; (1603/4) 132; (1605) 136-7; *Lear,* 135-9

Venus,   53, 69
Vergil, Polydore,   35, 75

Warham, William (archbishop of Canterbury),   2
Watson, William,   95, 97
Wentworth, Peter,   89-91, 95, 131
Westminster Palace,   40 n2
Whetstone, George,   29, 66-7
Whitehall,   40, 48; (1561/2) 45; (1564/5) 49; (1594/5) 85-7; (1606) 135
Wickham, Glynne,   136